D1526807

The Cambridge Introduction to
Performance Theory

What does 'performance theory' really mean and why has it become so important across such a large number of disciplines, from art history to religious studies and architecture to geography? In this introduction Simon Shepherd explains the origins of performance theory, defines the terms and practices within the field and provides new insights into performance's wide range of definitions and uses. Offering an overview of the key figures, their theories and their impact, Shepherd provides a fresh approach to figures including Erving Goffman and Richard Schechner and ideas such as radical art practice, Performance Studies, radical scenarism and performativity. Essential reading for students, scholars and enthusiasts, this engaging account travels from universities into the streets and back again to examine performance in the context of political activists and teachers, counter-cultural experiments and feminist challenges, and ceremonies and demonstrations.

Simon Shepherd is Professor Emeritus of Theatre at the Royal Central School of Speech and Drama, University of London. He has written on performance, theatre and culture for over thirty years and his books include *Direction* (2012), *The Cambridge Introduction to Modern British Theatre* (Cambridge, 2010), *Drama/Theatre/Performance* (with Mick Wallis, 2004), *Studying Plays* (with Mick Wallis, 1998) and *English Drama: A Cultural History* (with Peter Womack, 1996).

The Cambridge Introduction to
Performance Theory

SIMON SHEPHERD

The Royal Central School of Speech and Drama

CAMBRIDGE
UNIVERSITY PRESS

CAMBRIDGE
UNIVERSITY PRESS

University Printing House, Cambridge CB2 8BS, United Kingdom

Cambridge University Press is part of the University of Cambridge.

It furthers the University's mission by disseminating knowledge in the pursuit of education, learning and research at the highest international levels of excellence.

www.cambridge.org
Information on this title: www.cambridge.org/9781107696945

First published 2016

Printed in the United States of America by Sheridan Books, Inc.

A catalogue record for this publication is available from the British Library

Library of Congress Cataloguing in Publication data
Shepherd, Simon, author.
The Cambridge introduction to performance theory / Simon Shepherd.
Cambridge, UK : Cambridge University Press, 2016. | Includes bibliographical references and index.
LCCN 2015040124 | ISBN 9781107039322 (hardback) | ISBN 9781107696945 (paperback)
LCSH: Social interaction. | Performance – Social aspects. | Acting – Social aspects. | Performance art – Social aspects.
LCC HM1111. S485 2016 | DDC 302–dc23
LC record available at http://lccn.loc.gov/2015040124

ISBN 978-1-107-03932-2 Hardback
ISBN 978-1-107-69694-5 Paperback

Contents

Preface

By the late 1970s the French and the Germans had taken a new word into their languages. This word was necessary because it enabled them to specify an activity for which there was otherwise no available term. The new word that entered their languages was the English word 'performance'.

The activity to which it was applied consisted of circumstances in which one or more people communicated in real time and shared space with another group of people. The method of communication did not explicitly refer to, and often made a point of rejecting, the conventions of what could be recognised as 'theatre'. It was a communicative activity seen to take place much more widely and variously than the practice of theatre. Indeed, although never before systematically recognised as such, it was identified as a regular occurrence in general human behaviour, capable of being done by most human beings in whatever society.

This insight came out of a widespread interest in analysing and explaining behaviour that had hitherto been assumed to be simply everyday, normal, natural. It gathered pace, across various disciplines, from the mid-1950s onwards. The first part of the book thus tracks the differing theories and definitions of human interactional behaviour which, beginning in different places, when taken together bring into being a concept of something which is called 'performance'.

By 1979 'performance' seemed to have gained so much currency, to have spread so far, that it was, some thought, a catch-all term, used to describe almost anything. Over a period of about twenty-five years, then, a concept comes into being, is felt to have such potency that it moves across academic disciplines and arts practices and gets formalised into degree programmes. That coming into being in part resulted from the work of scholars studying the world around them, but a lot of the potency that is attached to the concept of performance was put in place outside the academy, in the work of political activists and artists. A new concept of performance was formed in a new practice of performance, a practice shaped by its interactions with, its battles against the limitations of, the specific presiding economic and social structures, the institutions and violent hierarchies of capitalism, in post-1945 western Europe and the United States, and going on still. The emergence of the concept of performance is tangled up with, brought into being by, a set of particular historical circumstances, and it always carries their bruises.

To be accurate, what came into being was not a single concept so much as a set of closely related concepts, emerging from a set of circumstances. Together these circumstances all constituted a massive change in modes of thinking, but within that the concepts of performance developed as a variety of specific understandings and formulations, and they had generally specifiable genea-logies. That it's necessary to make this point is again to do with language. While the French and Germans may have needed to import a term they did not have, English-speaking peoples have the reverse problem. In English the word 'performance' has a range of applications that is promiscuous to the point of gaudy. At one end it can be a synonym for general words such as 'do' or 'achieve' or 'work'. At the other end it has specific application to the work of actors. If you say a machine performs efficiently, you don't imply that it is presenting a fiction for the delight of an audience. If you say a child performs well in school you are not usually talking about a drama class. For the machine the word 'work' would do, for the child the word 'achieve'. While attempts are made to blur these meanings together, it's an English-language game, and nobody seems to want to do it with other verbs, such as 'operate'. But we could, with similar logic, say that a train company operates efficiently and thereby claim that it's handy at removing gallbladders.

At the specific end of its English range of meanings, 'performance' is used of what actors and other entertainers do in theatre institutions. There is a large body of writing about this activity and it could all be taken to constitute a theory of how performing is done in various times and places. It could indeed be called 'performance theory' but it could just as legitimately be called 'acting theory', and its materials, generated over centuries, would mainly be of interest to those who work in or study theatre. The French and German languages can adequately label this body of work without needing the term 'performance'.

So the time is now well overdue that we ask me to come clean about the thing to which this book claims to be an introduction. The phrase 'perfor-mance theory' has two main problems in it: first, what is meant by 'perfor-mance' and, second, is it a 'theory'? As I have said, I intend to set limits on what is meant here by 'performance'. In doing so I have made a book which differs from a number of other guides to performance theory. For instance Elizabeth Bell's book offers a very full and accessible account of a large range of material, but I part company with her when she says that 'The challenges for performance theory are to account for all the resources . . . that we bring to the creation, participation, and study of performances' (2008: 22; my elision). Writing an account of the creation of performance would lead into acting theory – indeed Bell has a chapter on 'Performing Drama' – and 'participation' could be said to be in the territory of audience studies. These inclusions reveal Bell's disciplinary origins in a form of Performance Studies which emerged out of the text-based activities of 'oral interpretation'. By contrast my book does not come out of any particular disciplinary configuration of Performance Studies. It shuts the door on the set of theories that belongs with acting and theatrical performing, and it tiptoes cautiously around understandings of 'performance' that fit with the traditional work done by the university discipline of drama. So it takes a fierce line on excluding practices that I think belong elsewhere. Whether it is in Bali or Berlin, theatre or dance can be dealt with appropriately using models and terminology that pertain to theatre and dance. 'Theatre anthropology', for example, is not the same thing as and has a different remit from 'cultural performance', so I deal with the latter but not the former. We shall, however, regularly encounter the anxious attempts of performance to define its separation from theatre.

So that's what it's not. What it is (or tries to be) is a book specifically concerned with a set of related ideas that emerged from the mid-fifties onwards, and for which no other word but 'performance' would do. It endeavours to explain where those ideas came from, why they were necessary, who used them and what work they did. The journey takes us across a variety of academic disciplines from architecture, cultural anthropology and folk-lore to geography, sociology and theatre. It takes us from universities into the streets and back again, encountering on the way political activists and teachers, counter-cultural experiments and feminist confrontations, happenings and ceremonies, demonstrations and wanderings. The long middle section of the book looks at examples of the concepts of performance developing, and being put to use, in a range of contexts that include creative practice, pedagogy and politics.

As the term 'performance' evolves from its emergence into a position of dominance, different sorts of discussions happen around it. Its initial appropriateness may at first be tentatively inspected and then be fiercely guarded, histories may be told with different points of origin and shapes of development, lines drawn to discriminate oh-so clearly between what is and isn't. It is difficult to claim that all these discussions amount to one whole coherent 'theory'. Indeed the attempts to articulate a universal Theory often have the effect of flattening out the landscape in order to produce something slightly banal. In part this happens because the word 'performance' itself has become so baggy, has mopped up so many possible meanings and applications, that discourse about performance is becoming damaged. It is relinquishing its capacity, and willingness, to be specific and settling into a generalised, all-embracing vocabulary that is both oratorically grandiose and intellectually vacuous.

Many scholars have warned about letting the word become universalised in this way, and I have taken those warnings on board. That is why I have spent time looking at a number of different circumstances where the concepts that got called performance were coming into usage and developing their own vocabularies, though my attention has been limited to Europe and the United States. What the range of examples offers, I hope, is a sense of the specificity of these various concepts, which have their own particular histories and uses. So too they have their different modes of working in practice and are amenable to different critical approaches. Solo journey is not collective ceremony and is not group play. In tracking the development of concepts I have tried to show that the process of discussing performance, making discriminations, telling stories and adapting previous ideas is a series of theoretical manoeuvres usually produced by, and servicing, specific interest positions. Thus even within the boundaries that I have set for it, the entity of 'performance' shifts, mutates, knots itself up and gets into downright contradictions.

But 'performance theory' doesn't just imply a theory *of* something, a theory that might tell us what performance is and how performance works. It can also use the concepts of performance as ways of making sense of other materials. Performance theory can be a way of framing objects of study, viewing them as performances, thereby facilitating a new sort of thinking about them. Thus it can explain how interactions work by, for example, drawing on analogies with theatre, or ritual, or ceremony, or play. But alongside this, performance theory does one further thing. It can invoke an idea of performance that embodies particular values and rhetorically deploy this idea to justify projects and positions, even facilitating adjustment to the same presiding structures against which earlier performance practices came into being. It successfully provided the language for the institutionalisation of itself.

There are, then, various performances, various concepts and various ways 'performance theory' might work. Seeking to avoid gathering everything up into a catch-all term, the book tracks this diversity. In a couple of summary moments I attempt to situate performance within a general context of thought and explain why it became such a potent concept. So if you want the short-cut introduction to 'performance theory' you'd best read, after this Preface, the conclusions to Parts I and III, and the Closing Note. You would, though, be missing out on sensuous practice.

Part I

Definitions of performance

It was a new sort of activity. Well, actually, it was a very old sort of activity. Human beings appeared to have been doing it for centuries, but nobody had really called attention to it before. From the mid-1950s onwards, scholars in various academic disciplines began to get interested in how to describe and explain this activity. It was a little bit like theatre acting but didn't happen within the formal conventions and purposes of theatre. Instead it took place within what could be called everyday life, except that it could often be distinguished from other sorts of ordinary behaviour. While there were many different ideas as to how it was specifically distinguished, and to what sort of degree, from artistic theatre and ordinary behaviour, the various different scholars all ended up calling it the same thing, which was, of course, performance.

Although they were going on simultaneously I shall deal with these developments under two separate headings: first, the identification of a particular form of behaviour; second, the terminology of performance. In the first case, work by sociologists and sociologically influenced theatre specialists borrowed from each other to identify modes of interaction that were neither formal aesthetic drama nor casual everyday behaviour. In the second case, work by cultural anthropologists and folklorists developed terminology for, and understanding of the operation of, performed events in different societies. All of this together amounted not just to a new understanding of human interactions but also to a new way of doing understanding. The concept of performance was integral to both.

Chapter 1

Sociology and the rituals of interaction

The various stories about the origins of the concept of performance always tend to share one name in common: Erving Goffman. Goffman was trained in the University of Chicago School of Sociology, founded by Robert Park. The Chicago sociologists used the urban space and institutions around them to develop insights based on close observation of human interactions, a method sometimes called human ecology. But it was Goffman's work in particular that had an impact on the thinking about performance. Most accounts of the development of a non-theatrical concept of performance begin with a work he first published in 1956, *The Presentation of Self in Everyday Life*. This was a groundbreaking analysis of the structures and dynamics of interpersonal encounters, which built on an essay published the previous year. We shall look at what Goffman outlines in that essay before moving back to *Presentation of Self*.

'On face-work' appeared in 1955 in a journal of psychiatry. His other essays of this period appeared in journals of sociology and anthropology. It is that disciplinary fluidity which suggests something of the new territory being opened up by research based in observations of the 'glances, gestures, positionings and verbal statements' of regular, continuous human contact. 'On face-work' lays the groundwork for much that was to come, from Goffman and from others, by the simple shift of focus from individual person to group interaction. As he said later, in 1967, 'the proper study of interaction is not the individual and his psychology, but rather the syntactical relations among the acts of different persons mutually present to one another' (Goffman 2005: 2, 1). Needing to forge a new vocabulary, Goffman defined 'face' as 'an image of self delineated in terms of approved social attributes' and to 'have face' is to present an 'image that is internally consistent': 'At such times', says Goffman, underlining his demolition of the romance attached to that item of the human body which has so often been regarded as most personal, 'the person's face clearly is something that is not lodged in or on his body, but rather that is diffusely located in the flow of events in the encounter'. Because 'face' is dependent on socially approved attributes the individual is locked into a system of social expectation, which means that individuals are as much concerned with others' behaviour as their own, so that a person conducts him- or herself in an encounter 'so as to maintain both his own face and the face of the other participants' (Goffman 2005: 5–7, 11).

On this basis 'face-work' designates 'the actions taken by a person to make whatever he is doing consistent with face', such as maintaining poise when under pressure. And in studying those actions one becomes aware of what Goffman calls 'the traffic rules of social interaction': 'Each person, subculture and society seems to have its own characteristic repertoire of face-saving practices' (Goffman 2005: 11–13). The word 'repertoire' hints at the way the argument is tending, for once one understands the rules of social interaction as something learnt by individuals, as a way of always saving face, then it becomes possible to see face-work as a form of performance. This impression is sustained by the way a subsequent essay, 'The Nature of Deference and Demeanor' (1956), begins to deploy its terminology: 'most actions which are guided by rules of conduct are performed unthinkingly, the questioned actor saying he performs "for no reason"'. But, unthinking though it may be, we are looking at something more than incidental behaviour: 'An act that is subject to a rule of conduct is, then, a communication, for it represents a way in which selves are confirmed – both the self for which the rule is an obligation and the self for which it is an expectation' (Goffman 2005: 49, 51). Rule-bound acts that establish and communicate selves happen elsewhere than in front of painted scenery.

The analogy with scripted theatre that is being gently introduced turns out to have some explosive effects. For, rather than keep in place the idea that a learnt role is fully emotionally inhabited, Goffman's argument suggests that the role is constantly negotiated and is dependent as much on the reactions of others as on individual feelings. Indeed individual feelings are always imbricated with, and constructed by, the apparent responses of others. And these responses are governed by a repertoire that is learnt. In saying this Goffman is in a very different territory from the linguistic philosopher J.L. Austin who, the same year, conceived of the 'performative' utterance as an utterance that gets something done. Goffman might say that a performative utterance does get something done but only because it draws on and recycles elements of the available repertoire. The logic of this argument about the shaping force of the rules of interaction leads Goffman towards a wonderfully provocative attack on a deeply cherished ideological concept, where he asserts that human nature 'is not a very human thing. By acquiring it, the person becomes a kind of construct' (2005: 45).

In the book that followed 'On face-work', *Presentation of Self,* Goffman elaborated the analogies with theatrical performance, again with explosive consequences. The general argument is that a person's management of the impression they give to others may be likened to a performer working on an audience, with a 'front' presented for public view and a 'back' area, in interactions governed by 'dramaturgical' discipline. Early on he defines his use of the word 'performance' as meaning 'all the activity of a given participant on a given occasion which serves to influence in any way any of the other participants'. But he is clear that this differs from a 'theatrical performance or a staged confidence game' where routines are thoroughly scripted in advance. In everyday life the process of socialisation gives individuals the capacity to manage encounters and to recognise rules without necessarily knowing in advance what they are going to do nor how it works, so in that sense their performances are not 'acted'. Nevertheless an incapacity to manage demeanour in advance does not mean that individuals do not express themselves according to their own personal pre-formed repertoire (Goffman 1990: 26, 79–80).

After defining individual performance, the book moves on to look at the dynamics of interactions, taking a particular interest in moments when performance is disrupted or breaks down and the mechanisms used to avoid such moments. These mechanisms involve 'impression management' by both individuals and teams, where a sense of 'dramaturgical loyalty' or discipline has its effects on team behaviour. Taken together these observations could provide, Goffman suggests, a useful new approach to the analysis of social establishments as closed systems. Whereas hitherto establishments were viewed 'technically' (efficiency of the system), 'politically' (efficacy of command), 'structurally' (status divisions) and 'culturally' (operation of morals and norms), to these might be added a 'dramaturgical approach'. This would describe the 'techniques of impression management' that obtained in the establishment, which among other things would provide the basis for an analysis of power: 'Power of any kind must be clothed in effective means of displaying it, and will have different effects depending on how it is dramatized' (Goffman 1990: 232–34). Thus *Presentation of Self* firstly establishes a definition and working-through of what non-theatrical performance is and, secondly, suggests that non-theatrical performance can be used as a way of framing an object of study, offering a 'dramaturgical approach' that makes new sense of existing material. Performance is thus both a particular element of behaviour and a way of analysing. This double function remained associated with the term for ensuing decades, with its analytic capability giving it huge potency. This is illustrated in Goffman's passing note about power, which seems to suggest, a number of years before Foucault, that power is a dispersed effect maintained by discourse.

But given the way Goffman's work was used later on, we need to underline two of the early points. First, performance is not just any form of behaviour but is specifically behaviour which works to influence others: communicative behaviour. Second, everyday encounters are not consciously planned deceptions but they do proceed according to protocols deeply learnt through processes of socialisation. The analogy with theatre, instead of invoking an image of an individual in full control of an expressive apparatus that gives them power over others, works to do the reverse. It splits the individual into two parts: a performer, permanently under pressure to manage the impressions given in interactions; and the character, the entity created by the work of the performer. So while 'self-as-character' has been hitherto assumed to be 'housed within the body of its possessor', by Goffman's argument 'this self itself does not derive from its possessor' but is generated within the scene of the interaction with the effect that 'a self is imputed to him' by others. Lest there be any doubt the point is repeated: 'A correctly staged and performed scene leads the audience to impute a self to a performed character, but this imputation – this self – is a *product* of a scene that comes off, and is not a *cause* of it.' He then screws it home: 'The self, then, as a performed character, is not an organic thing that has a specific location, whose fundamental fate is to be born, to mature, and to die; it is a dramatic effect arising diffusely from a scene that is presented, and the characteristic issue, the crucial concern, is whether it will be credited or discredited' (1990: 244–45).

Although it has been noted that the dramatic metaphor had limits as a sociological tool (for example, Manning 1991), it also functioned to demolish myths of human nature and organic selfhood, which in turn had implications for hitherto dominant ideas about the nature of knowledge. The world Goffman envisages is one of constant negotiation of positions, always being adjusted. In this world the learnt and expected conventions of social interactions may be thought of as 'ritual order', governed by a ritual code that works to maintain equilibrium. Because this ritual order 'seems to be organized basically on accommodative lines', one has to think about it differently from other types of social order. In particular one has to understand that it is not governed by facts:

> Facts are of the schoolboy's world – they can be altered by diligent effort but they cannot be avoided. But what the person protects and defends and invests his feelings in is an idea about himself, and ideas are vulnerable not to facts and things but to communications.

Communications belong to a less punitive scheme than do facts, for communications can be by-passed, withdrawn from, disbelieved, conveniently misunderstood.   (2005: 42–43)

In demoting the importance of facts, emphasising their vulnerability to communication, Goffman's argument challenges the basis of the sort of positivist approach which assumes the stability of facts. And instead of 'fact'-based thinking he seems to encourage us towards a mode of thinking that assumes continual adjustment to always changing specific circumstances: relativism. The formulation of a relativist approach to the world has, as an integral part of it, the realisation that everyday human interactions can be described as performance.

But not perhaps as theatre. In the second edition of *Presentation*, in 1959, Goffman inserted a concluding note admitting that his extended elaboration of the theatre analogy was a 'rhetoric and manoeuvre'. His book was not, he clarified, about 'aspects of theatre that creep into everyday life' but instead about 'the structure of social encounters'. That said, the staging of theatrical characters involves 'the same techniques by which everyday persons sustain their real social situations'. To allow it to be imagined that the book was about theatre in everyday life would have the effect of softening the implications contained in the idea that the everyday is itself performed. The unsettling nature of those implications is clear in a slightly earlier passage where Goffman gathers up all his theatrical metaphors, the back region, the front with its props, the onstage team, the audience, all the apparatus of the social interaction, to conclude: 'The self is a product of all of these arrangements, and in all of its parts bears the marks of this genesis' (1990: 245–47). Not only has the self nothing to do with the essence of an individual, but as a constructed entity it always bears the marks of its particular history. On these terms Goffman's particular concept of performance contrasts remarkably with some of the assumptions later to be made by artistic performance makers who assumed that by stepping away from the artifice of theatre and embracing the 'everyday' they would come closer to a mode of performance that could express the real self, where they could escape mediation and illusion to produce authentic emotion. Goffman on the other hand suggests that the everyday is itself a site for the production of impressions and dramatic effects, and that there can be no self outside of mediation. Thus, while artistic performance makers may have persisted in their own particular fictions, Goffman's formulations about performance had their most profound impact and were developed considerably further in the work not of artists but of social scientists.

For example, Goffman's distinction between 'self' and 'character' was used by Messinger, Sampson and Towne in their 1962 exploration of 'the uses of the "dramaturgic approach" to social experience', which is, they say, 'a mode of analysis finding increasing use in social-psychological circles'. They describe 'a perspective that renders life a kind of "theater"', as a mode of analysis, but they are also interested in where this places the analyst. As they see it, 'the actor's view of what he is doing, is not relevant to the dramaturgic analyst', whose job instead is to focus on the impression the actor is actually making. It's a model of analysis that, in contrast with what ethnographers in this period thought they should be doing, consciously keeps a distance when it reads social performances. Indeed this 'dramaturgic approach' is a long way removed from theatre dramaturgy. Certainly Goffman's influence is there but Messinger and his co-authors say that their approach specifically draws on Kenneth Burke's 'dramatism'. This term was coined by Burke as a name for the method he employed in his book *A Grammar of Motives* (1945). The book does what it says, in that it is an attempt to provide a 'grammar' of the 'basic forms of thought which . . . are exemplified in the attributing of motives'. To produce this 'grammar' Burke adopts some overarching terms that will enable him to describe a range of examples. These terms are 'act', 'scene', 'agent', 'agency' and 'purpose', and he explains their function: 'In a rounded statement about motives, you must have some word that names the act (names what took place, in thought or deed), and another that names the scene (the background of the act, the situation in which it occurred); also, you must indicate what person or kind of person (agent) performed the act, what means or instruments he used (agency), and the purpose.' Although there may be disagreements as to their interpretation, these words allow him to answer questions about what, when, who, how and why. But his interest is in the 'purely internal relationships' between the terms, seeing how they 'figure in actual statements about human motives'. And although his terminology, being derived from analysis of drama, intends to treat language and thought as 'modes of action' (1945: xv, xxii; my elision), the work is explicitly philosophical and based in analysis of written texts and words such as 'constitution'. As Elizabeth Burns says, Burke is not primarily concerned with social action 'but with basic forms of thought which underlie it' (1972: 20). In that respect it was to be Goffman who would be much more influential on modelling a concept of performance.

Contemporary with Goffman's attempts to describe the syntax and dramaturgy of human interaction other scholars were trying to apply the mathematical theory of games to analyses of human, and specifically economic, behaviour, as in von Neumann and Morgenstern's *Theory of Games and*

Economic Behavior (1944) and Martin Shubik's *Game Theory and Related Approaches to Human Behaviour* (1964). Shubik has said that in the fifties he put too little emphasis on 'conversational game theory' and that the actual activities of human beings don't easily admit of mathematical modelling (Shubik 2011), but it nevertheless held a promise of being able to describe the mechanisms of human interaction which stripped away traditional assumptions about character and interaction and thus appealed, if briefly, to those exploring new modes of performance. Philip McCoy did groundbreaking work on theatre and games theory, which came to the notice of theatre academic Richard Schechner. At the same time performance artists such as Vito Acconci and Anthony Howell developed performances based on rules of interaction, as an alternative for example to character motivation. When they appeared in published texts for performance by those associated with Fluxus, these rules took the form of enigmatic and all too brief instructions: 'Arrange to observe a sign / indicating direction of travel / travel in the indicated direction / travel in another direction' (George Brecht); 'drink from a baby bottle and pee' (Walter Marchetti) (in Stegmann 2012: 377, 380). In this form they became a sort of challenge to the imagination of performers, or perhaps an invitation, and in this respect they tied in with another popular topic of the period: play. Studies of 'play', following on from the work of the Dutch sociologist Johan Huizinga, became interesting as another instance of identifiable forms of human behaviour that seemed to be governed by agreed conventions and indeed rules. In a work originally published in 1938 Huizinga suggested play is 'productive of culture' but that this is threatened in 'highly organised' society by the operations of religion and science (Huizinga 1949: 75, 119). This model, in which the role of poet remains in touch with play, was attractive to those who made aesthetic performance but it was criticised in 1958 along lines characteristic of the period. Roger Caillois said that play produced nothing, that its place in ordinary life was demarcated by 'precise limits' and that it had a range of its own rules, observable in games (Caillois 1961: 7). In his suggestion that the analysis of rule-bound games gave insight to the shapes and pleasures of social interaction, Caillois was in similar territory to Goffman. But Huizinga's original formulation became highly influential on the thinking of political activists, as we shall see in Part II. For them play was related to another activity which both Huizinga and Goffman invoked as a model, namely ritual behaviour. Although ritual had for a long time been studied as a way of understanding religion, following the work of Marcel Mauss in the early twentieth century, ritual came to be seen as a form of social activity that produced religion. When culture emerged as a specific category of analysis, ritual activities became particularly important for study, as seen in the work of Victor Turner, Clifford Geertz, Edmund Leach and Marshall Sahlins (see Bell 1992: 14–15). Taken together, face-work, game, play and ritual all seem to be modes of human behaviour that are somehow intensified beyond the accidental or casual. The sense of intensification comes from the fact that these modes of behaviour all have understood, if not necessarily conscious rules, and second, they all operate as modes of communication. What they communicate is the sense of the selves of those participating in the activity. Because these are modes of communication which work specifically to communicate ideas of self, it seems reasonable and convenient to group them as forms of non-theatrical performance.

A further elaboration of this concept came from a different direction when in the mid-1960s in Birmingham, UK, a group of scholars whose disciplinary origins were mainly in the analysis of literary text picked up on Goffman's general sense of human interactions as 'syntactical'. They began to read as 'text' social interactions and cultural display, in all their modes, even between football fans: 'The aggro fans talk of is in effect a highly distinctive, and often ceremonial, system for resolving conflict.' Observing match-day behaviour in 1978 Peter Marsh gives as example an interaction between Sheffield and Oxford fans in which there's a provocation to fight. Rather than leading automatically into actual physical conflict the stand-off is defused by those involved. What goes on, says Marsh, is typical of football grounds everywhere: 'the patterns of conflict and hostility . . . are so routine and commonplace that they are taken-for-granted and unremarkable. The apparent inconsequentiality, however, masks the fact that it is in these rituals that "honour" is satisfied.' They provide 'useful pieces of self-presentation' (Marsh 1978: 65, 67; my elision).

While this reference to 'ritual' might throw back to Goffman, the interest in ceremonial 'system' and 'pattern' of conflict is typical of an approach that was developed in the early seventies in the Centre for Contemporary Cultural Studies at the University of Birmingham (hereafter CCCS). Founded in 1964 by Richard Hoggart, who wrote *The Uses of Literacy* (1957), CCCS had its roots in a socially aware literary studies. While some of its academics were also influenced by American studies of social interactionism, with an essay on Howard Becker appearing in a Centre publication (CCCS 1975), the interest in literary and cultural objects gave CCCS both a direction and a method. The mode of literary studies done by Hoggart, F.R. Leavis and Raymond Williams was one that in different ways – for these people had different political positions – commented on class division and cultural segmentation, and it did so from a position that was actively opposed to the dominant order. That same opposition was vigorously displayed by the young academics of CCCS when they participated in student actions against the University, for example the sit-in of 1968. And it also directed their selection of objects of study which were, in the main, the operation of the news media and popular television as sites of ideological production and, second, the activities of groupings who were outside the dominant and often seeking to resist it, such as youth subcultures. All of this cultural work, we should note, was regarded by sociologists as being 'unscientific' (Dworkin 1997: 117).

In attending to both the media and subcultures the preferred method was to analyse them as 'texts'. But in the case of subgroups, the 'text', rather than being a written cultural product, was more likely to be the clothing worn by members of the group. The adoption of particular modes of dress and pre-ferred pastimes came to be seen as constituting 'code' and 'style', and by reading 'style' members of CCCS were able to analyse the outlooks and values of such subgroups as bikers, skinheads, teddy boys and punks. The job of the academic researcher could thus be summarised as being to 'discover the hidden meanings inscribed in code on the glossy surfaces of style' (Hebdige 1979: 18). Such reading of the code of the subgroup styles was formulated first by Phil Cohen in 1972. His innovation was that, in Dick Hebdige's words: 'Rather than presenting class as an abstract set of external determinations, he showed it working out in practice as a material force, dressed up, as it were, in experience and exhibited in style. The raw material of history could be seen refracted, held and "handled" in the line of a mod's jacket, in the soles of a teddy boy's shoes' (Hebdige 1979: 78).

The activity of reading subculture as 'text' had more behind it than the traditions of literary study. There was also borrowing from anthropology. Anthropologists proposed that they could understand more about the people they studied by learning to identify and interpret their symbols and sign-systems. For example, in his study of the hippy subculture Hoggart's deputy, Stuart Hall, referred to Victor Turner's work on the sign-systems of the Ndembu tribe. But perhaps the more significant influence was that of Claude Lévi-Strauss, from whom scholars of CCCS took the term 'bricolage', the word Lévi-Strauss gave to systems of classi-fication and connection by which so-called primitive peoples made sense of their worlds. The term was adopted by John Clarke to enable sense to be made of discursive systems such as fashion: 'Together, object and meaning constitute a sign, and, within any one culture, such signs are assembled, repeatedly, into characteristic forms of discourse. However, when the *bricoleur* re-locates the significant object in a different position within that discourse … a new discourse is constituted, a different message conveyed' (Clarke 1975: 177; my elision).

In reading subcultures the scholars of CCCS were doing something more than simply analysing how particular groups behaved. The work of reading was important to them because it could explain the operations of ideology and thereby reveal how dominant social structures maintained themselves in being. And this in turn could reveal how they might be resisted. Precisely by positing cultures as texts, social analysts opened the way for de-familiarising that which had seemed hitherto natural or commonsensical. Finding the text and then reading it had a political imperative. In the case of subcultures a CCCS reading could complicate the simplistic terms of media condemnation and demonstrate instead what the activities of a subculture indicate as to the operation and efficacy of dominant order.

One of the best known, and most extended, of the CCCS readings is Dick Hebdige's book, *Subculture: The Meaning of Style* (1979). Here Hebdige proposes that a subculture's choice of clothing and commodity objects, its 'style' can be read as a language. This works to a specific purpose: 'The communication of a significant *difference*, then (and the parallel communication of a group *identity*), is the "point" behind the style of all spectacular subcultures' (1979: 102). Behind that formulation lie the ideas contained in Roland Barthes's 1972 book *Mythologies*. Here Barthes sets out to describe the mechanisms by which the meanings and values specific to a particular social group are generalised in such a way that they come to seem like 'common sense' and 'natural'. In short the argument displays how a dominant ideology is sustained and reproduced. But it was the method that demonstrated this argument which had the lasting influence. What Barthes was doing was to show that any cultural phenomena, whether 'low' or 'high-class', whether art or rubbish, could be read as a language. Applied to subcultural groups, then, the language interpreted from their clothing and objects could be shown to be speaking back against dominant society, deliberately enacting their difference.

I use the phrase 'deliberately enacting' deliberately. In Hebdige's model the adoption of subcultural style involves conscious choice and activity: 'It is basically the way in which commodities are *used* in subculture which marks the subculture off from more orthodox formations.' In case studies of punks or teddy boys or rastas, Hebdige argues that subcultural style is seen as part of a 'struggle' between competing discourses, 'a struggle for possession of the sign'. Within this struggle ordinary commodities are 'open in a double inflection: to "illegitimate" as well as "legitimate" uses. These "humble objects" can be magically appropriated; "stolen" by subordinate groups and made to carry "secret" meanings: meanings which express, in code, a form of resistance to the order which generates their continued subordination' (1979: 103, 18).

Against any notion that a subculture is something to be read, a passive text to be opened up by the activity of the scholar, Hebdige's argument is that members of the subculture themselves have agency. They actively use commodities, exhibit style and relocate significant objects. They do things with clothes and objects as part of an activity of negotiation, indeed struggle. Goffman might have seen this as a negotiation around self-presentation, conceived in terms drawn from drama, and twenty years or so later he turns up in a Hebdige footnote: 'there is also a more mainstream tradition of research into social encounters, role-play, etc. which proves overwhelmingly that social interaction (at least in middle-class white America!) is quite firmly governed by a rigid set of rules, codes and conventions (see in particular Goffman, 1971 and 1972).' Referring here to a re-publication of Goffman's *Presentation of Self* and *Relations in Public*, Hebdige steers clear of terminology derived from drama but notes instead the importance of 'rules, codes and conventions' that govern 'social interaction'. For him, as we know, the codes are those of 'style', and the rules and conventions relate to choices within a system, 'the conventional modes of sartorial discourse' (Hebdige 1979: 161, 101). These are all elements of which members of a subculture make a language. The function of that language within their social interaction, while it is not seen as the text of a 'drama', works nevertheless, as Hebdige sees it, to 'express . . . a form of resistance'.

Alongside Hebdige's expressive codes and communicative 'style', CCCS scholars had other favoured words that denoted forms of behaviour which, while not being recognisably dramatic, were rule-bound. We met these in the stand-off between football fans recounted by Marsh: 'ceremony' and 'ritual'. The function of the football rituals, Marsh suggests, is not only to construct, and then defuse, actual violence but also to offer opportunities for individual display: 'Fans demonstrate aspects of character which meet with acclaim and social approval within their social world. Fighting and being part of any aggro that's going on are useful pieces of self-presentation in this respect because, whatever else his failings, a fan who stands his ground is one of the boys' (Marsh 1978: 67). These ritualised interactions, like style, function to communicate group identity. But they are also 'pieces of self-presentation'. Marsh's phrase lets us know that, not very far behind his modelling of football fan interaction, stands Goffman's account of everyday human mechanisms for presenting self. But the language has altered.

In 1964 Peter Worsley had criticised the effect of Goffman's 'dramaturgical' metaphors:

> The concept of role is the central concept of the social sciences. Its
> analytical utility is immediately obvious . . . As in the theatre – from
> whence the metaphor is taken – the script is written for the actor: he does
> not invent the role. Yet it is precisely at this point that the limits of the
> analogy reveal themselves. Too often the social role is conceived of as
> absolutely fixed.   (in Burns and Burns 1973: 23)

For those in CCCS the cultures they were looking at involved negotiations, appropriation of meanings, so they looked for language that would not bring with it the associations of the theatrical role. Like Goffman, however, the project was to find a way of making supposedly natural everyday behaviours available for analysis. Rendering these behaviours as text or drama or ritual is a way not only of de-naturalising them but also, in consequence, of opening them up to a form of scrutiny which can reveal both their values and the nature of their interactions with their contexts. This is where such words as 'style', 'ritual' and 'ceremony' enter the frame. While remaining clearly outside established art practices, they aim to confer on certain sorts of everyday behaviour a sense of that which is rule-bound, learnt, imitable, deliberate, functional and expressive. In doing so, the work of cultural studies was in effect making these behaviours available for reading as performance.

But they went a step further than developing a vocabulary for describing, and thus reading, everyday behaviours as a form of performance. CCCS scholars were also interested in the contexts of the performance, where such contexts may both give the performance meaning and extend it, where it is the relationship between performance and context which is the object of knowledge. Thus, in the study of football fans, it was not simply a matter of identifying the ways in which their interactions were ritualistic. It was also productive to look at their behaviour in relation to the game itself. A properly socially engaged study of football fans thus meant developing an awareness of the relationship between the formal rule-bound activity – the football game – and the less clearly rule-bound activities that surround it. The way of proceeding was mapped out by John Clarke in his suggestion that, in order to explain why football hooliganism happens, we have to formulate a more complex understanding of where it happens, a context

> in which there are connections between the game, how it is watched, who
> it is watched by, and the activities of football hooligans. This involves
> taking the way in which football is organised and played, and the ways in
> which football is watched as *social* activities. This means being sensitive
> to two main aspects of social activity. First, it means looking at the types
> of social relationships involved in how the game is organised and

watched: the connections between the game itself and the society of which it is a part (eg. why football has come to be such an important part of the country's leisure time); the connections between the game and those who watch it and the sorts of relationships among those people and groups who form the audience. Secondly, it means looking at the *meanings* of these relationships – at the traditions and values around which football and being a football supporter are organised. This is to say, that watching football involves certain unwritten codes about what football 'means', about 'how' to watch it, and about how to behave at football matches, and so on. (Clarke 1978: 38–39)

In effect the cultural researcher here is taking the analysis into the domain of what we might call spectatorship or audience studies.

But it moves audience studies further on when the analysis suggests that the audience – the fans – were themselves doing a mode of performance. That move establishes that what we are looking at is a series of interrelated performances, from the clearly rule-bound one of the football game itself through to those which are less explicitly rule-bound, the ritualistic encounters of the fans. And from here one can now envisage an even less apparently rule-bound activity, the assumed behaviours of watching, with all its unwritten codes. These interrelated performances are conceived as a set of 'connections', to use Clarke's word, where a proper reading only comes from discovering what the connections are. The analysis of football thus proposes that we see its 'performance' not as a singular activity but as a set of performances. These can be arranged on a spectrum from the most intensively rule-bound to the least rule-bound. Elsewhere, as we shall see, a similar approach was proposed to the study of drama.

While Clarke focussed mainly on the game at the centre, in the work of his contemporary Dick Hebdige there was a move beyond the study of the rule-bound performance together with a development in understanding how performance works socially. A look at this will provide a summary of the various elements that comprised the CCCS thinking about role and ritual and ceremony.

Hebdige's publication came out in about 1974 as one of the (often undated) 'stencilled occasional papers' which CCCS used as a cheap and flexible mechanism for disseminating its ideas. The project was called *Sub-Cultural Conflict & Criminal Performance in Fulham* and its aim was made clear in its subtitle: *Towards a Radical Theory of Role.* As a basis for re-thinking the by-now problematic sociological concept of role, Hebdige studied the behaviour and interactions of one of the deprived areas of post-war London. It was chosen in part because of the status it had acquired in the popular press: 'Fulham ... provided the backdrop against which the British media played out its vicarious fantasies of violent crime in the sixties, and the local population was not unaffected'. To find out how far, and in what ways, the population was affected by their characterisation in the popular media, Hebdige observed interactions in public spaces, particularly in the pub, 'the single most important area of play available to the working class individual in this country' (Hebdige c.1974: this publication has no page numbers; my elision).

The population of Fulham was particularly susceptible to media representation because they found themselves in a state of cultural crisis that had persisted since the war:

> The community as a whole faced peculiarly complex problems of self-definition, but solutions to the problems were most urgently required inside the deviant group which had to draw up fairly rigid lines of demarcation between itself and the outside world, between acceptance and denial if it was to retain any clear sense of identity at all. Unless the contrast between the criminal actor and his public was continually ratified in his everyday interactions with 'straights' and 'fellow crooks' nothing could make sense and the credibility of his performance was thrown into jeopardy.

That formulation 'criminal actor' is not a loose metaphor. It recurs in Hebdige's analysis of a fight that took place one Boxing Day: 'I postulated the existence of four separate codes of honour which had dictated the initial choices made by the actors in the Boxing Day fracas ... The various actors organised these codes in hierarchies which corresponded to their needs at the moment of crisis' (my elision).

This is something different from the academic outsider simply reading the codes of the subculture. Certainly Hebdige has postulated these codes, but his sense is that the people he is watching are not so much responding passively or merely instinctually as taking decisions, at some level, about how to handle the situation in which they find themselves. And the acting here is more than a temporary management of a crisis. As Hebdige sees it, acting, or indeed performing, is a constituent factor in the identity of those he was studying: 'The "performer" defines himself against the reaction of his public – he *is* only in so far as he is *seen to be* and he must find his self image reflected in the eyes of his spectators'. Far from being the adoption of a fixed role, the personal performance is seen to be both provisional, dependent as it is on the responses of others, and yet necessary, as a way of establishing self-definition in an alienated society.

The interest in this sort of performance took Hebdige into analyses of smaller constituent elements. He describes the conversational wind-up as a type of speech act, drawing here on the work of Gregory Bateson. And to specify the particular activity of the 'social deviant' who 'performs the clownish functions' of the 'in-group deviant', he uses Goffman's book *Stigma*. In the case of one of his subjects, a man called Frank, Hebdige found himself dealing with a personal performance that doubled up on itself: 'myth (and dramaturgical metaphors!) are unavoidable in Frank's case for he had invested in his own alienation, and had appeared in several films'. Frank becomes an example of Goffman's explanation of how a 'private person' transforms into a 'public figure', but he does so in a way which shows that he is in control of the process. And here is where we have to note the departure of Hebdige's version of role from that which had previously obtained both in sociology and in theatre studies. Worsley, we recall, said 'the actor does not invent the role': it is written for him (or her). This implies a passive sense of inhabiting role, fitting in with what is, sometimes literally, pre-scribed. By contrast Hebdige sees the criminals in Fulham in a continual process of negotiating their role, making choices about codes and speech acts, looking for their image to be affirmed. Of course in a different respect they are also fixed somewhere, within an area of London hit by a chronic social and cultural crisis of identity, which determines how they act. But in dealing with the conditions in which they find themselves they have a certain amount of agency. The 'radical theory' of role is coming up with a dialectical concept of social performance.

That radicalism Hebdige felt really resided in his choice of methodology. He explains, later on, that his preferred methodology 'retains, in marked contrast to conventional structuralist techniques, a commitment to qualitative and evaluative distinctions (i.e. a moral commitment), and . . . it remains undisguisedly subjectivist and is therefore ultimately fallible' (my elision). Further, 'it was by dealing directly with the question of aesthetics, that I hoped somewhat paradoxically to prevent this thesis from degenerating in to the aesthetic game towards which the "science" of structuralism seems naturally inclined.' The use of the methodology therefore 'was also meant to be concerned *directly* (i.e. to be *about*) the problem of meaning which the phenomenological study of subcultures habitually raises'.

Despite what he and his colleagues say elsewhere about reading the 'texts' of subcultures and interpreting their 'codes', Hebdige is clear that the study of subcultures has to be 'phenomenological'. A proper method for dealing with their everyday performance has to be aligned with the qualitative and subjective. And, perhaps precisely because it is dealing with real, as opposed to aesthetically scripted, identities, there is an ethical urgency to understanding not just the mechanisms of role negotiation but also why, qualitatively, they matter. An awareness of the elements of performance has helped Hebdige do, as he sees it, better and more necessary sociology. But in developing this awareness of performance, within a non-theatrical everyday context, Hebdige has in fact added substantially to what performance might be understood to be.

Chapter 2

Theatre, ceremony and everyday life

With its roots in literary study the Centre for Contemporary Cultural Studies at the University of Birmingham (CCCS) picked up the idea that ritualised human interaction could be seen to have a 'syntax', a set of rules, that could then be analysed as text. Another way of approaching these sorts of human interaction was to see them as offering roles to their participants. Once again this approach implies that the interactions are performed, and once again it grows out of sociological interests, but this time its development moves through the formal discipline of theatre studies.

The point of origin takes us back to that crucial period, the mid-1950s. Following a conference on Theatre and Society at Royaumont, in 1956 the sociologist Georges Gurvitch published their agreed findings as to a new direction of research. These identified the following topics: 'the diversity of audiences, their different degrees of relative homogeneity and cohesion'; analysis of the 'performance' itself 'as worked out within a specific social framework'; study of those doing the 'performance' as 'a social group, both as companies and more widely as an occupation'; study of 'the functional relationship between the *content* . . . and the actual social system, particularly structural forms and social classes' (in Burns and Burns 1973: 76–77; my elision).

This approach is based on, and justified by, an assumed affinity between theatre and society. This affinity holds true whether one begins by studying theatre or society, and it can thus give new understanding not only of aesthetic production but also of society itself:

> For even the most naïve observer, nothing is more striking than the
> *ceremonial elements* in collective life, and the ways in which the social
> roles of the individuals and groups which constitute it are acted out. Do
> not the social ceremonies, and the individual and collective roles which
> we play in them (sometimes without knowing it), present an astonishing
> analogy with what we call the theatre? (in Burns and Burns 1973:
> 71–72)

On the basis of that analogy Gurvitch finds himself, in the very same year as Goffman's *Presentation of Self*, thinking afresh about the concept of social role: 'the acting out of social roles constitutes part and parcel of the social order. To begin with, each individual plays several social roles, which normally do not correspond with each other completely, which often come into conflict and can become so acute as to create genuine contradictions.' Such contradiction may be seen, for example, in the political leader who plays a 'subdued role' in his own family (in Burns and Burns 1973: 72). Like Goffman's in 'Facework' Gurvitch's argument suggests that, rather than being a coherent or fixed subjectivity, individuals act – or even are – different in different social or, we might say, discursive or citational contexts. This is a step further on than the proposition that human agents perform their lives through style and ceremony. It gets us very close to the idea that, by thinking in terms of the acting out of roles, or shall we say performance, we necessarily have a model of the unfixed, conflicted, human subject.

But for Gurvitch it was less in individual behaviour than in collective activity, in 'social ceremonies', that the 'theatrical element' of society was most clear. He opened the way for a range of cultural analyses when he asserted that 'theatricality remains a far more persuasive and fundamental aspect of social life than all the organizations, procedures and practices, symbols and even normative patterns which are operating within the social framework. The most spontaneous activities of social life in general are not without some theatrical characteristics' (in Burns and Burns 1973: 72). That open door was walked through in 1965 by Jean Duvignaud, who more or less repeated Gurvitch's formulation: ' Social life, however', says Duvignaud, 'displays aspects that are identical with ceremonies. Moreover, it seems that they assume considerable importance in collective life and that they assert themselves with a distinctiveness greater than the organizations, the practical activities and the symbols that are at work in society. Thus there may be a truly *spontaneous theatre* at the levels of experience.' He then qualifies this by noting that 'Social life is not, of course, reduced to these theatrical aspects alone. It includes non-ceremonial and even anti-ceremonial aspects. But the existence of this active collective participation brings society close to the theatre and suggests some continuity between social and dramatic ceremony' (in Burns and Burns 1973: 82). Hidden behind Duvignaud's prose there's Gurvitch: 'Obviously, social reality cannot be reduced to ceremonies alone ... it also contains what is non-ceremonial, even anti-ceremonial ... Nevertheless, theatricality remains a far more pervasive and fundamental' and we are back into the text I quote above (in Burns and Burns 1973: 72; my elision).

This shared language emphasises the closeness at this period between the work in sociology and that in theatre. Each was material for the other. Gurvitch was principally a sociologist; Duvignaud principally an analyst of theatre. Duvignaud was later translated by Tom Burns, who was a university colleague of, and doing similar work to, Goffman. If we are looking for originary points for 'performance theory', we would do well to attend to this disciplinary dialogue for it not only produces, in the mid-1950s, a proposition about the pervasive theatricality in everyday social life but also, in doing so, comes up with a model of the unfixed person which modern thinking about performance might recognise.

From here, on the basis of Gurvitch's ideas, Duvignaud takes forward the thinking around two terms that became fundamental in developing a concept of performance: 'role' and 'ceremony'. A year after Worsley's critique of the limitations of the concept of role in sociology, Duvignaud circulated and developed Gurvitch's ideas for a new audience, contributing his own different emphasis. For him, the thinking about role was tangled up in what he called social ceremonies: 'A tribunal, a jury, the unveiling of a monument, a religious service at a mosque or synagogue, a festival, even a family birthday are all ceremonies at which people play parts according to a scenario which they are in no position to modify because no one can escape the social roles he is obliged to assume.' Taking up Gurvitch's picture of multiple and possibly contradictory roles, Duvignaud presses further to suggest that individual roles are always caught up into something larger than themselves:

> The fact that each person in a complex society can play many different social roles (that of foreman, goalkeeper and trade unionist at the same time) shows that individual lives may be engaged in many networks of role playing, and take part in a variety of ceremonies which at each stage imply a different form of pre-determined collective action. In the course of these ceremonies, which embody social activity at its most obvious level, individuals take on characters fixed by tradition and act accordingly.   (in Burns and Burns 1973: 83)

Viewed from a culture in which Butler's theory of gender as citational behaviour (see pp. 186–88) has become more or less naturalised, the concept of individual lives being 'engaged in networks of role playing' becomes a very interesting formulation. It implies that the individual takes on different, but always rule-bound, behaviours according to the networks – or perhaps discursive communities – which they enter. A version of this position is something that we might now say is a stock-in-trade of thinking about performance.

The other key term in which Duvignaud had an interest was 'ceremony'. While Gurvitch, sketching the foundations for a sociology of theatre, moved fairly easily from society as theatre to theatre as society, Duvignaud chose to spend more of his time differentiating between social and theatrical ceremonies. This step also set him apart from the work of Goffman and his followers where language taken from drama was simply applied to everyday life. By discriminating between theatrical and social ceremonies Duvignaud suggests a whole category of event which may function differently from theatre but which has a similar sort of status. He argued that, unlike the characters in theatrical drama, social ceremonies represent 'symbolic or allegorical "*personnages*" who, themselves, represent and designate the *coherence* of the group while emphasizing the unanimity of its members'. They evoke a 'static' time outside history and change, and hence are a mechanism for the process whereby, as Emile Durkheim put it, a society 'realizes its collective existence through performing the drama of its mythical cohesion' (in Burns and Burns 1973: 83–84). One other reference could have appeared here, and that is to Milton Singer's formulation of the 'cultural performance' (see pp. 42–43) by which a particular social organisation encounters the structure of tradition.

The fact that Singer's name does not appear here may be to do with disciplinary specificity, but it may also be connected to a problem that recurs through all the material we are considering across this book. Different national cultures have their own particular frames of reference. The French sociology of theatre, notes Elizabeth Burns, was not known in Britain or the United States. And it is just one of the many remarkable features of Burns's excellent book *Theatricality* that she knew what was going on beyond her own backyard. Indeed she followed its publication in 1972 with an anthology of writing on sociology of literature and drama, edited with her husband Tom Burns, in which they made available for the first time the texts of Gurvitch and Duvignaud in English (and from which I have been quoting). But Elizabeth Burns was doing a lot more than replaying the French work. Her book draws on both the French sociology of theatre and the 'micro-sociology' of Chicago to produce, from their combination, a theorisation of the relationship between theatre and everyday life more profound than almost any before or since.

This theorisation explores the ways in which apparently ordinary behaviour may be said to be theatrical. The brief version of this exploration given at the start of the book begins its argument by suggesting that if you compare the mummers' play, late-nineteenth-century theatrical realism, and contemporary participatory improvisations, you have three different proposals as to how to define the reality of what's going on: 'let's pretend this is reality'; 'this is a plausible alternative, [*sic*] reality' closely akin to what you accept as norm; 'let us together make this a reality that overrides any other possible reality.' Each is an exercise in illusion but achieving it depends less on aesthetic techniques than on agreement between actors and audiences as to which level of reality is being used or, in other words, on the definition of the situation. This phrasing allows Burns to introduce sociological research into the definition of the 'situations' of everyday life, where 'To take part in any social occasion, to assume membership of the relationships which go with it, the participants accept an initial commitment to keep things going, "to keep within bounds". There has to be a common perception of those bounds, an acceptance of a definable normality of conduct, purpose and intent.' Perception and acceptance are two different elements: 'The actor sees, then he interprets and then he acts.' While this may be the basis on which, in theatre, the illusion of a particular sort of reality is created, it's important to note that, given what has already been said about social situations,

> illusion is only a specifically theatrical term for a process inherent in all social interaction. It is the process of confining attention to those involved in a specific situation, of limiting activities, given that situation, to what is appropriate or meaningful or consequential, and of observing a defined level of reality. The process is essentially that of providing a frame for action. The important thing is to signify the degree of seriousness or fatefulness that is to be attached to an event.

She gives the example of a party where there is agreement that the purpose of the event is enjoyment and so people deliberately behave as if they are all equals. But: 'Not only is the "as if" of equality a temporary fabrication – an illusion; so also are the "as if" of the importance of the occasion, the necessity to "keep things going" until the end, to prevent awkward silences, open hostility or sheer boredom which may cause people to leave.' Even in ordinary life, therefore, different levels of reality are deliberately selected, and these can be likened to the levels of reality agreed to in the theatre: 'the "pretend" reality of games, sports, parties, ceremonies, the "alternative" reality of occupational worlds and ritual, or the "overriding" reality concerned with the deliberate efforts to change or defend definitions of the situation' (Burns 1972: 15–17). At this point Burns does not merely produce a wide range of activity which may be said to be performed, but she finds a way of distinguishing between the sorts of work the performance is doing. Her theorisation seeks to foreground specificity rather than to universalise. This contrasts strikingly with what was to follow elsewhere.

Burns goes on to argue that the parallel between theatre and everyday life is not the whole story, because the theatre is an institution. But this institution begins in everyday life: 'Acting antedates drama. Ordinary conversation often incorporates the representation of other people's words, attitudes and gestures. .... This capacity, inherent in spontaneous interaction, is a prerequisite source from which fresh embodiments of convention can be contrived to develop the institutional form of drama.' But while acting may be an intrinsic part of daily interaction, ritual and drama alike, the particular institutional development of drama saw a separation of audience from actors which in turn put a particular pressure on the sort of acting that was done. 'Spectators and performers were learning to assume different, though, at times, interchangeable roles' (Burns 1972: 25–27; my elision). This precision about the forms and effects of institutionalisation is also a key part of any exploration of performed activity.

From here, having laid out the scheme of her argument, Burns then goes into much more detailed explorations, which include an examination of the ways in which everyday behaviour may be said to be acting. Because this is such a thorough attempt at bringing together sociological thinking and aesthetic practice, it is appropriate, for an overall understanding of the concept of performance, that we thus follow Burns a little further. Her analysis of everyday performance begins with the sociological concept of role, which goes back to Marx but becomes more closely inspected and problematised by scholarship of the 1950s and 1960s, on which she founds her argument: 'The social system is in fact a system of roles which are defined by the negative and positive sanctions of law, custom and norms of behaviour. Individual members of society have to learn a succession of roles, usually by the informal educational process of socialisation.' This learning begins by perceiving, for expectations of roles may change in different societies. Thus roles are a means of 'placing ourselves in society' but at the same time 'they are also perceived as a means of consolidation of the self'. Through role the individual learns how to be effective in society by behaving in the appropriate ways in different situations. This observation, familiar from Goffman's work, means that we have to let go of a notion of a defined knowable self: 'Actions, gestures and speech provide the evidence from which motives, intentions and a central core of selfhood can only be inferred. Thus a performed self is created with which the performer himself may be uneasy' (Burns 1972: 128–30).

That formulation invites the obvious parallel: 'the performed self, distinguishable and yet not separate from the performer, is comparable to the character presented by the actor in a play. Yet the way in which this character is formed is significantly different. The script is replaced in ordinary life by an ongoing process.' That process consists of objective demands, the expectations of the role and subjective aims and desires. The individual becomes conscious of, and learns to accommodate to, what is expected of role through a process that, according to G.H. Mead, begins with childhood participation in play. Play allows for the temporary taking on of roles of which there is no expectation, whereas in the games characteristic of adulthood there are rules which establish that participants know what is expected of them. Nevertheless the social or occupational roles of adulthood can still retain the expressive elements of play, and through these individuals may become aware of the ways in which ordinary life is 'theatrical'. That theatricality will not, and cannot, confirm coherent individual identity: 'in contemporary western societies, the experience of varia- bility of occasions, of role-switching, of the novel and unexpected, connotes an awareness of the fracture of social identity . . . We are commonly aware of a difference between "self" and "role", and, indeed, of a multiplicity of selves, of a distinction between the self-as-performer and the self-as-audience, observer, and critic of the self-as-performer.' It is, of course, 'on this reconstruction of the self and of social reality that the whole conception of drama and theatre is founded' (Burns 1972: 132–37; my elision).

While Burns's book appeared in the United Kingdom, a different attempt to think about relations between performance and social science was pub- lished the next year in a special issue of *The Drama Review* (*TDR*), guest edited by Richard Schechner. In his headnote he pointed out that for a couple of decades studies of society and performance had been coming to share similar territory, with a 'shared basic principle' that 'people in groups . . . in some ways "ritualize" their behaviors; "present" themselves rather than just be.' On the way to this shared understanding the social sciences developed terminology 'adapted from the vocabulary of theatre: role playing, scenes, setting, acting and/or action', and theatre borrowed in the other direction, taking terms such as 'interaction, ritual, ceremony, confrontation'. The result of this sharing of concepts was the development of a new idea of what performance might be said to be. Rather than simply aesthetic activity asso- ciated with theatres, performance could be regarded as 'a kind of commu- nicative behaviour that is part of, or continuous with, more formal ritual ceremonies, public gatherings, and various means of exchanging information, goods, and customs' (Schechner 1973: 3; my elision).

While this was an astute enough summary it remained at a fairly superficial level, and indeed the contrast with the depth of Burns's work is striking. In particular Schechner's work here is debilitated by the problem noted above, namely a lack of awareness of the international scene. It seems from the volume's other essays, as Schechner acknowledges, that scholarship on theatre sociology was barely developed in the United States at this time. He himself, though always attentive to possible new developments, had attempted to use the sociological work in an essay a few years before. His 'Approaches to Theory/Criticism' (1966) picks up on the work of Goffman, but its overall emphasis nevertheless remains fixed on aesthetic theatre rather than behavioural performance. The essay's primary aim is to develop an appropriate method for analysing scripted drama. On the way it signals the shape of things to come by recommending that scripted drama be placed alongside other modes such as ritual, play, games and sports, but at this point he is only feeling his way towards a 'theory'. His note on Goffman registers the hesitancy: 'Performance is an extremely difficult concept to define.' Goffman's view implies that 'performing is a mode of behavior that may characterize *any* activity. Thus performance is a "quality" that can occur in any situation rather than a fenced-off game.' He ducks away from the implications of this by quite properly stating that his own focus in the essay is more limited: 'I thought it best to center my definition of performance around certain acknowledged qualities of theatre' (1966: 27).

Four years later, in 'Actuals: A Look into Performance Theory', he reported on the 'anthropological, sociological, psychological, and historical materials' in which he found 'an incipient theory for a special kind of behaving, thinking, relating, and doing. This special way of handling experience and jumping the gaps between past and present, individual and group, inner and outer, I call "actualizing".' Although he calls it a 'special kind of behaving', Schechner's essay is, again, drawn to aesthetic theatre: 'Understanding actualizing means understanding both the creative condition and the artwork, the actual' (Schechner 1988: 40, 41). By 1973 he had got to a coherent model which was able to define performance as a separate entity from, and larger than, drama. This is set out in the long essay, placed first in the issue of *TDR* on 'social science' which Schechner edited. The argument of 'Drama, Script, Theater, and Performance' is that, since the ancient Greeks, western theatremakers and commentators have given their primary attention to the handling of the words to be spoken in the show. How they were to be spoken and gestured was of lesser importance, and subject to individual variation. Yet prior to this, and outside western theatre, what dictated the activity of a performed event were agreed 'patterns of doing', unalterable specifications as to what needed to take place, that remained constant from one enactment to another. The focus on handling of words, which Schechner calls 'drama', is a local and specialised instance of the larger patterns of doing which he calls 'script'. Similarly there is the relationship of 'theater', designating specific aesthetic activity, and 'performance', designating the full range of activities which surround the theatrical activity. In Schechner's words; 'The drama is the domain of the author, the composer, scenarist, shaman; the script is the domain of the teacher, guru, master; the theater is the domain of the performers; the performance is the domain of the audience.' Acknowledging the slipperiness of the terms, he fixes them visually in a diagram of concentric circles, with 'drama' in the middle and 'performance' as the largest circle which accommodates all the rest. While it has to be noted that there is much overlap and that 'the boundary between the performance and everyday life is shifting and arbitrary, varying greatly from culture to culture', where 'the boundaries are set, it is within the broad region of performance that theater takes place, and at the center of the theater is the script, sometimes the drama.' This then allows for the generation of two binaries: with drama as 'a specialized kind of script' and theatre as 'a specialized kind of performance' (1988: 71).

Clearly here 'performance' is seen as different from 'everyday life', although the 'boundary' between the two changes. What comprises 'performance' is 'The whole constellation of events, most of them passing unnoticed, that take place in/among both performers and audience from the time the first spectator enters'. Now it should be noted that Schechner's focus here is primarily upon the formal aesthetic event, rather than the social 'ceremonies' that interested Duvignaud or indeed the rule-bound behaviours of football fans. Like Duvignaud, however, he is trying to unsettle the focus on dramatic text which had been the primary area of attention in literature, if not theatre, departments. But by contrast with Schechner's argument the contemporary work of sociologists of theatre and culture might suggest that, given that they are not 'everyday behaviour', the 'constellation of events, most of them passing unnoticed' at the gathering, were themselves scripted so to speak, in that audiences learn conventions of behaviour, as do off-stage performers. For instance Schechner says, later on, discussing one of his own productions, 'The audience quickly learned the conventions of the production' (1988: 72, 81). These conventions are not always invariable, and can be locally nuanced, but they do operate from one enactment to another. But those conventions of behaviour are clearly not what Schechner has in mind when he says 'script' is the domain of the guru. So we are left with a notion of convention-governed behaviour that is not everyday life, but that also is not learnt from gurus. Furthermore, those learnt conventions of behaviour allow audiences to distinguish between how they behave on public transport before they get to the theatre and how they behave inside the theatre; they have something to do with identifying, as is necessary, that variable boundary between 'performance' and 'everyday life'. So, although Schechner doesn't have a word for it, one might say there is a potential extra outer circle, beyond 'performance', which is the circle of learnt conventions, a sort of non-guru script, which itself enables the boundaries between the other elements to be identified.

That these various words remained problematic is evidenced from elsewhere in this somewhat rambling essay. If we look at the summary offered after Schechner's reflections on his own production, it says: 'the drama is what the writer writes; the script is the interior map of a particular production; the theater is the specific set of gestures performed by the performers in any given performance; the performance is the whole event.' Earlier on he had said that 'script' 'pre-exists any given enactment, which persists from enactment to enactment', and that 'maintaining it intact contributed to the efficacy of the rite'. As western theatre developed, however, this 'active sense of script' was 'almost entirely displaced by drama', and 'the script no longer functioned as a code for transmitting action through time'. In another summary he says: 'Drama is a tight, verbal narrative; it allows for little improvisation; it exists as a code independent of any individual transmitter; it is, or can easily be made into, a written text. A script – which can be either tight or loose – is either a plan for a traditional event . . . or it is developed during rehearsals to suit a specific text as in orthodox western theater' (1988: 85, 70–71, 91; my elision). By now it is getting quite difficult to hang onto a clear idea of what Schechner means by 'script' or, for that matter, theatre. Script pre-exists any particular show and yet it is developed in rehearsal; it has to be kept intact but yet it is made to suit a specific production. It is displaced by drama and continues to function alongside drama. Theatre is performers' gestures. Which leaves one wondering as to the nature of the activity of 'technicians'. And 'text' doesn't seem to have a place in the circles. But if this is all confusing, then it gets worse in a subsequent essay from the next year, where we're told: 'In drama the script is already fixed in its details, the precise gestures of the role are rehearsed for a particular occasion.' But this blurring can be sorted out if we cease trying to define things according to their internal characteristics: 'A performance is called theater or ritual because of where it is performed, by whom, and under what circumstances' (1988; 114, 120). Here Schechner's eyes are firmly fixed on a binary of 'theatre' and 'ritual', which has to do with 'entertainment' and 'efficacy'. When he was thinking about his concentric circles, in the earlier essay, he told us that 'Ritualized behaviour extends across the entire range of human action, but performance is a particular heated arena of ritual, and theater, script, and drama are heated and compact areas of performance' (1988: 95). The clanging of the overworked central-heating boiler tends to be rather distracting, so for the sake of clarity we could try limiting the play of terms: if 'performance' can be theatre or ritual, then we could say that, rephrasing the sentence above, 'theater or ritual is a particular heated arena of ritual, and theater, script, and drama are heated and compact areas of theater or ritual.' Which still leaves us with the conundrum of whether theatre is contained within ritual or is in binary balance with it, and where script sits.

And indeed, what on earth is 'performance'? This word slides around, often because it is under pressure created by Schechner's interest in writing about his own productions and demonstrating how they make a new sort of theatre by unsettling the privileged position of written text and changing the relationship of performers and audience, allowing the audience to play more of a role in the event. Although his model of concentric circles is based on his own production practice, however, its value is that it can be applied elsewhere, across the range of completely traditional theatre production. For example, one can say that early-modern tragedians knew how tragedies were meant to end, and the same could be said of melodramas where the shapes of the performance and its gestures pre-existed any individual script, which is why a villain that died incorrectly got booed. The concentric circles thus offer a potentially interesting way of thinking about theatrical genres, more productive I think than the bizarre application to theatre history of the 'efficacy-entertainment braid', with what Bottoms (2003: 184) calls its 'near-puritanical' binary (which, as is noted elsewhere, conveniently – perhaps too conveniently – demonstrates that the sort of thing Schechner was directing was part of the richer phases of theatre history; Shepherd and Wallis 2004). But it's a model that would need using with care, for, as we've seen, Schechner's key words slide around in a confusing way. That confusion originates, I suspect, somewhere deeper than the desire to legitimise, and celebrate, his own productions. While the argument properly acknowledges the development and changes of history, the diagram and summary formulations attempt to come up with generalisations that claim to work across time, transhistorically. But that drive to generalise, by ignoring historical specificity, comes up with unreliable terms in a slippery model, a symptom perhaps of things to come. And in the key area of our concern here, unlike Clarke's more precise mapping of the relationship between the football game and its contexts and meanings, Schechner's argument doesn't get us much closer to defining 'performance' in relation to 'everyday life'. That boundary seems flexible not only from culture to culture but within Schechner's own work. And that boundary turned out to be the fault line that ran through the work, threatening to bring its structures, its tables, circles and braids all tumbling down. Suffice to say that the repeated use of the word 'performance' does not itself constitute performance theory.

In these early essays by Schechner 'sociology' is servicing the development of, in the main, a new critical approach to drama, experimental and otherwise. Meanwhile Gurvitch, Duvignaud and Burns suggested that theatre art should be studied in the context of its production processes and labour force, its institutions and its consumers. In doing so they cultivated an interdisciplinary approach which opens out toward the wider society, looking at its group interactions and the social roles of individuals. Ahead of Schechner, when Duvignaud sought to describe the specific functioning of social ceremony he drew on anthropological work from the late 1950s. His interest in classical tragedy led him to explore what role the activity of performing tragedy played in the life of a town. Like Duvignaud's model of 'social ceremony', Burns's work on 'conventions' is an attempt to describe that which has symbolic and representational resonance but which is clearly differentiated from theatre practice. In offering to account for various modes of cultural and social behaviour that could include, on the same spectrum, both civic gatherings and aesthetic entertainments these models formulate a meta-language that is locked neither into theatre studies nor into sociology.

The meta-language, trying to describe qualities held in common by theatre and daily behaviour, may be said to be defining an activity that can be called 'performance'. But, as we know from Goffman and others, there is a different way of looking at the relationship of theatre and daily behaviour. In this relationship theatre acts as a metaphor, or an analogy, providing a way of framing daily life in order to think about it in a different way. This use of it came to constitute what some sociologists called 'performance theory'. An example of this second relationship, of 'performance theory' in operation, may be seen in an extended reflection on performance as a way of doing thinking that was published in 1975.

Lyman and Scott's *The Drama of Social Reality* maps out a long line of quasi-sociological engagement with theatre and suggests a critical method that arises from the analogy of theatre and everyday life. For them the study of drama was fundamental to doing social science, since 'reality is a drama, life is theatre, and the social world inherently dramatic.' Behind those phrases you can hear a queue of thinkers, reaching back, at the earliest point, to Evreinoff's book *The Theatre of Life*, published in 1927. Here Evreinoff claims to have discovered a persistent theatricality in all of life, including among animals. A time is coming, he said, 'when we will at last realize that there is just as much "theatre" in "nature" as there is of "nature" in "theatre"' (2013: 21). For Lyman and Scott, Evreinoff's text contained 'the fundamentals for a new political sociology' (1975: 2–3, 112). It also offered an introduction to the way of thinking, the 'dramatistic ontology', proposed in Kenneth Burke's *Grammar of Motives* (1945). This, as we know, tried to establish general rules for the ways in which motives are attributed to human actions. It is in the work of Evreinoff and Burke – and also Gustav Ichheiser – that Lyman and Scott see the influences of Goffman's 'dramaturgical' approach to everyday behaviour.

Their critical method is tried out on selected plays of Shakespeare. But Lyman and Scott also insist that it provides a theoretical apparatus for social science: 'Social scientists who theorize within the framework of performance theory must behave, in the first instance, like an *audience* at a drama.' Theatre audiences, say Lyman and Scott, bracket off the stage 'in a special frame'. When the social scientist does likewise, 'he refuses, in effect, to take for granted the meanings-in-the-world that are typically and regularly available to and enacted by his human subjects.' The analogy with drama works because it de-naturalises the everyday and makes it available for reading. It also attends to a more phenomenological understanding of the observable world. At this point Lyman and Scott then progress beyond Goffman, who 'is committed to the notion of drama as mere metaphor, a heuristic tool for delivering the various strategies for "impression management"'. By contrast Burke's 'dramatism' is 'both a method of analysis and an ontology', a claim which they underpin with a quotation from Burke: 'drama is employed, not as a metaphor but as a fixed form that helps us discover what the implications of the terms "act" and "person" *really are.*' Their reaching back to Burke enables Lyman and Scott to suggest something that went much further than 'drama-turgical' sociology, indeed something that would become the stamping ground, so to speak, of 'performance' scholars: 'In using such phrases as "dramatistic approach" and "performance theory", we are pointing to a perspective that involves both ontological and heuristic features associated with the notion of drama.' By way of demonstrating their perspective they analyse slave resistance in the United States. What interests them in particular is the tactic of resistance whereby the slave developed 'dual personae (i.e., masks) for presentation to the different audiences he faces'. This enabled the slaves to 'take over the masters' definitions of and attitudes toward Negroes and use them to undermine the masters' power'. In the 1990s this might be seen as having something to do with citation and performativity. For Lyman and Scott in 1975 it evidences what they call 'dramatic artistry' (1975: 3, 163–64, 168–69, 131–32).

In getting to this point Lyman and Scott have shown something more than the operation of 'performance theory' as a frame for thinking. They have also shown that the frame can be deployed not simply to explain modes of behaviour but to highlight significant features. The frame can be placed on any material of the analyst's choosing, and therefore reading a performance becomes a way of examining or, perhaps more forcefully, dramatising ethical and political selection. In a similar way Burns proposed that the imposition of the performance frame had effects in the real world. She opens her book by talking about the common use of the word 'theatrical' to describe certain sorts of behaviour. But, she says, you can only describe behaviour as theatrical if you know what drama is, that's to say if you are in the position of an observer who 'recognises certain patterns and sequences which are analogous' to those familiar in theatre. So we have to acknowledge that 'theatricality' does not denote 'a mode of behaviour or expression, but attaches to any kind of behaviour perceived and interpreted by others and described (mentally or explicitly) in theatrical terms. These others are more aware of the symbolic than of the instrumental aspect of any behaviour which they feel they can describe as theatrical.' By way of example, later on, she instances Conor Cruise O'Brien's account of the activity in the United Nations building: 'The drama-tisation and moralisation of the interplay . . . speeds up the process in the real world. The playing out of roles before the gallery evokes a need to sustain them into real life' (Burns 1972: 12–13, 135; my elision). But while Lyman and Scott describe their use of the performance frame as 'performance theory', Burns of course uses the word: 'theatricality'. The two applications do the same job of work and seem to amount to the same sort of process. The irony is that 'performance' becomes the dominant term. For if Goffman is the ultimate father of the concept of performed behaviour, Burns, assimilating micro-sociology and French theatre sociology, achieved a comprehensive theorisa-tion under the name of 'theatricality'. This was done in advance of much that followed under the name of performance. How that name got there interests us next.

Chapter 3

Ethnography, folklore and communicative events

Between them Chicago sociology and French sociological theatre studies extended the range of what could be considered to be performed human behaviour. In order to think about this activity, they initially drew analogies from aesthetic theatre, but this work was then moved away from explicit theatrical models by the Centre for Contemporary Cultural Studies at the University of Birmingham's (CCCS) study of culture as text and by Burns's work on conventions. While this all began to put in place an object of study that was neither theatre nor everyday behaviour, it tended not to be called 'performance'. The development of the use of that term came instead from elsewhere, from a specific branch of ethnography which studied folklore. 'During the past quarter century', said William Hugh Jansen, in 1957, 'there has been growing concern among folklorists about a rather imponderable quantity called performance – particularly performance of the folktale and folksong.' In order to make it somewhat less imponderable Jansen proposed a system for classifying the performance of verbal folklore. He also recommended that, in addition to the study of the content of folklore, 'there should be more consideration of the manner of folklore, of that dual but inseparable process of performance and reception.' In making this recommendation he was at the same time extending what might be meant by the word 'performance'. He acknowledges that in speaking of oral verbal folklore 'one must employ the term *performance* in something like its theatrical or dramatic definition', but then he notes that folklore compels a new application of the word:

> the element that I can find no term for except *performance* does not exist until the 'doer,' the speaker, or the reciter of the bit of folklore steps outside himself as an individual and assumes a pose toward his audience, however small, that differs from his everyday, every-hour-in-the-day relationship to the same audience. Integral in this posing is a purpose. The poser is *as poser* a teacher, a monitor, or an entertainer; he may be any one or any combination of the three.

From here Jansen offers some illustrative situations showing the potential range across what we might call performance's functions as efficacy and entertainment, and he then suggests 'three ways to weigh the degree of performance or the anticipation of performance': the form of the performed item, its particular function, the actual performer (Jansen 1957: 110, 112–13).

While Jansen's thinking about folklore methodology pushed him to extend the concept of performance in a direction that would have been quite normal in the 1990s, back in 1957 it seemed that the word was under too much pressure to be useful: 'another term for this quantity is badly needed' (Jansen 1957: 117). Indeed in an essay a few years later, in 1964, Dell Hymes proposed the adoption of the phrase 'ethnography of communication' for describing communicative events very like those that concerned Jansen. For Hymes the prevailing methodology of linguistics was not adequate to describe 'the place of language in culture and society', and there needed to be, besides linguistics, 'a second descriptive science comprising language', a proposition he sees as supported by Goffman's work on face-to-face interactions (see pp. 3–5). This 'second descriptive science' is the ethnography of communication, which has as its main aim the refusal when considering the communicative event of any separation between 'message-form (sign type) and context of use'. This refusal is in line, he suggests, with the general change in anthropology 'away from the study of cultural content as product toward its study as process, away from study of abstracted categories, departments of culture, toward study of situations and events'. So too it is in line with the shift that broadened linguistics to include 'communicative means other than language' within its scope. Within this context, the ethnography of communication will lead to a set of changes which are, in summary, 'emphasis and primacy of speech over code; function over structure; context over message; the ethnographically appropriate over the ethnologically arbitrary; but the interrelations always crucial, so that one can not only generalize the particularities, but also particularize the generalities' (Hymes 1964: 3, 6, 11).

Hymes is dealing with something more than folklore studies, but his proposal is in the same spirit as Jansen's recommendation that one study not just the content but the 'manner' of folklore, 'the inseparable process of performance and reception'. He goes further than Jansen, however, in attempting to categorise the various elements that should be addressed in studying a communicative event. Basing these on communications theory and Jakobson's linguistics, he suggests:

> (1,2) the various kinds of participants in communicative events – senders and receivers, addressors and addressees, interpreters and spokesmen, and

the like; (3) the various available channels, and their modes of use, speaking, writing, printing, drumming, blowing, whistling, singing, face and body motion as visually perceived, smelling, tasting, and tactile sensation; (4) the various codes shared by various participants, linguistic, paralinguistic, kinesic, musical, and other; (5) the settings (including other communication) in which communication is permitted, enjoined, encouraged, abridged; (6) the forms of messages, and their genres, ranging verbally from single-morpheme sentences to the patterns and diacritics of sonnets, sermons, salesmen's pitches, and other organized routines and styles; (7) the topics and comments that a message may be about; (8) the events themselves, their kinds and characters as wholes.

This list of elements would form a useful starting point – and regularly do – for analyses of all sorts of performances. It is notable, given later concerns, that Hymes includes both addressors and addressees within the category of 'participants', that he allows for the potential flexibility of 'settings', and that verbal language is only one item amongst a variety of 'channels'. And, although he doesn't call these communicative events 'performances', he is as concerned as Jansen to note that they have to be distinguished from 'behavior and interaction in general' (Hymes 1964: 13, 17). This is why he itemises the elements that constitute the communicative event.

The other reason it is important to list these elements is to demonstrate the difference of an approach that looks at, for example, 'the structures, degrees of elaboration, distinctiveness, values and genres associated with channels, codes, message-forms and settings'. These 'aspects of communication', says Hymes, would not receive much attention in studies of communication that were more interested in it 'as a problem of achieving, through situations and others, purposes of one's own'. By contrast the anthropologist 'is likely to look at communication from the standpoint and interests of the local community itself, as well as from the outside, and see its members not as objects of persuasion and manipulation, but as potential sources of knowledge and insight' (Hymes 1964: 11–12). It is tempting to see this as a swipe at Goffman's 'dramaturgical' analysis of social interaction in which 'impression management' figures large. Whatever, this is certainly an explicit assertion that anthropology is on the side of community. And it is that ethical position-ing, alongside the analytical methodology, that will become another key element in anthropology's shaping of the concept of performance.

But performance was not Hymes's word in this essay. Discussions among cultural anthropologists in the late 1960s and early 1970s indicate how the concept of performance begins by being mainly entangled with, and some-times obscured by, the general idea of 'communication'. It gradually crystallises out as a concept in its own right as the seventies progress. This comes before the transformation of the academic discipline of communication as 'oral interpretation' into Performance Studies which has been well charted (see pp. 151–52), so we need to clarify how folklore study developed its own idea of performance.

At the opening of their book called *Folklore: Performance and Communication*, which was published in 1975, Dan Ben-Amos and Kenneth Goldstein tell us that their book grew out of a session they organised for the annual meeting of the American Folklore Society in 1969. Their session was called 'Folklore and Communication', and included papers by Dell Hymes, Richard Bauman and Barbara Kirshenblatt-Gimblett. Commenting on the changes in their discipline, Ben-Amos and Goldstein note a shift from focus on text to context, a shift that perhaps began with Malinowski's insistence in 1926 that the fairy-tale text has to be related to the manner in which the tale is told, its time setting and even the context of the function of the event and private ownership. From here this shift in folklore studies introduces 'communication and performance' as 'key terms', thereby freeing folklore from its 'literary bonds'. This shift in approach to folklore has a clear point of origin. It 'derives much of its theory and method from the field of sociolinguistics. It owes a direct debt to Hymes' idea of "the ethnography of communication". This application of linguistic theories and methods to the social dimensions of speaking recast communication in culture into a new mold.' It gave folklore scholars new tools for analysis, enabling them to uncover 'rules for social verbal behavior'. And although 'text' was still important they needed also to draw on 'proxemic, kinesic, paralinguistic, interactional descriptions'. To develop a new vocabulary and methods, scholars such as those in *Folklore* look to 'literature and linguistics, anthropology and sociology, and more specifically to recent studies on human communication, interactional analysis, semiotics, proxemics, kinesics, ethno- and psycholinguistics'. Folklorists are thus deliberately multi-disciplinary (Ben-Amos and Goldstein 1975: 3–4). Indeed *Folklore* was published in a series on Semiotics.

The link of performance and communication does, however, contain dangers according to Dell Hymes. His essay for the volume was not the paper he gave back in 1969 but a more recent work in which he reviews developments in the field. What concerns him initially here is the sloppy use of the concept of 'performance'. 'Performance is not merely behavior, but neither is it the same as all of culture (or conduct, or communication).' While 'some grammarians have confused matters, by lumping what does not interest them under "performance", as a residual category', and one wonders if he is thinking about the philosopher J.L. Austin here, cultural anthropologists and folklorists 'have tended to lump what *does* interest us under "performance", simply as an honorific designation'. Performance, he says, is not a 'wastebasket' term, but has to be regarded as a very specific activity, a 'quite special category', because it is 'a key to much of the difference in the meaning of life as between communities'. While, as he adds, analytical categories may of course change as research develops, there are some basic distinctions which should be kept clear:

> There is *behavior*, as simply anything and everything that happens; there is *conduct*, behavior under the aegis of social norms, cultural rules, shared principles of interpretability; there is *performance*, when one or more persons assumes responsibility for presentation. And within performance itself, as the doable or repeatable, there is the pole that can be termed performance full, authentic or authoritative performance, when the standards intrinsic to the tradition in which the performance occurs are accepted and realized.   (Hymes 1975: 13, 18)

Hymes's strictures are echoed by Kirshenblatt-Gimblett who insists that instead of broadly indicative descriptions of contexts there should be focus on '*actual* narrative events' where folklore 'in its immediate context of use' will be seen as 'a highly structured, integrated form of interpersonal behavior' (Kirshenblatt-Gimblett 1975: 107).

Just as does Kirshenblatt-Gimblett, Hymes moves into detailed analysis of a set of case studies to show how 'authentic or authoritative performance occurs only at a certain point or in a certain respect'. Where it is not 'authentic or authoritative' the performance is merely 'illustrative' or 'reportive', and that difference is made by such things as 'knowing tradition and presenting it; between knowing what and knowing how'. Where for example the 'language of telling is not the language of the tradition, but of interpretation', it is not authentic performance of a myth. To get at the differences with which Hymes is concerned requires the innovation in folklore of 'serious stylistic analysis', indeed 'the literary criticism', of native traditions (Hymes 1975: 18, 66, 69). While Hymes turns to 'literary criticism' methodology, for her analysis Kirshenblatt-Gimblett draws on Erving Goffman in order to consider her topic, parable speaking, as an example of 'a highly structured, integrated form of interpersonal behavior'. Using Goffman's definition of a 'unit' of spoken interaction she analyses the performance, the report of it and the informant's answers to questions, where the performance is a distinct element. Important for later developments in the ethnographic interest in performance is Kirshenblatt-Gimblett's adoption here of Goffman's sense of the *function* of '"interpersonal ritual behavior" which attempts to restore harmony after someone has "made a scene"' (Kirshenblatt-Gimblett 1975: 107-08).

A couple of years after Hymes noted the increasingly sloppy use of the term, in 1977 Richard Bauman noted that 'In recent years, the concept of performance has begun to assume central importance in the orientation of increasing numbers of folklorists and others interested in verbal art.' His specific reference point here is a 1972 conference of folklorists. As used by these scholars the word 'performance' conveys 'a dual sense of artistic *action* – the doing of folklore – and artistic *event* – the performance situation'. Such usage points to a disciplinary shift, which we also saw described by Hymes, 'from folklore-as-materials to folklore-as-communication'. Bauman's 1977 book, *Verbal Art as Performance*, is, however, much more than an account of new scholarship within cultural anthropology and folklore studies. Its main aim is to 'develop a conception of verbal art as performance, based upon an understanding of performance as a mode of speaking' (Bauman 1977: 4, 3), and in doing so it makes a very significant contribution to the articulation and extension of what might be meant by 'performance'.

Although Bauman's original 1975 essay of the same name was published in the *American Anthropologist* his approach, he says, is not just that of a folklorist and linguistic anthropologist but also comes from his 'earlier training in literature'; indeed his 'commitments are fundamentally interdisciplinary'. This interdisciplinarity, with literary study as an early training, may recall the approach of those who founded the CCCS (see above pp. 10–11). Through the seventies the academic discipline of English literature, at least in the United Kingdom, was in crisis as to its identity, but other disciplinary changes were also afoot. The upheavals led, among other things, to mutations into cultural or linguistic anthropology (Dwight Conquergood is another who took Bauman's path) and to challenges to established practices. In several of the growth areas there was a sense that interdisciplinarity was underpinning a necessary break with tradition, where the traditional was often characterised as the verbal 'text'. Bauman says that where 'text' is taken as the unit of analysis this severely constrains 'the development of a meaningful framework for the understanding of verbal art as performance, as a species of situated human communication, a way of speaking'. Later in his essay he proposes that even the text can be reconceptualised when taken away from its abstraction on 'the written page' and resituated within the context of performance. In a remark that echoes Raymond Williams, amongst many others, he notes that such a move will place the text 'within an analytical context which focuses on the very source of the empirical relationship between art and society' (Bauman 1977: vii, 8, 40).

It is the task of understanding performance as a very particular way of speaking, as against any other ways of speaking, that leads Bauman towards an attempt to define the 'nature' of performance. Unlike other commentaries, though, this project does not involve the search for an 'essence' of performance but instead seeks to identify recurrent formal features. His first step is to suggest that performance 'sets up, or represents, an interpretative frame within which the messages being communicated are to be understood, and that this frame contrasts with at least one other frame, the literal', even though, as he later says, in spoken communication there is probably 'no such thing as naked literalness'. The introduction of the idea of 'frame' is borrowed from Gregory Bateson and Erving Goffman, and the discussion of literalness, where Bauman is arguing against the normative approach of the linguistic philosopher Austin, draws on the literary scholar Stanley Fish and the theatre theorist Elizabeth Burns. This is the range of disciplinary mix which informs Bauman's attempt to describe the 'kind of interpretive frame performance establishes' and to specify its 'interpretive guidelines'. 'Fundamentally', performance, he suggests, is 'a mode of spoken verbal communication' in which the performer takes on 'accountability to an audience for the way in which communication is carried out'. The importance of this definition is that in a stroke it broadens the concept of what performance might be: 'it is no longer necessary to begin with artful texts, identified on independent formal grounds and then reinjected into situations of use, in order to conceptualize verbal art in communicative terms' (Bauman 1977: 9–11).

Having demoted 'artful texts' and broken free of them, Bauman then empirically illustrates his point with a set of specific cultural examples drawn from various ethnographers. This leads him, via Goffman's suggestion as to how frames are invoked or 'keyed', to the observation that

> each speech community will make use of a structured set of distinctive
> communicative means from among its resources in culturally
> conventionalized and culture-specific ways to key the performance
> frame, such that all communication that takes place within that frame is
> to be understood as performance within that community.

He then works through a list of the various 'communicative means' whereby performance is keyed in different cultures. This list makes very clear that we are not simply dealing with language but also with 'paralinguistic features' such as those identified by Dennis Tedlock in 1972: 'rate, length, pause duration, pitch contour, tone of voice, loudness, and stress'. Observation of paralinguistic features indicates that 'what is important is the contrast between performance and other ways of speaking' (Bauman 1977: 16, 20).

Once you take performance as 'an interpretive frame', art ceases to be a special category but sits within a range of other modes of performance:

> conceived as performance, in terms of an interpretive frame, verbal art may be culturally defined as varying in intensity as well as range. We are not speaking here of the relative quality of a performance – good performance vs. bad performance – but the degree of intensity with which the performance frame operates in a particular range of culturally defined ways of speaking.

The separation of 'art' and 'life' vanishes; 'art' is an effect of intensification; and intensification varies. If you combine this observation with the notion of performance as 'situated behavior' then you can add to the intensifications of communicative means the effect of 'settings', 'the culturally defined places where performance occurs'. Having said this, Bauman then makes a step which puts him in the territory of Jean Duvignaud's comments on social ceremonies: 'Institutions too – religion, education, politics – may be viewed from the perspective of the way in which they do or do not represent contexts for performance.' Similar also to Duvignaud is his later note about 'performance roles' where it is necessary to analyse 'the relationship, both social and behavioral, between such roles and other roles played by the same individual' (Bauman 1977: 24, 27, 31).

Beyond setting, the most important 'organizing principle in the ethnography of performance is the event (or scene) within which performance occurs'. Bauman here references the 1974 work of Barbara Kirshenblatt-Gimblett. He then explains that the word 'event' is used to 'designate a culturally defined, bounded segment of the flow of behavior and experience constituting a meaningful context for action'. Used that way, the interactions of football fans outside the stadium may be said to be 'events'. The most obvious examples, however, are those 'for which performance is required', and here Bauman invokes Singer's 'cultural performances'. But, and this is the killer blow,

> As interesting as cultural performances are, performance occurs outside of them as well, and the most challenging job that faces the student of performance is establishing the continuity between the noticeable and public performance of cultural performances, and the spontaneous, unscheduled, optional performance contexts of everyday life.
> (Bauman 1977: 27–28)

In effect Bauman has here written a key part of the curriculum of those who, years later, were to see themselves as performance studyers. And obviously, without calling it such, he has, in 1977, formulated that defining article of faith for such students, the 'broad spectrum' approach to performance study.

Having evolved over twenty years from being an 'imponderable quantity', the concept of performance modelled by folklorists set in place some of the foundations assumed by later studies of performance. It enabled an approach to performance that doesn't bind it in with artworks; it kept performance separate from other modes of spoken communication and behaviour; it drew out general features while insisting on cultural specificity of practices.

Chapter 4

Cultural performance, social drama and liminality

While the folklorists were trying to identify the ways in which 'performance' could be related to and distinguished from everyday behaviours, other cultural anthropologists were interested in the social functions of events that were clearly framed as performances. This area of inquiry took anthropology very close to analysis not merely of non-theatrical performances but also of aesthetic theatre itself. For our purposes here, this development is interesting because it works towards a concept of performance as an overarching category which includes a variety of different kinds of event.

The research in this area is usually assumed to start with the work of Milton Singer in Madras in the mid-1950s. It had come out of the same School of Sociology at Chicago as produced the work of Goffman and Becker. At Chicago Singer worked alongside Robert Redfield and other colleagues to explore the role of cities within social and cultural modernisation. This role was particularly interesting in the case of a city which was so thoroughly governed by traditional beliefs and practices as was Madras. Singer came to believe that he could understand the operation of these beliefs, and their role in resisting or negotiating change, by watching religious ceremonies, which he categorised as 'cultural performances'. He developed this approach on the advice of an Indian colleague, the great Sanskrit specialist, Venkataraman Raghavan. So we should note, in passing, that, insofar as 'cultural performance' is one of its foundational concepts, the extended notion of performance that we now accept has one of its points of origin in the Indian academy.

Singer, be it said, placed great value on his Indian colleagues even though his was the only name that went into the western publishing machine, with his first book, *Traditional India* (1959), consisting of essays by various authors, including Raghavan, and published by the American Folklore Society. The concept of cultural performance was more fully developed in a later book, *When a Great Tradition Modernizes*, in 1972. Here Singer explained how Indian friends thought of their civilisation as 'encapsulated' in the performances of religious ceremonies: 'The performances became for me the

elementary constituents of the culture and the ultimate units of observation.'
Each of these units has 'a definitely limited time span, a beginning and an end,
an organized program of activity, a set of performers, an audience, and a place
and occasion of performance' (1972: 71). While other Chicago colleagues may
have observed and categorised 'everyday' social interaction, moving from the
detail of gesture and facial expression to larger concepts as to how individuals
present themselves to others, Singer took the routine ceremonies of southern
Indian society and, by closely analysing their detail, moved to an understanding of 'more abstract structures within a comprehensive cultural system'.
The ceremonies at which he was looking comprised weddings, temple festivals, recitations, plays, dances and musical concerts. Together these comprised 'cultural performances' because, through analysing their detail, 'it is
possible to arrive at the more comprehensive and abstract constructs of
cultural structure, cultural value system, and a Great Tradition.' The method
of the analysis worked in two directions: not only did it describe 'the structure
and organization of particular kinds of performances' but it also moved across
performances, comparing them one with another, 'tracing the linkages among
these structures and organizations' (1959: 145). The model of cultural performance thus was founded on the idea that one performance is not an isolated
event but part of a system of interlocked enactments that together constitute
the mode of operation of a whole society. Furthermore the analysis of these
performances was in effect a process of reading, where that process did not
necessarily fix on what the performance was trying to represent but instead
sought to describe the way it was structured and organised.

As a model, as opposed to the way the model is used, cultural performance
has much in common with Victor Turner's model of 'social drama'. This
Turner explained in his 1974 book *Drama, Fields, and Metaphors* as a unit of
social process that arises in a situation of conflict. It typically contains four
phases: breach of the norms, crisis, redressive action to solve the crisis and
social reintegration. As he later said, 'such social dramas revealed the "taxo-
nomic" relations among actors (their kinship ties, structural positions, social
class, political status, and so forth)' together with personal networks and
bonds. We are not only talking of simple tribal societies here. By 1982
Turner was arguing that 'the social drama is a well-nigh universal processual
form' (Turner 1982: 9, 71), but there are two important qualifications to this.
The first is that the 'cultural ways' in which we apprehend social drama 'vary
with culture, climate, technology, group history, and the demography of
individual genius', so there are limits on generalisation. The second qualifica-
tion insists that 'social drama' was 'hardly a "natural" form, since it was
heavily dependent on the cultural values and rules by which human conduct,

as distinct from behavior, was assessed' (Turner 1984: 20). That distinction between conduct and behaviour indicates that we are still in the world of the Centre for Contemporary Cultural Studies and Burns, with its learnt, and culturally specific, rules and conventions.

Up to this point, however, the model of 'social drama' may look as if it is doing little more than applying to social interactions and processes the metaphor of theatre, in a similar way to Goffman. Indeed Turner was criticised on just these grounds. But in defending his use of the theatre analogy, he demonstrated that he was talking about activity that went beyond, and subsumed, aesthetic performances: 'My contention is that social dramas are the raw stuff out of which theater comes to be created as societies develop in scale and complexity and out of which it is continually regenerated' (1984: 24). The justification for this argument was already implicit in Turner's earlier analyses of 'social drama'. Back in 1974 he said that the mechanisms used to contain the potential damage from breach of norms may include 'formal juridical and legal machinery' or 'performance of public ritual' (in Turner 1992: 75). To explain how ritual works Turner uses the idea of 'liminality'. This he takes from the Belgian anthropologist Arnold van Gennep's description of the three-phase process, the *rite de passage*, by which societies and their members negotiate change. Phases one and three consist of separation from society and reincorporation, and between them comes an in-between or liminal state (literally, in Latin, a threshold). In a *rite de passage* that, for example, initiates boys into manhood, the boys are separated from the village and enter a space where the previous norms no longer apply and the new norms are not yet in place. The attempt to describe this ambiguous state generates much symbolism, a creative effect in which Turner gets increasingly interested.

In a relatively early work, in 1969, he was focused on liminality within the process of initiation, where the neophytes were totally obedient to whatever was happening even while they developed intense comradeship among themselves (Turner 1995: 95). In the context not of initiation, however, but of the public life of the community with its big public festivals, liminality is a mechanism which enables that community to reflect on and understand itself. It can do this precisely because it is not governed by normal order and thus allows for possibility, supposition, experiment and play, like a verb in subjunctive mood. Thus, 'for every major social formation there is a dominant mode of public liminality, the subjunctive space/time that is the counterstroke to its pragmatic indicative texture.' The public liminal mode might be ritual in simpler societies and carnival and theatre in more complex ones. Set up in binary contrast with the 'indicative', all subjunctive modes, ranging across ritual, theatre, play and philosophical speculation, can be grouped into one category, and the name they can be given is the dominant mode of 'public reflexivity', namely performance (Turner 1977: 33–34).

But liminality here is working as something that goes beyond a categorising device. Generating more than symbols, liminality is 'often the scene and time for the emergence of a society's deepest values in the form of sacred dramas and objects'. It may also be the place for 'the most radical skepticism' (1984: 22). It is not just a state where norms are suspended but a mood or quality which is expressed in all forms of performance, and it also has an effect on those doing the performance. Liminality, says Turner, facilitates 'the liberation of human capacities of cognition, affect, volition, creativity, etc., from the normative constraints'. Writing in 1982 he sees liminality as 'an instant of pure potentiality when everything, as it were trembles in the balance' (1982: 44). This is somewhere rather different from the image in 1969 of liminality as, in part, obedient, 'passive or humble', accepting 'arbitrary punishment without complaint' (1995: 95). The difference is accounted for, at least as Turner has it, in the contrast between tribal societies and others. Whereas in tribal society everything within the liminal phase is done under obligation, even breaking rules, in a different society, say New York in the 1970s, liberation becomes much more possible, apparently. Now it is perfectly feasible to suggest that this different emphasis comes after Turner spent a period of time, in the late seventies, working with the experimental theatre director Richard Schechner and, because of his own love of drama, got excited by the potential seemingly offered by the new experimental work, with its emphasis on group interaction, improvisation, joint creativity and political engagement. But whatever the cause, the effect was to make a version of liminality that seemed in line with, if not shaped by, seventies' experimental theatre. And this is the version that tended to be cited by performance specialists for decades to come. It was a liminality that no longer hovered ambiguously. To do performance was to be 'liminal', and to be 'liminal' was to be creative and liberated, and, indeed, purely potent.

But liminality, we must recognise, is only an element of the 'social drama', having to do in particular with the crisis phase. And however convincingly aesthetic performance may seem to put you in touch with society's deepest values this is not to be confused with the 'social drama' itself: 'A social drama is the major form of plural reflexivity in human social action. It is not yet an aesthetic mode, for it is fully embodied in daily living. But it contains the germs of aesthetic modes, both in its jural and ritual operations' (1984: 25). Later on some people, perhaps in the heady circumstances of New York in the 1970s, were going to confuse aesthetic performance with all sorts of daily living, but Turner insists on the precision of the separation. And indeed, at the conference where he delivered this argument, there were colleagues who insisted on being even more precise.

That conference was devoted to 'cultural performances'. In his essay in the conference book, Turner says that what links all cultural performances is that they belong to the 'subjunctive' mood, and he lists 'Ritual, carnival, festival, theater, film, and similar performative genres' as 'clearly' possessing its attributes (1984: 20). The problem with the list, though, is that despite all his carefulness about aesthetic modes such as theatre, when categorised as 'cultural performances' they all slip into equivalence with one another. That equivalence is what John MacAloon, the editor of the volume, disputes in his own essay, which is about the spectacles associated with the Olympic Games. In the course of it he develops a theory as to what defines a 'spectacle' in order to distinguish it from other 'performative events'. The insistence on making the distinction is a way of combating the drive to generalise across different kinds of event which MacAloon sees as a problem for performance analysis. It will not do, he says, 'to subsume the entire Olympic phenomenon under one traditional rubric – for example "ritual". If it is true that genre theory is today moribund in literary studies, Raymond Williams is surely correct that this sort of "cramming" is in large measure to blame' (1984: 242).

By this stage we can make two observations. The first is that the concepts of cultural performance and social drama seem to offer an insight into how a society manages itself and, in particular, negotiates change. As Catherine Bell put it, Singer and Turner make a break from seeing ritual performances as projections of existing social relations, instead seeing them 'as modes of expressing cultural ideas and dispositions'. Going further, they point the way to viewing 'such cultural expressions as the very activity by which culture is constantly constructed and reproduced' (1998: 208). The second observation here is that, in order for this insight into culture to be precise, the constituent elements of social drama, the performative events, have to be regarded as serving particular purposes. As several people have said so far, a generalised notion of performance which works the same way across all events will not be sufficiently precise to be useful. So while performance emerges as a way of describing and thinking about special sorts of human behaviour it also requires that we understand the detailed ways in which these performed behaviours differ from one another.

Chapter 5

Performance as a new sort of knowledge

Goffman's 'dramaturgical' analysis, the readings of social rituals done by the Centre for Contemporary Cultural Studies and the understanding of role and convention established by theatre sociology all seek to establish information about particular sorts of human interactions. In a similar way Singer's and Turner's models claim to establish information about how societies work, as whole societies. What they all have in common is that they are producing this information by treating their objects of investigation as forms of performance. This information is very different from the largely statistical, and measurable, data that were previously gathered in order to understand social processes. An approach which frames and analyses its objects of study as performance thus seems to give access to new sorts of knowledge.

For example, it could bring about a change of emphasis from 'systems of representation' to 'processes of practice and performance', from texts to actions, from 'symbol structures' to 'physical habitus'. This is how two cultural geographers, Dirksmeier and Helbrecht, describe the impact on their discipline from viewing life 'as a performance'. For them this new way of looking and thinking offered an alternative to 'a growing discontent within the traditional social sciences and their understanding of practices as texts or representations of genuinely symbolic concepts' (2008: 4). Cultural geographers had become aware that a focus simply on representation could not give access to that which was not representable, leading to the development of so-called non-representational theory. In his overview of this 'theory', Lorimer notes that a range of different positions concur by insisting on 'expanding our once comfortable understanding of "the social" and how it can be regarded as something researchable', where the research is interested in 'how life takes shape and gains expression in shared experiences, everyday routines, fleeting encounters, embodied movements, precognitive triggers, practical skills, affective intensities, enduring urges, unexceptional interactions and sensuous dispositions'. He then focuses on research into gardens, homes and work (Lorimer 2005: 84).

The single mechanism which facilitated this change of interest was the notion of 'performance'. In 2000 a special issue of *Environment and Planning D* was devoted to this notion 'whose hold is becoming general across much of the social sciences and humanities', from architecture to history of science. In their editorial essay Thrift and Dewsbury list the domains in which the notion of performance has changed thinking: 'it expands our knowledge of how we know what we know about the world', 'it provides a way of talking and writing in much greater depth about how cultural attributes are passed on', 'it provides all manner of means of understanding space as lived', and it 'can create access to different kinds of times, and especially times of enchantment which resist the process of historicisation'. This impact on thinking has produced two major changes in the practices of geographers. First, it has opened up academic method, for although 'qualitative methods are often noised abroad as both comprehensive and sensitive to circumstances', they 'boil down to semistructured interviews, focus groups, and generally short-term ethnographies'. Instead performance offers a range of techniques for 'making the world come alive', leading both to research into such things as emotions and to academic presentations that are more theatrical. Second, performance has changed practices 'by stressing that performance is itself a form of knowledge, an intelligence in-action', leading, for example, to explorations of somatic action and musical improvisation (Thrift and Dewsbury 2000: 411, 420–26).

To Thrift and Dewsbury's list of areas engaging with the concept of performance can be added law and religious studies. In an extraordinary, and long, essay from 1992 Bernard Hibbitts addresses what he sees as a deficiency in analysis of the communication of legal meaning by non-verbal means in non-literate societies. The method for addressing this deficiency is taken from the concept of 'performance culture'. Although Hibbitts says this is in effect 'oral culture' his essay nevertheless attends to fluency in 'speech, gesture, touch, smell, and taste' as well as the 'theatrical' combination of different media when communicating a message in preliterate societies (Hibbitts 1992: 8). In religious studies, by 1998 'performance' had become a necessary 'critical term'. Just as cultural geography was enabled to break from focus merely on texts and representations, so too in religious studies 'the language of performance is usually invoked to counter the scholarly tendency to approach religious activity as if it were either a type of scriptural text to be analysed or the mere physical execution of a pre-existing ideology.' By framing and approaching its object of enquiry differently the concept of performance enables new understanding: 'the rubric of performance has been indispensable to the articulation of the specifically cultural dynamics involved in religious activity, thereby recognizing religious life as more than a functional expression of conceptual beliefs or social relationships.' Getting beyond that which is merely functional or mechanically reactive, 'Performance approaches seek to explore how activities *create* culture, authority, transcendence, and whatever forms of holistic ordering are required for people to act in meaningful and effective ways.' In this account of the term 'performance', which is surely one of the very best accounts available, Catherine Bell moves on to show the sorts of insights produced by the performance approach. These include analysis of the formal devices that produce efficacy, showing that 'ritual action does what it does by virtue of its dynamic, diachronic, physical and sensual characteristics'; engagement with 'human agents as active creators', not simply being moulded into the status quo by ritual but fashioning 'rituals that shape their world'; use of analytic vocabulary that attends to the 'emotional, aesthetic, physical, and sensory aspects' of religion; reconsideration of the impacts of orality and literacy, with performance theories encouraging scholars to attend to 'those practices which have no scriptural basis'; and, finally, greater awareness of 'the scholar's own position', where the reflexivity inherent in performance problematises 'claims to simple objectivity', and indeed sometimes leads to scholars of rituals making their own performances. After listing these areas of knowledge produced by a performance approach, Bell illustrates them from a specific example of Chinese incense burning (Bell 1998: 206–10).

The new approach based on the concept of performance is given a name by Dirksmeier and Helbrecht: the 'performative turn'. This they say 'is a strong signal in the wider cultural sciences that action is not merely to be considered as practical and script following' (Dirksmeier and Helbrecht 2010: 40). Others call it a 'performance turn', but both replicate a formula that has been applied to various shifts in academic thinking over the last two or three decades, which have seen, among others, 'the cultural turn', 'the theory turn' and 'the social turn'. Strangely, though, turns seem only to have happened since the 1950s. Very few people talk about the 'baroque turn', or the 'mechanisation turn' or the 'melodramatic turn'. The popularity of the term seems itself to be a fashion, a turn for turns if you will. It is not surprising therefore that Tracy Davis opens her introduction to the *Cambridge Companion to Performance Studies* by exploring the concept of the turn. Since the 1970s, she says, there have been 'linguistic', 'cultural' and 'performative' turns. Each has a philosophical inspiration, being opposed to 'more "orthodox" approaches', and may be linked to the effects of social movements. Analysing in more detail what constitutes the 'performative' turn, Davis says it is a 'pirouette, detour, revolution, deflection, tack and yaw', a play on words, if play be the word, to indicate 'how performance itself is a tool for innovative exploration, flexing under many circumstances, transforming when necessary, and apt to flow from one instantiation to another. It is both the *subject* of study and often the *means*' (2008: 1–2). Despite the conscientious working through of the word-play, nothing very specific is established. It is not clear how the 'performative' turn actually differs from other turns, which all are eligible for the same thesauric elaboration, in that the flexing is done with the word 'turn' rather than with the word 'performative', nor is it clear what specific procedural problems are posed when something is both the subject and the means of study. Above all, it is not clear why the 'performative' turn happens when it does. This is rather vital. Erika Fischer-Lichte says the 'performative turn' happened during the 1960s, and gives lots of examples to illustrate, including the performed reading of literary texts (2014: 148–49). It is not clear how this relates to the post-1970s' turn, nor whether the philosophical inspiration and connection to social movements constitute a different characteristic. Nor is it clear how either relate to the modelling of behaviour as performance that began in the mid-1950s. Suffice it to say that if it began back then, by the time Performance Studies was formally instituted the 'performative' turn was already well round the bend.

The terminology of the turn seems to be a way of sidestepping full historical explanation. Fischer-Lichte goes a certain distance, but the listing of various arts practices isn't quite enough to do the job. This abstracting effect of the terminology duplicates the effect of another term: performance as 'metaphor'. When people speak of viewing something 'as' performance there is an incli-nation to assume that the viewer can simply choose to impose performance as a 'frame', without being bound by any other analytic protocols. As States says, 'since the vehicle never specifies the intended meaning or application, one is free to call the similarities as one sees them' (1996: 1). This is a jolly enough game. It can also be played by choosing to regard the world as cabbage, but it's not quite clear what function this procedure has. The consequence is that viewing 'as' performance is regarded as nothing more than a game played by an analyst. On the other hand when Goffman and the others drew on the language of performance they thought they were identifying actual forms of behaviour. These forms of behaviour do not vanish if they cease being likened to performance. Performance is more than metaphor here.

As against the pirouettes and abstractions of the performance scholars, therefore, the more social science–based scholars seek to explain the emerging usefulness of the concept of performance in a way that is more historically and analytically grounded. Catherine Bell notes, as do Thrift and Dewsbury, that 'The notion of performance became popular in the late 1960s', and suggests that it emerges out of the logic of enquiries already being pursued: 'these new methods employed the language of performance to try to decode action as action by going beyond the textual framework standard to decoding analysis. That is, the challenge was to grasp the logic of the provisional, instinctual, and performative in social action without translating it into something else in the very act of analysing it' (Bell 1998: 206). But it was not simply performance that provided a new method. There were other analogies at work, all with a similar purpose in mind. The so-called performance turn belonged, as we've seen, to a felt need for a language of 'turns', including the cultural turn, the textual turn, and so on, and all these so-called turns may be seen as part of a larger shift in social science which can be called 'the interpretive turn'.

That last phrase is from Clifford Geertz who, in 1980, described what he saw as the changes happening in social science in general: 'Something is happening to the way we think about the way we think.' What was happening was that the analogies by which theoretical thinking operated changed away from those of craft and industry: 'In the social sciences, or at least in those that have abandoned a reductionist conception of what they are about, the analogies are coming more and more from the contrivances of cultural performance than from those of physical manipulation.' The effect is that 'The instruments of reasoning are changing' and with them society is understood no longer as a machine but as 'a serious game, a sidewalk drama, or a behavioral text'. From here Geertz explores these three analogies for thinking about society: we shall follow what he says about the second one (1980: 166, 168).

Noting that the analogy of social life to drama has a very long history Geertz observes that what is new is both the systematic application of the analogy and its use in a 'constructional', non-deprecatory way. But although the application may be systematic, it contains a contradiction. The analogy with drama is drawn on the one hand from 'ritual theory of drama' and, on the other, from what he calls the theory of symbolic action, the 'dramatism', of Kenneth Burke, which, Geertz notes, is both very influential and obscurely elusive. These two sources of the analogy pull in 'opposite directions', to 'drama as communion, the temple as stage' and 'drama as persuasion, the platform as stage'. The problem with the ritual approach, of which Geertz says Turner is the foremost proponent, is that its strength is also a weakness: 'It can expose some of the profoundest features of social process, but at the expense of making vividly disparate matters look drably homogeneous.' So while ritual theorists can perceive 'great dramatic rhythms' in all sorts of social instances, they cannot specify what makes one instance different from another. They are indeed unable to say what the performance means. The ability to specify meaning rests, by contrast, with symbolic action approaches. Both approaches, Geertz says, are necessary (1980: 168–74).

For our purposes there are two general points arising from Geertz's overview. The first is that it enables us historically to position the popularity of the performance concept as part of a general shift, in the decades after the Second World War, against reductionist or positivist thinking in the social sciences, a turn among turns, perhaps, a cognitive *corps de ballet*. Analogies with machines and a respect for 'factual' data gave way to new approaches to thinking. Performance supplies one such analogy. Hebdige, for example, argues eloquently that performance framing is necessary and valuable as a method because it avoids being spuriously 'scientific' and biased to the quantitative. In making that claim he lines up 'performance' with a way of doing research that is qualitative, evaluative and subjectivist.

The second point is that the impulse towards generalisation, thinking that the job is done when everything is seen as performance, has to be resisted. All may be performance but one performance does a different job of work, operates differently, means differently, from another. Not to see this is not only to produce yet another version of a drab homogeneity but also to make mistakes about the object of study. At each stage of the journey through this Part we have heard academics talking about the need to be specific about the events being analysed. MacAloon, recall, in 1984, criticised the scholarly activity, or rather unscholarly activity, of 'cramming' everything under the same heading. So too Bell warns, more than a decade later, that

> the greatest challenge to current performance theory lies in its tendency to flirt with universalism, that is, to substitute performance for older notions of ritual in order to create a new general model of action. This tendency toward universalism and essentialism spawns many of the smaller problems afflicting performance analyses, such as the tendency to assume that performance is a single, coherent thing, sufficiently the same everywhere, that to approach something as 'performance' implies a general formula for explaining it.   (1998: 218)

That flirtation with universalism is easier in circumstances where the word 'performance' has settled into place, apparently fixed in meaning. It also demonstrates a drive towards constructing coherence, extending the rule of the same. But in the work we have been looking at here the word 'performance' was only gradually coming into being as a general term, and it was doing so in conditions where it revealed or created instability, incoherence. Victor Turner describes his early years as a scholar: 'Within anthropology there was a tendency to represent social reality as stable and immutable, a harmonious configuration governed by mutually compatible and logically interrelated principles. There was a general preoccupation with consistency and congruence.' The same might be said of a version of performance study that drives towards universalism. But, against that vision of logical coherence, what Turner found in his fieldwork was a social system as 'a set of loosely integrated processes . . . controlled by discrepant principles of action' (1992: 73–74: my elision).

If Turner's encounter with what he was studying forced him to think differently, certain parts of the academy found different thinking thrust upon them from outside. In 1968 the Anti-University of London attempted to destroy distinctions not only between disciplines and art forms but also between teacher and student. It drew together, among others, performance artists Yoko Ono and John Latham, the situationist novelist Alexander Trocchi, the feminist Juliet Mitchell and the socialist historian C.L.R. James. It lasted only a few weeks, imploding in recriminations. But it was symptomatic of a longer process whereby under sustained pressure by students and teachers universities developed new programmes. These included of course some teaching of 'performance'. When Mark Taylor explains the changes in religious studies he points, in part, to the change in sensibilities following 1960s' civil rights campaigns and anti-war movements, but it was often explicit direct action that led to change. The universities, among other institutions, were subjected to the force of a new sort of activist behaviour, somewhere between art and politics, which emerged from the streets outside. The universities, we might say, only learnt the need for teaching performance once they had been subjected to a strange uncategorisable action that later on came to be called performance. It is the emergence of that strange disruptive and uncategorisable activity to which we now turn.

Part II

The emergence of performance as sensuous practice

From about the mid-1950s onwards there were people doing political, cultural and artistic things that seemed to be unlike things that had been done before. Much of what they were doing was consciously experimental, seeking to avoid or challenge already available categories. Politics and art were being made in a different way. But through this range of work there were some consistent ideas and connections. We shall trace these as we encounter the emergence of practices, and ideas about those practices, to which we might now give the name of performance.

Chapter 6

Situationism, games and subversion

Through the latter half of 1964 and on into 1965 small groups of young people would converge at midnight every Saturday at the foot of a statue in Amsterdam. The statue was that of an anonymous small boy, the Lieverdje. It was a gift to the city from a tobacco company, and, as far as the Saturday night gatherings were concerned, it was less the statue itself than these donors who were important. For this was the spot chosen by Robert Jasper Grootveld to promote his campaign against the use of tobacco. Each midnight event would consist of a speech by Grootveld followed by the burning of something. On at least one occasion it was the statue itself which went up in flames.

Provocations in Amsterdam

The events at the Lieverdje were part of a one-man campaign. It started with Grootveld defacing cigarette advertisements with the word 'Kanker' or the letter 'K'. As a consequence of legal action by advertising agencies for this vandalism he was repeatedly gaoled. From this first phase of his campaign he moved on to establish an 'Anti-Smoking Temple'. Here he

> led his collaborators, primarily artists and local teenagers, in ritual performances against smoking and tobacco. Vast quantities of smoke were produced to exorcise evil spirits, with Grootveld leaping around the fires in ceremonial dress, his face painted and his spellbound audience circling the flames behind him. His tongue-in-cheek sermons ended with the anti-smoking coughing song: 'Ugge-ugge-ugge-ugge' ... The Publicity Song followed: 'Publicity, publicity, publicity, moooooooooore publicity'. (Kempton 2007: 25; my elision)

Then in April 1964 Grootveld launched a citywide game called Marihuette. Although this name was based on 'marijuana' Grootveld claimed 'marihu' could consist of anything that smoked – straw as well as grass, so to speak – apart from tobacco. Teun Voeten says the idea of the game 'was to demonstrate the establishment's complete ignorance on the subject of cannabis' (1990). Its rules were distributed by means of a chain letter (a pre-Internet mechanism of viral communication), leaving receivers able to add to the rules as they wished. As part of the game Grootveld filled cigarette packets with marihu, of any burnable sort, and smuggled the packets into vending machines. The rules themselves, characteristically of this sort of game, were fairly inscrutable, largely having to do with getting numbers of points in relation to being arrested, rather than avoiding arrest, for marijuana usage.

Marihuette was followed by 'Acetone Miep'. Dressed as a woman, Grootveld entered tobacco shops and 'accidentally' dropped a bottle of acetone so it smashed on the floor. The fumes of the chemical contaminated the tobacco that was on sale, rendering it valueless. From here he went on, now dressed as a man, to stage his Saturday night events, his 'Happenings', at the Lieverdje statue. The 'sermons' at the statue attacked the tobacco industry, the liquor industry, those who advertised tobacco and liquor and, from here, the whole interlocked network of advertising and press media, together with the social classes that not only worked in these particular industries but also used their intoxicating products. The audience at the sermon, mainly students and teenaged youth, would chant his slogans along with the coughing song.

In among that chanting audience was Roel van Duyn. In his youth he had been active in the anti-nuclear weapons campaigns. At the time of Grootveld's Saturday night events he was planning to set up an anarchist paper, in order to shape and disseminate a new sort of anarchism that could respond more closely to the circumstances of modern Dutch society. So he modelled the strategy of this anarchism on the behaviour of a Dutch youth subculture that resembled British Teddy Boys. In a study of it which appeared, with much press attention, in 1965, the members of this subculture were referred to as 'Provos', on the basis that their behaviour was designed to provoke. Inspired by both Herbert Marcuse and the Marquis de Sade (Voeten 1990), van Duyn recognised in provo behaviour the energy and attitude which could provide the basis of a new anarchism, so he called his paper *Provo*. At the same time he was establishing contact with others who held similar views. As both a paper and a group Provo appeared on the Amsterdam scene at the end of May 1965. From here Provos would leap into the centre of, that's to say would cause, a political maelstrom which dragged not only Amsterdam but also most of North Western Europe into its energy field. As van Duyn's paper said: 'Provo realizes eventually it will be the loser, but won't let that last chance slip away to annoy and provoke this society to its depths' (in Voeten 1990).

The rhetoric and tactics of both Grootveld and Provo did not appear out of the blue. Behind Grootveld's Saturday night events can be felt the presence of another political group. That presence made itself felt in the chants of the crowd. Alongside the slogans and the coughing song the assembled students and teenagers chanted 'Image image'. That word, used in that context, had probably made its way to Amsterdam from Paris, whither we shall shortly follow it.

Before doing so, however, I should make clear why we began in Amsterdam in the mid-1960s, and why we are about to go to Paris. In Part I I traced the roots of new ways of looking at various modes of so-called everyday behaviour. By framing such behaviours as 'performance' it was possible to open them up to a new sort of analysis. The material most commonly opened up in this way was everyday social interaction, the self-presentation of subcultural groups, religious and secular ritual, the ceremonies of personal and civic life. While the new concept was being formulated that civic life and some of its modes of interaction were being challenged and disrupted. As prosperity in western Europe began to increase after the war there were critiques of the structure of interlocked commercial interests. Alongside these there developed, in particular, an awareness of the power of communications media to reinforce established interests and shape people's attitudes, and hence of the need to interfere with mechanisms for disseminating dominant ideas and values. The activity of disruption developed a form and language for itself, shaped in part by what it was trying to disrupt. This new disruptive behaviour was difficult to categorise. It was not formal theatre, nor was it supposedly normal behaviour, nor was it political demonstration on the traditional model. With its events and sermons and games something like Provo could be seen as performance.

Fifty years later performance as a practice and concept has come to be associated with, indeed often seen as a champion of, a set of attitudes and values. These include, to varying degrees, radical critique, breaking of boundaries, process and energy rather than stasis and product, liberation rather than containment. Performance comes to be associated with feelings, flow and freedom. This Part aims to explore how the concept of performance comes to be positioned in this way. With that aim in mind, we now head for Paris.

Situations in Paris

Used as it was in the chants in Amsterdam, the word 'image' connects to a philosophical and political position that was opposed to the dominant economic organisation of society. That position was developed by Guy Debord and his associates. Together they publicised and put their ideas into practice first under the name of the Lettrist International and then, more famously, as the Situationist International (SI).

The target of situationist action was the 'spectacle'. Debord's book *The Society of the Spectacle* begins: 'In societies where modern conditions of production prevail, all of life presents itself as an immense accumulation of *spectacles*' (2010: § 1). The problem with 'modern conditions of production', as Debord saw them, was that they create a world dominated by, and turned into, the circulation and exchange of commodities. The effect of this commodity domination is that social relationships between people are, as Marx put it, conducted and understood, 'mediated', through things. Caught up into relationships of this sort, human beings themselves become thing-like. The fullness of human potential is reduced, feelings are abstracted, 'being' is replaced by 'having' and human existence is experienced as alienation.

Up to here this is the position of Marx in *Capital* where it is argued that the mechanisms of commodity exchange turn the relationships between people into abstractions, being given material form as money. Debord now goes a step further, slightly altering Marx's language, as Jappe notes (1999: 19), to propose that 'The spectacle is not a collection of images, but a social relationship among people, mediated by images' (2010: § 4). At base the spectacle functions in a way that prevents people realising the actual alienation produced by commodity society. The effect of that alienation, in making relationships abstract, is to create separation between people. The tricksy work done by the 'spectacle' thus, in Jappe's words, 'consists in the reunification of separate aspects at the level of the *image*' (1999: 6). That's to say, the sense of connectedness between people is only ever one of the spectacle's illusions. It's an illusion because it is only within the spectacle where it becomes possible that, as Debord puts it, 'images detached from every aspect of life fuse in a common stream' (2010: § 2). The appeal of the 'common stream', of the illusion of connectedness and unity, is attractive to those who feel isolated in their separation from others. They need what the spectacle can give them. And, hence, their relationship to the spectacle is one of passivity. Of course the spectacle itself has produced this passivity, through the alienation of lives, and indeed its operation requires it. It brooks neither critique nor answering back. As Debord says the major consequences of the spectacle are 'generalized secrecy; unanswerable lies; an eternal present' (in Jappe 1999: 7). So, as Jappe says:

> The spectacle is thus not a pure and simple adjunct to the world, as propaganda broadcast via the communications media might be said to be. Rather, it is the entirety of social activity that is appropriated by the

spectacle for its own ends. From city planning to political parties of every tendency, from art to science, from everyday life to human passions and desires, everywhere we find reality replaced by images. In the process, images end up by becoming real, and reality ends up transformed into images.   (Jappe 1999: 7)

To counteract the passivity which is produced by the spectacle, particular tactics are needed. These involve the deliberate construction of 'situations':

> The construction of situations begins on the ruins of the modern spectacle. It is easy to see to what extent the very principle of the spectacle – nonintervention – is linked to the alienation of the old world. Conversely, the most pertinent revolutionary experiments in culture have sought to break the spectator's psychological identification with the hero so as to draw him into activity by provoking his capacities to revolutionize his own life. The situation is thus made to be lived by its constructors.   (in Knabb 1981: 25)

It is in the way that the situation is lived that it reveals its own radical potency:

> The really experimental direction of situationist activity consists in setting up, on the basis of more or less clearly recognized desires, a temporary field of activity favorable to these desires. This alone can lead to the further clarification of these primitive desires, and to the confused emergence of new desires whose material roots will be precisely the *new reality* engendered by the Situationist constructions.   (in Knabb 1981: 43)

In his insistence on the importance of the emergence of new desires as a mechanism for changing the society of the spectacle Debord departed from the traditional emphasis of French Marxist theorists who, in Jappe's words, 'have chosen to confine themselves to the social sphere and to the "super-structure"' (Jappe 1999: 126). Indeed Debord's analysis actually had much in common with that of Sartre, even though Sartre was roundly denounced by the Situationists. The analytical position taken up by Debord came from following his interest in alienation, which led him to the aspects of Marx influenced by Hegel, and, in this respect, as Jappe argues, his thinking was linked to that of Georg Lukács, for Lukács likewise placed importance upon the effects which resulted from the fetishism of the commodity, a viewpoint summarised in this way by Jappe:

> More and more, man becomes a mere passive observer or spectator (*HCC [History and Class Consciousness]*, 90, 100, 166) of the independent movement of commodities, which to him seems like a kind

> of 'second nature' (*HCC*, 128) – a phrase also used by Debord in *The Society of the Spectacle* (§ 24).   (Jappe 1999: 23)

For Situationists the freeing of desire was always part of a larger political struggle, and indissoluble from it. As they saw it, this proposition separated them from previous art movements and from the activity of artists in their own society. That's not to say that Debord did not welcome some aspects of the preceding surrealist project, but that project was an 'ideological failure' because of 'its belief that the unconscious was the finally discovered ultimate force of life.' This belief led it back 'to traditional occultism' and enabled it to be accommodated by dominant order (in Knabb 1981: 19). Debord was not alone in this critique, which was echoed by artists and critics elsewhere. For with surrealism, as with other art movements, there was the demonstrated liability of being absorbed into, rather than actually changing, the spectacle.

If previous art movements were well intentioned but compromised, contemporary artists, in situationist eyes, were already incorporated to the system of commodity exchange:

> A large part of the situationist critique of consumer society consists in showing to what extent contemporary artists, by abandoning the richness of supersession implicitly present albeit not fully realized in the 1910–1925 period, have condemned themselves to doing art as one does business. Since that time artistic movements have only been imaginary repercussions from an explosion that never took place, an explosion that threatened and still threatens the structures of the society. The SI's consciousness of this abandonment and of its contradictory implications (emptiness or a desire to return to the initial violence) makes the SI the only movement able, by incorporating the survival of art into the art of life, to speak to the project of the authentic artist. We are artists only insofar as we are no longer artists: we come to realize art.   (in Knabb 1981: 139)

As is clear, the situationist stance was not opposed to art as such but to art as commodity. The task therefore was to move forward, by dissolving the boundary of art and life, not to destroy art but to re-conceive it: 'We are against the conventional form of culture, even in its most modern manifestation, but that is not to say that we prefer ignorance, the petty-bourgeois common sense of the shopkeeper, or neo-primitivism ... We place ourselves beyond culture. Not before it, but *after*. We say it is necessary to *realize* culture by transcending it as a separate sphere' (in Jappe 1999: 69).

To interrupt the glittering dance of the spectacle, without at the same time being absorbed into its rhythm of commodity exchange, the Situationists developed a set of practices the general outcome of which was, perhaps not surprisingly, to produce not things but attitudes. The intention was to create 'a new mode of behavior' (in Knabb 1981: 24). Their first experiment in this line, if line it may be called, was the *dérive*, 'the practice of a passional journey out of the ordinary through rapid changing of ambiances', 'a technique of transient passage through varied ambiances' (in Knabb 1981: 24, 50):

> In a dérive one or more persons during a certain period drop their usual motives for movement and action, their relations, their work and leisure activities, and let themselves be drawn by the attractions of the terrain and the encounters they may find there.   (in Knabb 1981: 50)

While a *dérive* can be done by one person,

> the most fruitful numerical arrangement consists of several small groups of two or three people who have reached the same awakening of consciousness, since the cross-checking of these different groups' impressions makes it possible to arrive at objective conclusions.   (in Knabb 1981: 51)

That note about 'objective conclusions' suggests that the practice of the *dérive* is not just a random stroll. Indeed Debord takes pains to distinguish it from random strolling. Its focus is directed at an encounter with, and understanding of, another key term: 'psychogeography': 'The study of the specific effects of the geographical environment, consciously organized or not, on the emotions and behavior of individuals' (in Knabb 1981: 45). Given this focus, the *dérive* is a very different matter from random walking about: 'The dérive entails playful-constructive behavior and awareness of psychogeographical effects; which completely distinguishes it from the classical notions of the journey and the stroll' (in Knabb 1981: 50). It is an activity which is both playful and constructive; which depends on people deliberately letting themselves be drawn into a terrain about which they also form 'objective conclusions'. It is an activity neither of work nor of leisure, and indeed resists that binary. It is outside the purposes of the systems of the spectacle but it is not without purpose. It is not a performance in the old sense, not a commodity; but it is perhaps a sort of artistic project. Let's call it for now a mode of constructed behaviour.

As a practice the *dérive* sits alongside others, of which the best known is exemplified by a scheme dreamt up by the Provos in Amsterdam, their white bicycles. Along with a series of schemes for social welfare, the 'white plans', by which the Provos tried to interfere with, if not change, the way people behaved in and thought about the city, the white bicycles were a scheme for free public transport (several decades later the Conservative mayor of London developed such a scheme, which of course required the sponsorship, and advertising, of a major bank). Through painting the bicycles white, the Provos took a very familiar object and changed its status and meaning. The mode of private transport, the private property, once painted white becomes public transport, property held in common. This transformative action which puts established or traditional materials to new, unexpected or even perverse uses is a version of the situationist practice of *détournement*. They define this as 'The integration of present or past artistic production into a superior construction of a milieu. In this sense there can be no situationist painting or music, but only a situationist use of these means' (in Knabb 1981: 45–46). A classic case, within the domain specifically of art, is Asger Jorn's practice of painting over oil paintings bought from junk shops. But *détournement* does not have always to involve conventional art objects. A press clipping can be detourned by placing it in a new or unexpected context. Debord's adaptation of Marx's opening to *Capital* as the opening sentence of his own *Society of the Spectacle* can be regarded as *détournement*.

But where it becomes most interesting in the story I am telling here is in its manifestation as 'ultradetournement, that is, the tendencies for detournement to operate in everyday social life. Gestures and words can be given other meanings and have been throughout history for various practical reasons.' In developing their account of this sort of *détournement*, and specifically apropos the subversions of language and of clothing, Debord and Wolman invoke a concept which pops up in various political and cultural locations, and not merely situationist ones. 'The need for a secret language, for passwords', they say, 'is inseparable from a tendency toward play.' So too 'we find the notion of disguise closely linked to play' (in Knabb 1981: 13).

Play for the Situationists was a rich resource of resistance to the alienating exchange system of the spectacle. 'In our time functionalism, an inevitable expression of technological advance, is attempting to entirely eliminate play, and the partisans of "industrial design" complain that their projects are spoiled by people's tendency toward play.' In a world which needs to eliminate it, 'The only progressive way out is to liberate the tendency toward play elsewhere and on a larger scale' (in Knabb 1981: 44–45). The work, as it were, of liberating play is done by games, and 'game' is how the Situationists described their activity: 'Our action on behavior, linked with other desirable aspects of a revolution in mores, can be briefly defined as the invention of games of an essentially new type. The most general goal must be to extend the nonmediocre part of life, to reduce the empty moments of life as much as possible' (in Knabb 1981: 23–24). They were clear about what was 'new' about these types of games: 'The situationist game is distinguished from the classic conception of the game by its radical negation of the element of competition and of separation from everyday life. The situationist game is not distinct from moral choice, the taking of one's stand in favor of what will ensure the future reign of freedom and play' (in Knabb 1981: 23–24). Grootveld, we recall, carried forward his campaign against tobacco by means, in part, of an extended game, Marihuette. It had the artificial structure of rules, however bewildering, yet involved real arrests. Indeed the indeterminacy of its rules allowed for a blurring between that which was everyday and that which was game. It was not completely separate from everyday behaviour, but it was a different way of framing everyday behaviour. It was thoroughly functional, in a way which contested the assumptions of functionalism. It was less a noun, perhaps, than a detourning adjective. What Grootveld and the Situationists did was to construct a gamed world.

And their major game, 'the ultimate goal of all our activity', even though it might have never been carried out, was the construction of situations (in Knabb 1981: 14). We have already touched on the proposed purpose of constructing situations, namely to break through and reverse the effects of alienation. But it's now time to have a closer look at the language Debord uses to describe the activity of constructing situations. When he says that a situation is 'made to be lived by its constructors', he explains: 'The role played by a passive or merely bit-part playing "public" must constantly diminish, while that played by those who cannot be called actors but rather, in a new sense of the term, "livers," must steadily increase' (in Knabb 1981: 25). Although he wants to avoid the term 'actor', the structure of the traditional theatrical company haunts the distinction he draws between bit-part players and (lead) actors. That language recurs a year later, in 1958, in the essay 'Preliminary Problems in Constructing a Situation'. It begins by explaining that a 'constructed situation' is: 'a unitary ensemble of behavior in time. It is composed of gestures contained in a transitory decor. These gestures are the product of the decor and of themselves.' But although the constructed situation is 'necessarily collective in its preparation and development', a familiar figure now puts in an appearance: 'at least for the period of the first rough experimentations a given situation requires one individual to play a preeminent role as "director."' The allocation of roles does not stop here, however:

> If we imagine a particular situation project in which, for example, a research team has arranged an *emotionally moving gathering* of a few people for an evening, we would no doubt have to distinguish: a *director* or producer responsible for coordinating the basic elements necessary

for the construction of the decor and for working out certain
interventions in the events ... the *direct agents* living the situation, who
have taken part in creating the collective project and worked on the
practical composition of the ambiance; and finally, a few passive
spectators who have not participated in the constructive work, who
should be *reduced to action*.

Although the roles of 'director', 'direct agents' and 'spectators' recall the
structure of early twentieth-century theatre, these are only provisional terms:

This relation between the director and the 'livers' of the situation must
naturally never become a permanent specialization. It is a purely
temporary subordination of a whole team of Situationists to the person
responsible for a particular project. These perspectives, or the
provisional terminology describing them, should not be taken to mean
we are talking about some continuation of theater.   (in Knabb 1981: 43,
44; my elision)

The guardedness about theatre, and its uses, is explained by Puchner: 'critique
of theatrical totality ... was part of a long tradition of Marxian thought that
used the theater or theatricality to describe the representational practices and
effects of capitalism.' The solution, as Puchner says, was to 'detourn' theatre
(2006: 231, 237; my elision). Brecht and Pirandello had already shown the way
towards a destruction of 'the theatrical spectacle'. From here the situationist
project needed to move into the domain where the separation of art and life
has been ended: 'It could be said that the construction of situations will
replace the theater in the same sense that the real construction of life has
tended more and more to replace religion' (in Knabb 1981: 44).

The 'constructed situation' is more or less a way of doing theatre that isn't
theatre. It occupies the space where theatre was. But it nevertheless seems to
use approaches that are associated more with theatre practices than with other
art forms. Even though the Situationists would say their principal effort was to
replace *poetry*, in their descriptions of projects such as the construction of
situations there is a heavy stress on creating dynamism. By contrast with
Freudian psychoanalysis, in 'situationist-oriented psychoanalysis' participants 'would have to discover precise desires for ambiances *in order to realize
them*'. By means of this method 'elements out of which situations can be
constructed can be determined, along with *projects to dynamize these elements*' (in Knabb 1981: 43). A situation is more than a 'form'. It not only
includes emotion but is also predicated on activity. And that activity is driven
not by pretence or obligation but by something more fundamental: 'really
experimental' situationist activity consists of 'setting up, on the basis of more

or less clearly recognized desires, a temporary field of activity favorable to these desires' (in Knabb 1981: 43).

Rejecting the theatre as part of the spectacle, as an art form already locked into the system of commodity exchange, the Situationists articulated the need for interventions that were dynamic, drew on emotion, liberated play and facilitated desires. With the concept of a deliberately constructed 'temporary field of activity', albeit constructed by temporarily using roles familiar from the rejected theatre, they were envisaging a practice that would transform if not potentially replace theatre.

Chapter 7

Hippies and expressive play

When the midnight crowd in Amsterdam were chanting 'image image' around Grootveld they were celebrating the revelation of, and attack on, the workings of the spectacle. And, when the Provos set about provoking the Dutch state to reveal the brutality behind the civilly organised commodity relationships, there was, again, an echo of the Situationists. The echoes were reverberating further afield. In Strasbourg a newly elected student union executive blew its entire budget in 1966 on printing a situationist pamphlet which had a significant set of words in its title: *On the Poverty of Student Life: Considered in Its Economic, Political, Psychological, Sexual, and Particularly Intellectual Aspects, and a Modest Proposal for Its Remedy* (discussed in Home 1991: 45; translations vary). The Strasbourg students were not alone. Student unrest was spreading across western Europe. And even as they watched it contemporary commentators became aware of a similar attitude to dominant order expressing itself, albeit in a somewhat different way, on the other side of the Atlantic. And just as was happening in European thinking there were new ideas about the thing that would end up being called performance.

It is 1967, in Haight-Ashbury in San Francisco:

> Two youths seat themselves on the sidewalk or in a store entranceway; bent beer can in hand, one begins scratching a bongo-like rhythm on the pavement while the other tattoos a bell-like accompaniment by striking a stick on an empty bottle. Soon they are joined, one by one, by a tambourinist, a harmonica player, a penny-whistler or recorder player, and, of course, the ubiquitous guitarist. A small crowd collects and, at the fringes, some blanket-bedeckt boys and girls begin twirling about in movements vaguely resembling a Hindu dance. The wailing, rhythmic beating and dancing, alternately rising to peaks of intensity and subsiding, may last for as little as five minutes or as long as an hour, players and dancers joining in and dropping out as whim moves them. At some point – almost any – a mood takes hold that 'the happening is over'; participants and onlookers disperse as casually as they had collected. (Davis 1970: 333–34)

An everyday event such as this typified the culture of the young people who gathered in Haight-Ashbury in the late 1960s, the hippies. Their culture very quickly attracted the attention of social commentators such as Fred Davis, for it seemed to be an experiment in a different way of living that was set in opposition to the values and behaviours of dominant culture. As Davis put it:

> Hippies are opening up new avenues of collective response to life issues posed by a changing sociotechnological environment. They are doing so by rejecting those virtuoso standards that stifle participation in high culture; by substituting an extravagantly eclectic (and, according to traditional aestheticians, reckless) admixture of materials, styles, and motifs from a great diversity of past and present human cultures; and, most of all, by insisting that every man can find immediate expressive fulfilment provided he lets the socially-suppressed spirit within him ascend into vibrant consciousness. The manifesto is: All men are artists, and who cares that some are better at it than others; we can all have fun!   (Davis 1970: 333)

The release of the 'socially-suppressed spirit' was often facilitated, or at least imaged, by a release of the body, shown in the adoption of behaviour and dress that refused the constraints of 'straight' society. One of the major discursive influences of this cultural moment was that the body, or should we say 'body', acquired status as a key medium for oppositional activity. For social commentators such as Davis the implications of the new youth culture had bearing on people's assumptions about norms of behaviour, and, connected to this, their attitudes to a dominant order which preserved and perpetuated those norms.

For our narrative here the interest is less in the hippies themselves than in what social commentators thought they were seeing. In particular we shall need to attend to the language in which they characterised hippie culture and its effects. To do this I am going to draw on the work of one commentator above all others, Stuart Hall. Hall was associated with Birmingham's Centre for Contemporary Cultural Studies (CCCS; see pp. 10–15), and he published an early account of hippie culture as one of the occasional stencilled papers by which CCCS cheaply disseminated its work. Hall's paper seems to have appeared in 1968, but the archive copy is incomplete, and there are textual notes which date from at least 1969. In that year Hall published his essay 'The Hippies: An American "Moment"' in Julian Nagel's book *Student Power*. In this he quotes Fred Davis's essay from 1967 with which we started.

As Hall sees it, hippie opposition to dominant order was expressed in several ways. The act of 'dropping out', of deliberately leaving education, employment and traditional family life, could be seen as a 'symbolic gesture of withdrawal from the commonplace, prescribed routines of their generation' (Hall 1969: 174). Next, the clothing of the hippies, an intentionally bizarre combination of mainly grubby elements, declared their identification with the victims of economically successful white America – the poor and American Indians (although the feeling was not necessarily reciprocated). This identification was more than dressing up, at least in the early days. Street begging was common in hippie cultures, for to live by begging was to reverse all the moral assumptions of affluent white America. In adopting these modes of dress and behaviour hippies were determinedly embracing, in a very public way, that which was labelled deviant, and, as such, they were displaying a refusal of the values of the dominant: 'To be labelled "deviant" is to accept a social identity and the possibilities of a social career which passes beyond the rules and conventions of "the system"' (Hall 1969: 175). This came at a price in that, in the wrong bits of small-town America, anyone with long hair and the wrong clothes might be branded 'hippie' and beaten up on the spot. The refusal was not a matter simply of clothing and behaviour. To refuse the norms of social conformity and economic success brought with it a refusal of the subjectivity required, and shaped, by those norms: 'Their emphasis on expressiveness is a counter-thrust to the bottling up of emotions and the role-doubling which they feel to be so central a part of the dominant personality types of modern American society' (Hall 1969: 182). That emphasis on expressiveness was seen to be particularly grounded in the apparent freedom to exercise individual choice or whim, in the words of the slogan to 'Do your [that is, my] own thing.' In Hall's analysis the commitment to individualism derived in part from 'the idealisation of the spontaneous' and was in part 'a protest against the over-managed, over-directed, over-routinised character of middle class life – a revolt against the model of the "organisation man" and the "organised life"' (Hall 1969: 189).

Once it is conceived in these terms, the hippie refusal of organised middle-class life can be aligned with other forms of protest. One part of this culture very readily reminded Hall of a group that we have met before. In Haight-Ashbury the Diggers constituted a politically aware group of hippies who gave out free food to those who were begging and provided accommodation to those who had arrived in town with nowhere to stay. What distinguished the Diggers from the rest, says Davis, were 'their ideological brio, their articulate-ness, good works, and flair for the dramatic event' (1970: 328). As such, thought Hall, quoting this from Davis and then making the link, the Diggers 'are really Hippie "Provos"' (1969: 179). In his earlier stencilled essay he also connected them to the German SDS, the radical student organisation which, through the first half of 1967, had been involved in major demonstrations and sit-ins against visits by the American vice-president and the shah of Persia, the Vietnam war and police brutality. Alongside these parallels there were references to some key intellectuals. The stencilled paper references Sartre and Goldman, a pamphlet by Constant Nieuwenhuys published in 1966 by the Provos, and Marcuse's *Essay on Liberation* (1969). From Marcuse, Hall got a perspective which enabled him to view hippie culture as 'the creation of an *aesthetic ethos*'. But Nieuwenhuys, and indeed the Provos, also point us towards a group not explicitly mentioned but perhaps there somewhere in the background, the Situationists. As we shall see in a short while, some of the hippie activities were not a long way far off from situationist practices.

But the positioning of hippies within a wider context of generally similar protest was not the main focus of Hall's work. His attempt was to describe the specificity of their behaviour and then to interpret it, or, in the language of CCCS, to identify what constituted hippie 'style' and then to 'read' it. Identifying 'Hippie ambience' as having 'the force of a conscious *avant-garde*', Hall announces that he will 'try to view the Hippie *style* as a *project* for a certain section of American youth'. The style has many elements: 'The symbols, expressive values, beliefs and attitudes, projects and aspirations of a grouping like the Hippies constitute, taken together, a significant, meaningful way of being-in-the-world for *them*. It is by learning to "read" the meanings of these "signs" that we come to understand the global vision of the world, the *weltanschauung*, the project, which organises and makes coherent the many disparate strands' (Hall 1969: 170, 172). In taking this approach Hall was consciously promoting a new sort of sociology, with a method that drew on phenomenology. In his stencilled paper he also refers, in an early use of him by another discipline, to the work of Victor Turner on 'Symbols in Ndembu Ritual'. For Hall there was something large at stake in the synthesis of these elements. In a footnote to the stencilled paper he tells us that his sociological position rejects the 'structural-functionalism' version of old sociology, rather like Turner perhaps rejecting traditional anthropology, and in making that rejection his new sociology not only comes to align with, but actually to practise, the 'new politics'.

That new politics was being demonstrated, as it were, outside the academy by groups such as the hippies. By reading their style on its own terms Hall aimed to show the ways in which the style itself practised a new type of political activism which placed its characteristic emphasis on 'involvement, on participation, on grass-roots organising, on *praxis* rather than ideology, on by-passing the bureaucracies of established power' (Hall 1969: 193). Whereas previous forms of activism would have confronted dominant order head-on, occupying its spaces and burning its buildings, the hippies 'mean to unravel it from within, destroying the *rationale*, undermining the legitimacy, the social ethic which is the moral cement which holds the whole fabric together ... The Hippies are second or third wave partisans in a new kind of cultural guerrilla warfare: a warfare of the social consciousness' (Hall 1969: 196; my elision). Or, as the Editors of *Ramparts* put it in 1967, 'The hippie choice of weapons is to love the Establishment to death rather than protest it or blow it up (hippies possess a confounding disconcern about traditional political methods or issues)' (Ramparts 1971: 4). Of course Hall has to concede that, given the typical attitudes of hippie culture, very few might have subscribed to any conscious plans of this sort, nor even have tolerated the notion that they might actually plan. But in a sense that's the point. For Hall the hippie 'phenomenon' works not as a conscious plan but as a 'manifestation': 'Drop-outs from the political struggle they may be: they are some of the first enlisted troops in a new kind of politics of postmodern, post-industrial society: the politics of cultural rebellion' (Hall 1969: 196).

We have already noted some of the elements of that rebellion – the dropping out, the clothing, the individualism. But let's now focus on one of them, the commitment to expressiveness: 'The Hippies', says Hall, 'reach for the expressiveness and intensity of the existential now by accenting the pleasure/play aspects of daily life.' Thus a typical mode of transport through daily life might be Ken Kesey's 'elderly school bus, painted like a fluorescent Easter egg in orange, chartreuse, cerise, white, green, blue and, yes, black'. This would travel the countryside at around fifty miles an hour, 'four loud-speakers turned all the way up, broadcasting both inside and outside Carl Orff's Carmina Burana and filled with two dozen people simultaneously smoking marijuana' (Ramparts 1971: 5). Someone who had gone into the countryside for a quiet walk would, whether they wanted it or not, have found themselves expressed on. Perhaps more common, and more locally confined to the areas of hippie occupation, were the activities Hall lists: the 'scenes of informal enactment, like a play or happening in broad daylight' (1969: 183), to illustrate which Hall lifts from Davis, without acknowledgement, the description with which this section began. Here, in the description of expressiveness, for my purposes Hall's language becomes rather interesting. In the early stencilled paper he noted parallels to the hippies' subcultural attitude, the 'new sensibility', in such other cultural activities as the theatrical 'happening' and similar events described in early issues of the *Tulane Drama Review*. So too he made connections across to the Living Theatre. He also at this point noted Jerry Rubin's manifesto which proposed 'revolution as theatre', a concept to which we shall return.

As we've seen, to illustrate typical 'scenes of informal enactment' Hall begins with the gathering described by Fred Davis. The only term Davis provides for this event is 'happening', and that in quotation marks. He does, however, attribute the emergence of such gatherings to a 'readiness to let go, to participate, to create and perform without script or forethought' (Davis 1970: 333). Performing is one of a set of verbs which include the notion of 'letting go', so it doesn't have much sense of aesthetic specialism or even deliberation. By contrast Hall compares the 'informal enactment' to 'a play or happening in broad daylight'. Similarly street begging, he says, 'has the spirit of play-acting behind it, of role-play or acting-out of an existential confronta-tion. Like street-players in costume, they have transformed the pavement into a sort of "living theatre". There is the same dramatic quality in the more organised "happenings"' (Hall 1969: 183). But although the reference point is the activity of art theatre, it is only ever a likeness rather than the thing itself. And that likeness is itself fairly imprecise – 'play-acting' interchanges with 'role-play' and 'acting-out'; it's 'dramatic quality' rather than drama. The language here is grappling with something that doesn't really have a workable label. But what Hall is very clear about is that this is not so much art as politics by other means, and at the same time it is a form of politics which requires that we re-define what doing politics is. Other commentators stressed it rather differently: Brake in 1985 said 'hippy culture evaded rather than confronted the state', but he also concedes, in a sentiment that echoes Geertz's rejection of fact-based knowledge, that it was part of a transformation of politics 'from arid economic determinism to a wider exploration of the relationships of differing forms of exploitation and their effects on people's lives' (Brake 1985: 98). Certainly all sorts of debates can be had about the extent to which hippie culture was annoyingly self-indulgent and egotistical, but my interest here is not so much in evaluating hippies for themselves as in looking at the language and approaches that were used to make sense of what they were doing. And here we have to return to Hall's shrewd, if perhaps also somewhat romantic, account.

To help us think about the nature of hippie politics Hall offers a paradigm, a dialectic of movement between two poles that 'may be defined roughly as the *expressive* and the *activist*'. Placing the hippies more at the 'expressive' pole he offers the contrast of emphases: 'The expressive "moment" gives emphasis to the development of a revolutionary *style*; the activist "moment" puts the emphasis on a revolutionary *programme of issues*.' While the expressive fore-grounds the 'personal, the psychic, the subjective', the activist 'stresses the political, the social, the collective'. The contrast is clinched in a neat antithesis: 'Hippies create *scenes*; activists build "the movement"' (Hall 1969: 198–99).

At the heart of that antithesis is a word derived from theatre but no longer theatrical. For the scenes created by hippies may be said to have more in common with constructed situations. Love as 'flower power' manifests as 'the gentleness and receptivity with which Hippies hope to confront and unmask the power and authority structures of civil society' (Hall 1969: 184). That duality between gentleness and unmasking is there in Marty Balin's account, decades later, of Jefferson Airplane's approach to their rock performances. They aimed, he said, to 'comfort the disturbed and disturb the comfortable' (*Born to be Wild* BBCFour: January 2013). Ken Kesey's garishly painted old school bus had a similar effect. The Editors of *Ramparts* tell the story of how the busload of stoned hippies found themselves being followed by a police car: 'The law was not unexpected, of course, because any cop who sees Kesey's bus just about has to follow it . . . It is part of the game: the cop was now playing on their terms, and Kesey and his Pranksters were delighted' (Ramparts 1971: 6). When the cop gives up, they are all disappointed. Had the cop not given up, however, they could have been arrested. Just as with Grootveld in Amsterdam the game takes place in real everyday life, with real consequences. It is as if it were a temporary field of activity, a moment of deliberate play that has the potential to reveal the ridiculousness of the dominant regime and its values. As a practice that produces a changed attitude it recalls the construction of situations, and so too situationist games. And, of course, that school bus, going anywhere on a (provocative) whim, might be said to be a version, in its journeyings, of *dérive*. Its fabric, re-painted in those garish colours, transforms it, with all the precision of *détournement*, from being a vehicle that gets kids to school in orderly fashion to a vehicle that promotes disorderliness and de-schooling. The most public hippie *détournement* was not, however, a vehicle but a piece of music. Coming to the end of his set at the closing moments of 1967's Woodstock festival, Jimi Hendrix started to play 'The Star-Spangled Banner'. Taking America's patriotic hymn he steadily dismantled it, and then, his guitar-playing expertise becoming more brilliant, he disembowelled it. From the familiar tune broken into fragments, a new work of art was created.

Operating to provoke and so reveal, these instances of the hippie style in action suggest we are not a very long way from the practices of the Situationists. And, just as with the Situationists, we seem to encounter the problem of vocabulary. There is a need to differentiate constructed behaviour both from artistic creation and from the assumed norms of everyday interaction, but there was no readily available language for making this differentiation securely. Hall solves it, provisionally, with a pun:

> The Hippies have not only helped to define *a style*, they have made the question of *style itself* a political issue. Secondly (and closely related), Hippies have helped create a repertoire of ways of confronting and contesting society which have a highly imaginative, provisional and improvisational flair. They have made their mark on the *dramaturgy* of the revolutionary movement. They take a delight in the semi-staged 'happening', especially if it can be carried off in such a way as to reveal the unrealistic or Dada-esque quality of middle class life. They have added obscenity, shock, play-acting, the 'put on', to the vocabulary of political confrontation. In doing so, they have given a new definition to the meaning of 'the political act'.   (Hall 1969: 194)

As we know Hall thought the new politics was part of the turn into a postmodern, post-industrial age. It didn't take long for that age to come up with a word that both differentiated acting from theatrics and suggested political efficacy without doing traditional politics. That word was 'performance' and on the other side of the Atlantic it was being put to political use in a particular classroom.

Chapter 8

Performance as a new pedagogy

Even while Hall was thinking about how to read hippie style, in a city not too far away from Birmingham, one morning early in November 1967 things began to kick off:

> A dozen students suddenly appeared on the steps of the Victoria monument in the centre of Bradford. They were all dressed in black – black jeans, black sweaters, black polythene capes tied round their necks, and they all wore red armbands. They climbed up the steps, turned round, and began to read in unison from the thoughts of Chairman Mao. A policeman at the foot of the steps tried to pretend that nothing was happening.
>
> At roughly the same time, two miles or so from the city centre, a procession of more than a hundred or so students, led by a chance band, came swinging through the gates of the park in which the city's main art gallery, the Cartwright Memorial Hall, is set. These students, too, were dressed in black, but with white armbands. The girls had boots and long skirts that swung around their ankles, and they carried wooden home-made rifles. Behind them, in the procession, were four huge, twelve-foot puppets, made out of cardboard boxes painted black. The students carried slogans on banners: 'Support Your Government', 'Down With Red Agitators', 'No Peace With Aggressors'.
>
> In the city bus station, a bus arrived from Barnsley. About twenty-five students in black with white armbands, got off the bus and looked round. A van drove up, crudely camouflaged. Out of it leapt a student with a red armband. He picked out the four prettiest girls, told them to get in the van, and drove away. Inside the van, the girls had their white armbands exchanged for red.
>
> Outside a bread shop in the city centre, a queue of two dozen students formed. They wore red armbands and carried the slogan 'Peace, Land, Bread'. Each student bought one teacake. Then they took their teacakes across the town to a disused post office that had been left to crumble in the middle of blocks of high-rise council flats. In the shop window were placards telling people they could take anything they liked from the

shop, for free, and could leave anything they liked except money. (Hunt 1976: 66–67)

These activities were all part of a larger event, *The Russian Revolution* – in Bradford. The participants – over 300 of them – came from art colleges across Yorkshire, but the central organisation was masterminded from a course at the Regional College of Art in Bradford led by Albert Hunt. Hunt was working within the education system, albeit on its fringes, and some of his previous experience had been in the commercial theatre, albeit its experimental end, so his work was more institutionalised and closer to aesthetic theatre than the products of Provos or hippies. Nevertheless the institutional arrangements at Bradford, like other art colleges in the United Kingdom in the late sixties and early seventies, allowed for modes of work that could cross boundaries and experiment. Indeed it's arguable that the shaping of a new sort of performance was in large part the product, in the United Kingdom and Europe at least, of a particular sort of institutional system.

Many artists were employed as lecturers, and they were expected to make work, although sometimes the work exceeded expectations and led to their sacking. For some artists teaching was a main focus of their work, the most celebrated example being Joseph Beuys, who was employed as a lecturer at Dusseldorf. Beuys claimed indeed that teaching was the only important part of his work, although that teaching was often done as performance. In a similar way Robert Filliou argued that teaching and learning were performing arts. But, as Roms and Edwards forcefully argue, examining the specific case of Cardiff, the importance of institutions goes beyond individuals. The institution not only allows for the provision of facilities and funds but also catalyses and then embeds the networks and festivals that support artists. This is why the exploration of pedagogic activity has to form part of our account of the emergence of a concept of performance. The reason that Hunt in particular is interesting is that he was not a performance artist. Certainly he had worked in 'traditional' theatre, but at Bradford he was employed simply as a lecturer, with a specialism, among other things, in film. In these circumstances the development of a language and methods for what he was doing becomes interesting. For while he called *The Russian Revolution* 'street theatre', it could just as well be seen, especially in its opening moments, as the construction of a 'situation'. In constructing a situation, and taking part in what also might be seen as a citywide 'game', his students learnt something about the dominant order and how it functions.

The project had its roots in Hunt's arrival at the Regional College in May 1965. Soon after arriving he found that the course he had designed on film was not engaging the students. They were attending only because they had to do one element of so-called liberal studies as part of their course, and they had little other interest in Hunt's films. So he gave them a short scene from Brecht's *Caucasian Chalk Circle* which they worked on physically, interpreting and then improvising from it. This led to animated discussion both about their own improvisation and about Brecht's rehearsal techniques and concept of the characters. 'What most struck me', says Hunt, looking back on it, 'was the way in which we'd begun to explore intellectual ideas through physical activity' (Hunt 1976: 9–10).

That 'physical activity' was something more than acting out the lines of a play-text. In a subsequent class Hunt asked them to turn a war poem into newspaper headlines. When they suggested acting it out they hit a problem with a character whose feelings of grief were not shown. After exploring several modes of approach they were introduced to the songs of Bessie Smith, so they tried doing the grieving mother's feelings as twelve-bar blues. Although this project was never completed, Hunt felt they had covered a lot of subjects and, most crucially, engaged with them 'not because they were down on a syllabus, which had to be covered, but because they were thrown up by physical work on a practical problem' (Hunt 1976: 12–13). Instead of being an 'acting out' of what is 'there' in the script or scenario, the 'physical activity' is a set of approaches to, ways of looking at, frames placed around a piece of text, all perhaps yielding up different insights and imaginings.

From here Hunt worked with his colleague Bill Gainham on a project that began simply as a game. Over a five-day period a blindfold game in a college annexe was turned into a coherent story without words. 'We called the event *Performance*. In the college community, it was a great success' (Hunt 1976: 35). This is not drama but an 'event'. It was developed out of the logic of a game combined with an exploration of the given conditions of the space – discovering for example how to use the fluorescent lighting to create after-images. The shaping of it into a story was done by inviting people regularly to watch and comment. For Hunt the 'real success' was that

> inside an educational institution, it had been possible to create a situation in which people could work freely together, bringing their individual skills to a collective situation, not because it was part of a syllabus, but because that was what they wanted to do.   (Hunt 1976: 35–36)

Performance was followed by a sequence of shows through 1966–1967. There was the *Vietnam War Game*, an event which was dispersed across the whole college site: 'the fact that we played the game openly, all over the college, using emblems, posters, wall-newspapers, turned the simulation game into a piece of theatre in which the audience – the college community – began to parti- cipate, quite spontaneously, and without being asked to do so.' Then there was the *Hot Gospel* project that brought together art students and pentecostalists. This was followed by Adrian Mitchell's *Making Poetry Public*, 'built around the idea that poems are presents you offer to friends'. The students toured Bradford with notebooks and cameras, returning to shape their material into a 'collective poem': 'For the performance, they invited only friends. There was no playing space or audience space: the group would perform one episode of the poem, then move to another part of the room and perform the next' (Hunt 1976: 47, 62, 63), This was followed in 1967 by *The Russian Revolution*, a game on an even larger scale.

What, though, did games enable the students to learn? Reflecting on the *Vietnam War Game* Hunt says:

> they'd learnt something about Vietnam and international politics; and about the way politicians behave; and about how language can be manipulated for political purposes. In learning to handle language unscrupulously themselves, they'd come to see through some of the processes of mystification. But also, in working together, in negotiating, finding solutions to specific problems, they'd been developing, in a practical way, skills they might later find useful in their jobs.   (Hunt 1976: 46–47)

To approach a text or a political problem through the apparatus of game is to come at a new way of thinking about it. We come back here to the idea of 'performance' as a concept that enables a new sort of thinking about appar- ently familiar material. That material might be a poem, or the definition of what theatre is, or a global conflict. To view it as something that can be 'performed' is not only to find a way of speaking about it but also to find a way of working together to do the speaking. But in Hunt's educational work performance was not merely a conceptual frame, an approach to material. It was also a way of bringing something into being. His aims in a new full-time diploma course in 1970 were: 'first, to extend the concept of theatre, as a concrete element in the educational situation . . . and, secondly, to extend the idea of fortnights of freedom based on common interest into the realisation of permanent freedom' (Hunt 1976: 129; my elision).

At Bradford in the late sixties the extension of theatre into a new domain was proposed not principally to explore the idea of theatre but to engage vocational students in thinking about art in relation to society, and from there to thinking about the structure of society, its languages and norms. Always for

Hunt the project was pre-eminently about enabling new understanding. As an approach to material performance was little more than an analytical tool. It could help students demystify the learnt languages of society and its public media, or – put another way – it could reveal the operations of the spectacle. By experiencing this analytical power, together with new ways of collaborative working, the students would discover, as Hunt saw it, a new sort of freedom within the given structure of their lives. Their street theatre was perhaps less about theatre than a way of being in the street.

The ambitions for the new course in 1970 didn't go anywhere. The institution 'reverted to the aim of achieving status through orthodox degree recognition'. In his final estimate of what had been achieved Hunt's language is very similar to that of the Situationists and the Provos:

> And this is what matters in the end about the work in Bradford: not that, as a result of decisions taken by sections of the 'self-certifying professional élite' remote from our working situation, that work never realised its full possibilities; but that the methods we invented to demonstrate, through play, fun and imagination, that élite's ultimate irrelevance are there, waiting to be used, by anybody, anywhere.   (Hunt 1976: 156, 166)

This final call to arms is a reminder that Hunt's book is a manifesto, telling the story of a pedagogic experiment after that experiment had finished. But I have let Hunt tell his own story in part because that story has been largely forgotten – and he'd presumably have guessed that would be the case, in a world lurching rightwards. But also it's interesting for the story I am trying to tell here to have Hunt's views expressed as he formulated them. Approaching that story via some of the activities surveyed in the rest of this chapter, we can meet familiar words and concepts, but now applied in an educational setting. Play and games had already become very fashionable in more experimental theatre, with Clive Barker's *Theatre Games* appearing in 1972. But in that context games are being used to help performers perform better. They are a tool for expression. For Hunt they are also, perhaps primarily, a tool for analysis. Games are a way of thinking about given material in order to think it a different way. The result in an educational institution might be an event that fits into no known genre and that you call *Performance*.

To make that event Hunt drew on the activity of game and play to invent a new pedagogy. This is not a specialist pedagogy, teaching theatre students how to develop themselves by playing. It is a pedagogy that can engage almost any sort of student. It works across disciplines and it calls into question not just disciplinary boundaries but the structures of formal education. The pedagogic work that made *Performance* was thus also making politics. Hunt's Bradford experiment found an organic way to create, as one unit, artwork, pedagogy and politics. The model of thinking and practice that facilitated this creation operated by ignoring, if not disrupting, assumed categories of knowledge and learnt practices of behaviour. Literally and metaphorically it occupied spaces in a new way. In this respect it was like the other ideas and practices that we have been surveying, but in this case it specifically gave itself the name of performance.

Chapter 9

Architecture and the performed city

While Hunt was working at Bradford, across the Channel spaces had been forcibly occupied in a new and spectacular way, offering an image of a new way of being. In May 1968 the streets and buildings of Paris were taken over by students and workers as a challenge to dominant order. To René Viénet it seemed that: 'Capitalized time stopped. People strolled, dreamed, learned how to live.' And with it the very fabric of the city was itself transformed: 'red and black flags gave a human appearance to the fronts of public buildings. The Haussmanian perspective of the boulevards was corrected and the green belts redistributed and closed to traffic. Everyone, in his own way, made his own critique of urbanism' (in Pinder 2005: 236).

'Urbanism' was from the start a topic of interest to those people whose ideas hovered behind – they would say shaped – the events of 1968, the Situationists. They saw the habitual structure and functioning of the city as a concrete manifestation of the alienating system of commodity exchange. In itself of course a concern with the city's effect on its inhabitants is neither new nor remarkable. Such concerns have probably existed as long as cities have. In the fashion for so-called city comedy in the London of the 1590s there was an interest in the sorts of behaviour that seemed to be produced by, and in response to, new mercantile wealth, behaviours facilitated by the spaces and living conditions of the city. In the mid-nineteenth century Engels suggested that the dynamic of the crowd was a characteristic feature of the city, and it was that presence which persisted into Walter Benjamin's early twentieth-century conception of a particular city type defined as an individual in separation from the crowd, the *flâneur*. More or less contemporary with Benjamin's sketching of the *flâneur*, Simmel characterised the mind-set of the crowd as a specifically urban product, shaped by the rhythm of city behaviours and interactions. In some ways, of course, this is not too far distant from the feeling that new rhythms were necessarily pressing on, and making themselves felt in, the late sixteenth century's rendering of the city as 'comedy'.

The difference of the situationist approach to the city is that they wanted to change how the city worked, changing it materially if necessary. The *flâneur* may be said to propose a different way of being in the city but at the same time accepts its spaces as given. By contrast the *dérive* was an activity that used the city in a way that it did not anticipate, moving against the rhythms of the spectacle. Less interested in producing the individualised personage of the *flâneur* it didn't merely try to experience the city in a new way but worked to collect data about instances of 'psychogeography'. Defined as 'The study of the specific effects of the geographical environment, consciously organized or not, on the emotions and behavior of individuals' (in Knabb 1981: 45), the main focus is not on the psychic states generated by the noise and business of the crowd. Instead it homes in, so to speak, on the relationship between built environment and human activity.

Dérives and psychogeography fell into place within an overarching project first articulated in Ivan Chtcheglov's manifesto from 1953, 'Formulary for a New Urbanism'. Chtcheglov had split away from the Lettrist movement in 1952 to found the Lettrist International. That splinter group then mutated into the Situationist International. Chtcheglov's 'Formulary' proposes that architecture is a way of breaking out of a current state of affairs where the disease of 'banalization' has 'swept the planet': 'Everyone is hypnotized by production and conveniences – sewage system, elevator, bathroom, washing machine.' A new architecture will not only enable people to dream again but also change their conceptions of time and space. 'The architectural complex will be modifiable. Its aspect will change totally or partially in accordance with the will of its inhabitants.' In this vision the new urbanism is part of the defining project of Situationism: 'We have already pointed out the need of constructing situations as being one of the fundamental desires on which the next civilization will be founded. This need for *absolute* creation has always been intimately associated with the need to *play* with architecture, time and space.' That playing actively modifies the built environment: 'The mobile house turns with the sun. Its sliding walls enable vegetation to invade life. Mounted on tracks, it can go down to the sea in the morning and return to the forest in the evening' (in Knabb 1981: 2–3).

Leaving to one side the troubling notion that he might also be to blame for inventing the caravan, Chtcheglov seems to have envisaged a more fundamentally unsettling version of one of the key situationist activities. In his new city 'The principal activity of the inhabitants will be the CONTINUOUS DÉRIVE. The changing of landscapes from one hour to the next will result in complete disorientation' (in Knabb 1981: 4). Borrowing Chtcheglov's big idea three years later, without acknowledgement, Debord and Wolman connect it to another key situationist practice: 'the *architectural complex* – which we conceive as the construction of a dynamic environment related to styles of behavior – will probably detour existing architectural forms, and in any case will make plastic and emotional use of all sorts of detourned objects: calculatedly arranged cranes or metal scaffolding replacing a defunct sculptural tradition' (in Knabb 1981: 13).

The 'new urbanism' became known in situationist theory as 'unitary urbanism'. It was an approach to building and planning that subverted their oppressive organisation of human activity and thinking, seeking to break down the structures of segmentation and striation 'to form a unitary human milieu in which the separations such as work/leisure or public/private will finally be dissolved. But before this, the minimum action of unitary urbanism is to extend the terrain of play to all desirable constructions.' It was also unitary in that it offered a programme for mass dissent from the false totality of the spectacle. Kotányi and Vaneigem describe the project in 1961, in terms that hideously anticipate 2016:

> The totality of the spectacle which tends to integrate the population manifests itself as both organization of cities and as permanent information network. It is a solid framework to secure the existing conditions of life. Our first task is to enable people to stop identifying with their surroundings and with model patterns of behavior. This is inseparable from a possibility of free mutual recognition in a few initial zones set apart for human activity. People will still be obliged for a long time to accept the era of reified cities. But the attitude with which they accept it can be changed immediately. We must spread scepticism toward those bleak, brightly colored kindergartens, the new dormitory cities of both East and West. Only a mass awakening will pose the question of a conscious construction of the urban milieu.   (in Knabb 1981: 66)

The built environment creates its effect not just by physically channelling human activity but also by creating identificatory feelings in those who more or less passively occupy the places as it were prescribed for them by that environment. Against this effect, learnt patterns of behaviour and the customary relationship to the environment can be disrupted by play. That environment can itself play, becoming unfixed and disorderly, and thus create new freedoms. In the basic shape of this argument produced by unitary urbanism there is the foundation for a concept of architectural performance.

The journey towards the concept of architecture as performance begins with the Lettrists and in particular with the work of their member Constant Nieuwenhuys. Constant, as he was known, was a Dutch artist also associated with the group CoBrA. In 1959 he began to exhibit models of a new sort of city. These, he said, were neither an architectural planning project nor a traditional artwork. Instead they 'maintain a creative game with an imaginary environment that is set in place of the inadequate, unsatisfying environment of contemporary life' (in Pinder 2005: 162). The name Constant gave to the city imagined in his models and sketches was the New Babylon.

At the heart of the New Babylon, driving its conception, was the importance of 'play', understood as a way of being in the world that escaped the structures of work. It involved imaginings that were able to reach beyond the assumptions and limits of functionalism. As Constant said in 1963: 'it should be clear that the functional cities that have been erected during the long period of history in which human lives were consecrated to utility, would by no means suit the totally different needs of the creative race of the *homo ludens*' (in Pinder 2005: 204). Although play was an important concept in general to those associated with the CoBrA group, that final phrase comes specifically from Johan Huizinga, whose work influenced Constant. His planning for New Babylon would thus create the conditions for the play that would reverse alienation. He outlined the principles in 1959: 'we believe that all static, unchanging elements must be avoided and that the variable or changing character of architectural elements is the precondition for a flexible relationship with the events that will take place within them.' In this vision the material fabric of the city interacts with those who live in it: 'Every transformation of space, no matter how minor, is understood as a direct intervention in social life that sets off a "chain reaction" of responses. New forms of behaviour evolve, only to be challenged by the next spatial move, and so on' (in Wigley 1998: 111, 14). In Constant's urban vision: 'social space is truly the concrete space of meetings, of the contacts between beings. Spatiality is social. In New Babylon social space is social spatiality' (in Pinder 2005: 220). To demonstrate those connections between the spatial and the felt he planned an exhibition at the Stedelijk Museum in Amsterdam in May 1960 in which the gallery space would open out into the city, and the city wanderer would become imbricated with the built gallery. The exhibition didn't happen, however, because the Situationists walked out.

Nearly forty years passed before the experiment of Diller & Scofidio's Blur Building, exhibited at the Swiss National Expo in 2002. The building consisted of a platform, suspended over Lake Neuchatel, which could accommodate up to 400 visitors. The rest of the structure was formed of an artificial mist created by a series of very fine water jets. Controlled by computers that responded to climactic conditions the cloud of mist changed its shape, moving outwards in cooler weather, leaving trails of fog in high winds or moving up and down according to temperature. The problem was that, unlike New Babylon, it would have made no difference to how people performed their lives. For in New Babylon the environment would create the conditions for 'psychological', 'societal' and 'erotic' games. It would promote chance meetings, unexpected experiences, different bodily states: 'One crosses cool and dark spaces, hot, noisy, chequered, wet, windy spaces under the bare sky, obscure corridors and alleyways, perhaps a glass grotto, a labyrinth, a pond, a wind tunnel' (in van Haaren 1966: 13). As Pinder correctly notes, this New Babylonian mode of movement through the city, with its somatic adventuring, anticipates the later twentieth-century thinking that informs 'nomadology' and programmes of 'de-territorialisation'.

In the New Babylon project we see a political imperative driving a conceptualisation of architecture as a mode of performance, where the architecture produces bodily and emotional experiences while interactively responding to what it produces. It's important to note, however, that this was not an isolated example. A similar position had been formulated somewhat earlier in a very different place. In the early 1950s the Congrès Internationaux d'Architecture Moderne (CIAM) began to fracture in arguments around modernity and functionalism. Two young British architects, Alison and Peter Smithson, helped form a new group, Team 10, which was invited to organise the programme for the 1956 CIAM conference, at which the breakup of CIAM became clearer. Team 10 continued to meet, and in 1960, the Smithsons published their ideas and sketches about urbanism. These had an impact throughout the architecture profession, introducing to it ways of thinking about the city which were not far distant from those which Constant was more polemically to state a few years later.

Since the early fifties the Smithsons had argued that the street was 'an arena for social expression'. This notion, they said, was missing from the houses being built in 1952, which 'were to high standards of construction and met the needs of society as outlined by official sociologists but they lacked some very vital quality; a quality which was undoubtedly necessary in order to achieve *active* and *creative* grouping of houses. This missing quality – essential to man's sense of wellbeing – was IDENTITY.' To restore this quality they modelled their Golden Lane Project, a multilevel housing development arranged along lines that were more social than 'rational', to meet 'the need for an environment active and creative socially'. Their plan 'would make for a new way of living in the city'. This Golden Lane scheme was then 'elaborated into a general theory and presented to CIAM 9 at Aix-en-Provence in 1953 at which the words ASSOCIATION and IDENTITY were introduced into architectural thinking'. So here, immediately contemporary with

Chtcheglov's more poetically polemical ruminations, were architects demonstrating to other architects how the built environment could produce behaviours and create identity. In turn these ideas influenced Constant, whose
thinking in 1955 echoed the Smithsons' language: 'The traditional distinction
between inside and outside established by a linear system of streets and
facades would have to be replaced with a more complex sculptural play
between masses and voids that sets up a new kind of urban rhythm' (in
Wigley 1998: 26). A year later, in language somewhat more sober than
Constant, the Smithsons 'put forward an alternative system in which the
"infra-structure" (roads and services) was the only fixed thing'. While
Chtcheglov was getting his inspiration from de Chirico, the Smithsons were
looking at Pollock and Paolozzi, finding 'an order with a certain structure and
a certain tension, where every piece was correspondingly new in a new system
of relationship'. So in their thoughts 'On Building towards the Community
Structure' the Smithsons urged that 'Buildings should be thought of from the
beginning as fragments; containing within themselves a capacity to act with
other buildings; be themselves links in systems of access and servicing'
(Smithson and Smithson 1967: 15–74). Breaking with functional totality
and 'rationality', the Smithsons' vision conceived of buildings in dynamic
relationships with buildings, always potentially tense and creative.

Their scheme is not too far from that of New Babylon, but it creates less of
an historical noise. Constant, on the other hand, not only had noisy friends
(and enemies), but also plugged into a discursive genealogy that still has its
effects in thinking about performance and spaces. For, along with other
members of CoBrA, Constant had been influenced by Henri Lefebvre's 1947
Critique of Everyday Life. Lefebvre, writing from a Marxist standpoint, published analyses of the relationship between urban space and behaviour
throughout the later part of the 1960s. He too suggested that town planning,
with its zones and sectors, was a way of structuring everyday life. It created
separation but imposed from above an illusion of unity. In his *Introduction to
Modernity*, published in 1962, he explicitly commended the situationist project of 'dis-alienation' as particularly relevant to and successful in towns:

> it is within the context of the urban milieu that the creative activity of
> situations, and thus of a style and a way of living, is best undertaken.
> Thus the group has concentrated its attention on describing towns, on
> urban space and its use for play, and on all the forms of participation
> which derive from it.   (Lefebvre 1995: 345–46)

Once again 'play' is a crucial concept. For play doesn't simply occupy the
available spaces; it changes the relations between people and the built

environment and, in changing those relations, implies that, far from being fixed and set in concrete, as it were, the built environment is an always developing process of construction. Furthermore it responds to its inhabitants: 'the city can appropriate existing political, religious and philosophical meanings. It seizes them to say them, to *expose* them by means – or through the voice – of buildings, monuments, and also by streets and squares, by voids, by our spontaneous theatricalization of encounters which take place in it, not forgetting festivities and ceremonies' (1996: 113-14). Just under a decade later, in 1977, and across the world, Tuan repeated the idea that 'the city was and is an elaborate conglomeration of innumerable stages for the performance of private and semi-public dramas' but he lamented that the modern city had lost the occasions of large public performance (1977: 174). But this argument itself had already lost the visionary, and politically motivated, drive of Lefebvre and his predecessors. For Lefebvre and the rest it was about a different sort of performance from dramas and ceremonies. The ideal city 'would involve the obsolescence of space: an accelerated change of abode, emplacements and prepared spaces. It would be the *ephemeral city*, the perpetual *oeuvre* of the inhabitants, themselves mobile and mobilized for and by this *oeuvre*' (1996: 172–73).

Buildings that produce identification, buildings acting with other buildings, a city that theatricalises encounters: all of this language has written into it a notion of interaction very similar to one associated with performed behaviour. But as with the other actions and thinking so far reviewed in Part II the word 'performance' itself barely features. This is perhaps not surprising. In the academic world of cultural anthropology and folklore of the late fifties the word 'performance' was a novelty, an 'imponderable quantity'. Nevertheless it is my argument here that the actions and analysis of groups such as Provos and Situationists contribute to the formation of a concept of behaviour that works with, indeed promotes, the dynamic of interaction as a means of unsettling fixed structures and ideas, replacing a material and discursive stability with constant negotiation and fluidity, managing not to be impressed, as it were, by dominant order, indeed impressing itself onto that order. It's a process that could be taken to be similar to Goffman's version of what goes on between people in everyday communication. But in the activities of the provocateurs and counterculture the performed behaviour became indissolubly associated with the energy, the demonstrably embodied recalcitrance, of invasive play and occupied streets. As Lefebvre put it, those associated with groups such as the Situationists 'are all in search of the *opening*, by which they may enter in a practical way into the "possible-impossible" dialectic, which in turn implies other dialectics: "foreseen-unforeseen", "necessary-aleatory", "seriousness-play", "revolution-conservatism"' (Lefebvre 1995: 348).

To make a practice of that which is possible is to use creativity in order to bring something new into being, within the circumstances, and against the limits, of the officially given. The new thing on and by which creativity works is human action. The creation of the possible, of the unforeseen, aleatory and playful, may be said to be one of the bases of performance. But it leaves hanging the questions as to who is doing the performance, in what associations and to what ends. While so far the thinking about the city has generally assumed activities done by groups or for groups, the discourse around behaviour in the city was also powerfully steered in another, highly influential, direction.

To follow this we return to that moment in Paris in 1968 and join a scholar who was energised by those events, although he commented on them without apparently taking sides. Michel de Certeau's account of 'Walking in the City' is part of his book, *The Practice of Everyday Life*, which appeared in English in 1984. Funded by a large research grant to investigate culture the book takes for analysis particular and local practices, and this it seems is where its ideological commitment lies. For in his account of the concept of the city, its discursive structure, de Certeau notes that, although it is a 'totalizing' concept, actual urban life 'increasingly permits the re-emergence of the element that the urbanistic project excluded. The language of power is in itself "urbanizing", but the city is left prey to contradictory movements that counterbalance and combine themselves outside the reach of panoptic power.' A literal version of urban movements that contradict the totalising force of the city might be exemplified in some of the groups we've met already, and what de Certeau has in mind here could well be illustrated by the situationist *dérive*. But he is not here invoking the actual *dérive*. Instead it is a metaphor which describes a research methodology that focuses on specific and local practices. And it not only describes the methodology but also rhetorically promotes it:

> one can analyse the microbe-like singular and plural practices which an urbanistic system was supposed to administer or suppress, but which have outlived its decay; one can follow the swarming activity of these procedures that, far from being regulated or eliminated by panoptic administration, have reinforced themselves in a proliferating illegitimacy, developed and insinuated themselves into the networks of surveillance.   (de Certeau 1988: 96)

To focus on specificity of practices is to be on the side of proliferating and swarming life as against 'panoptic administration', 'surveillance', 'observational organization'.

De Certeau positions his research project alongside – and as extension of – Foucault's analysis of disciplinary apparatuses. For de Certeau 'spatial practices in fact secretly structure the determining conditions of social life.' That formulation could also be said to have behind it the situationist proposition that the physical arrangements of the city organise social life, but there's a slight shift of emphasis in it. The 'present conjuncture', he says, 'is marked by a contradiction between the collective mode of administration and an individual mode of reappropriation' (de Certeau 1988: 96).

By way of illustrating how that mode of reappropriation works de Certeau begins by considering the act of walking in the city. Although this is a basic feature of city existence it cannot readily be mapped. For the map would only record the routes, the places, says de Certeau, where walking has happened. A map cannot record the 'operation of walking, wandering, or "window shopping," that is, the activity of passers-by' (de Certeau 1988: 97). Unable to be recorded in maps, walking nevertheless has an impact on the felt environment: the 'intertwined paths' of walkers 'give their shape to spaces. They weave places together.' This unofficial creativity not only eludes the official eye but it resists it as well: 'The long poem of walking manipulates spatial organizations, no matter how panoptic they may be: it is neither foreign to them (it can take place only within them) nor in conformity with them (it does not receive its identity from them)' (de Certeau 1988: 97, 101). Above all, perhaps, the practice of walking manages to be both an activity done by many and yet individual. 'Their swarming mass is an innumerable collection of singularities' (de Certeau 1988: 97).

To help him describe city walking, as Buchanan (2000) points out, de Certeau draws on an eclectic range of models. These produce various claims for it – that walking lacks a place, that it substitutes for legends, that it is a rhetoric that undercuts 'immobile order'. Of these the one of most interest here is the speech act:

> At the most elementary level, it has a triple 'enunciative' function: it is a process of *appropriation* of the topographical system on the part of the pedestrian (just as the speaker appropriates and takes on the language); it is a spatial acting-out of the place (just as the speech act is an acoustic acting-out of language); and it implies *relations* among differentiated positions.   (de Certeau 1988: 97–98)

Conceived on the model of the speech act, walking can be regarded as a physical rather than verbal performance. While the walker may be said to 'actualize' the possibilities of the built environment, for example when a wall blocks a particular direction, at the same time 'he also moves them about and he invents others.' He makes an analogy with Charlie Chaplin doing different things with his cane. Like the performer, the walker is both transformative and creative:

> the walker transforms each spatial signifier into something else. And if on the one hand he actualizes only a few of the possibilities fixed by the constructed order (he goes only here and not there), on the other he increases the number of possibilities (for example, by creating shortcuts and detours) and prohibitions (for example, he forbids himself to take paths generally considered accessible or even obligatory).

The value of this walking performance, in terms of opposition to a dominant panoptic organisation, is that it 'creates a mobile organicity in the environment' (de Certeau 1988: 98, 99).

Now, as we know, what makes walking as a 'speech act' resistant to panoptic mapping is that its 'enunciatory operations are of an unlimited diversity'. But in relation to this proposition there are some who would say that the limit to the diversity is set by the extent to which the 'enunciatory operations' might be intelligible. If they are to work as a language then they have to align with the elements of a system. But such a system does more than provide the resources for individual enunciation: at a fundamental level it establishes the organisation not just of speech but also of thought. The acquisition of language, the capacity to make a speech act, is dependent on not only entering but also accepting – becoming part of – the organisational system of language. Hence it could be said that individuals are already scripted, insofar as they have acquired language and ideology, before they make their individual speech act. This then prompts some questions: within what framework of thinking and discourse does the walker invent new possibilities? And to what end are these invented? For example, when Charlie Chaplin multiplies the possibilities of his cane on film, he has already decided which ones 'work' and which don't. The end towards which he is working is to create laughter, which comes in part from recognition as well as surprise. The range of possibilities is controlled by what the audience will recognise and what they will expect of him as Charlie Chaplin (as opposed to Buster Keaton). The cane must retain its identity as, basically, a cane, with all its associations, and the games with it must not exceed or disrupt the dramaturgic sequence in which it features. We are not, therefore, in the presence of totally free expressive creation. In the same way, when the walker makes a 'selection' of the paths to be followed, this walker is already positioned both within language in general and within the specific structures of the city, workplace, family and partnership. Walking is done by walkers, biological agents who function within determinate historical conditions and subject to ideological organisation.

The walker, however creative, is not actually a free agent. De Certeau instances a friend who opts to go 'along paths that have no name or signature' and observes that 'her walking is thus still controlled negatively by proper names.' Now these proper names, if not the human beings, seem to have an agency all of their own. They become detached from material spaces and exist simply as names. As such 'They become liberated spaces that can be occupied.' And their indeterminacy gives them power: 'They insinuate other routes into the functionalist and historical order of movement' (de Certeau 1988: 104, 105). The reappearance of the familiar binary of liberated/playful versus functionalist/organised here bestows a somewhat magical appearance of agency on mere names. It is claimed that names can become spaces and insinuate routes, that they, presumably, have a capacity for spatial practice. Once again we are starting to float free of material activity: with what agency, we might ask, is this spatial practice done?

Although I started out by observing the ghosts of situationist thought behind de Certeau's argument, here we discover how far he is away from that thought. While the Situationists may have used words to unsettle or provoke the functionalist dominant, this was shaped as *détournement* or game, with human agency doing the work of detourning. Similarly a *dérive* was not merely a wander on whim down streets the names of which one fancied. The *dérive* also gathered data about psychogeography, and it was best done by a group. De Certeau, on the other hand, sets the city's totalising force in opposition to individuality. He notes the contradiction between 'the collective mode of administration and an individual mode of reappropriation'. And while he might be thinking here of repeated individual appropriations the tendency is still to highlight the single rather than the group: the 'swarming mass' is a 'collection of singularities' (de Certeau 1988: 96, 97). This doesn't suggest the group action to which even that anti-social bunch the Situationists aspired. And there is one further contrast with them. The 'poem of walking', says de Certeau, 'is itself the effect of successive encounters and occasions that constantly alter it and make it the other's blazon: in other words, it is like a peddler, carrying something surprising, transverse or attractive compared with the usual choice' (de Certeau 1988: 101). It is because of its contrast with the 'usual choice' that the peddler gets paid for her or his commodity. The fact of its unusualness does not set it automatically in opposition to the system of commodity exchange; it simply gives it greater market value. Underneath the apparent binary contrast here the totality of the exchange system persists. And it is not only at this moment that it becomes evident. For remember that, when de Certeau contrasted the activity of passers-by with the map that failed to record that activity, he appeared to be celebrating walking as against graphic administration, a specific practice as against a totalising organisation. But a part of the activity that was thus to be celebrated, you will recall, is 'window shopping'. Our radically reappropriative city walker is already, it seems, caught up in the thrall of the society of the spectacle and its world of deliciously individualised commodities.

The image ideologically invokes all the subversion of the situationist city project while actually transforming it into a solipsistic saunter. The walking may be a form of performance but being a performance doesn't always guarantee that you're not just window-shopping the spectacle. It depends what the performance is being done for, what is at stake. There are other voices outside.

Chapter 10

New forms of activism

There was yet another person observing the events in Paris in May 1968. In his own commentary on them Jean-Jacques Lebel used an interesting word: 'The first stage of an uprising (the barricades, the mass demonstrations, the street fighting between the government forces and the radicals, as well as such events as the burning down of the Stock Exchange, which occurred on May 24th), the first stage of *any* revolution, is always theatrical' (1969: 112).

He was not alone in his sense that political action was 'theatrical'. Famously one of the founders of the Youth International Party, the Yippies, Jerry Rubin, talked about 'revolution as theatre' and the Bolivian revolutionary Che Guevara spoke, in a self-consciously 'lyrical' fashion, of how he learnt to see revolutionary situations in terms of 'protagonists in the drama' (in Baxandall 1969). Now it is clear that, across history, revolutions, uprisings and even limited protest actions have used apparently dramatic or theatrical devices and actions. Nottingham radicals in 1802 marched through the city with a figure of the Goddess of Reason; Westminster radicals in 1809 disrupted theatre performances by shaking rattles, holding placards and dancing jigs; members of the National Unemployed Workers Movement brought central London traffic to a standstill in 1939 by staging a mock funeral procession of coffins for the unemployed. These sorts of political demonstrations have been subject to much academic analysis, often in the context of research on new social movements, with the cumulative work of Charles Tilly establishing a framework for discussing political demonstrations as performances, with their own systems of reference and language (see Tilly 2008). For our purposes here, however, the interest is in the moment at which a concept and language of performance need to come into being in response to, and as shaped by, those demonstrations.

In the sixties and seventies there seemed to be a lot more of them. Not just the wave of student actions across the west but industrial disputes, strikes and demonstrations, civil rights and anti-war protests filled the cities and the news. Quite apart from quantity, however, what appears different in this period is the discourse about the events, the interest in describing not just what they do but how they function. To at least one contemporary commentator the explosion of these new sorts of political event seemed to constitute a point of precisely definable historical change: 'October 20, 1967 could be said to mark the end of the mass sterile protest parade and the start of an open-ended era of mass, infectious radical dramaturgy' (Baxandall 1969: 69).

A modern commentator, Craig Peariso, draws on a 1970 essay by drama critic Robert Brustein to suggest that the cause of this new radical dramaturgy lay in the culture of apparent permissiveness in the United States. In Brustein's view radicals took advantage of mass media that willingly reported radical ideas and action so that in effect every political action was simply staged for the camera. Peariso disagrees both with Brustein's politics and with his inclination to assume that aesthetics, planned displays, do not work. But he shares with Brustein an acceptance of the analysis famously made by Herbert Marcuse in 1966 which identified the US state as operating through 'repressive tolerance', allowing all voices to be heard but allowing nobody the capacity to make or act on decisions (Peariso 2014: 7–11). Whereas Marcuse was pessimistic that anything could be achieved, radical students, among others, thought differently. In 1969 a postgraduate student noted the distinctive new forms of student protest, 'public trials of professors (Italy), mock funerals (Germany)'. He argued that they resulted, ultimately, from the resolution of the Cold War into 'peaceful coexistence'. Whereas in conditions of Cold War western democracy was celebrated as a contrast with Soviet repression, after that mind-set dissolved the political left discovered the real truth of their own society where the 'formal freedoms' of parliamentary democracy are actually 'an instrument for deadening popular consciousness and dissent'. Thus students, a large group trained in intellectual labour, adopted forms of protest which 'obliged the authoritarian institutions of advanced capitalism to reveal themselves for what they were, and so to show the true nature of "repressive tolerance"' (Stedman Jones 1969: 36–38). This of course was precisely what the Provos were doing in Amsterdam or the hippies in their bus. Or indeed the activists of Gay Liberation, although other parts of the political left might not have wanted to admit it. For example, Dennis Altman instances so-called radical drag as 'an extravagant send-up of all that is normal and respectable', including assumptions about gender. 'Don't call us drag queens', said one of San Francisco's Cockettes, 'call us freaks' (Altman 1971: 173).

It is characteristic of sixties' radicalism that it analysed what it was doing while it was doing it. It was generating discourse and concepts. While it attempted to explain the cause of new forms of protest it also sought to explain how they functioned, and it is the development of this language which is interesting for our purposes here. While Lebel said revolution was 'theatrical' the man who celebrated the arrival of 'infectious radical dramaturgy' thought it was important precisely because it was different from being theatrical. This seemed very clear in that historic moment in October 1967 when a mass action was mounted against the Pentagon as part of the opposition to the war on the Vietnamese:

> Scaling ropes, flanking maneuvers, inundation by sheer numbers were but part of the repertoire of this humoristic, motley, and audacious legion. The yellow submarine of the hippies, 12 feet long, was passed over heads toward the doors. Smaller contingents of troops were surrounded, talked to, pressed in so tightly they could not use their weapons, allowed to retreat only in disorderly flight, perhaps with helmets swiped or a flower in a rifle barrel. Posters and slogans remembering Che appeared on abutments. Tens of thousands alternated 'America the Beautiful' with an ironic 'Sieg Heil!' salute chanted to commanding officers on the battlements. Yippies, banners proclaiming solidarity and a victory more than pyrrhic (**We Have One**), moved upon the portals chanting 'Out, Demon, Out!' to a strange music. Before the Pentagon under a golden sun in a crisp breeze, the flag of the Vietnamese National Liberation Front fluttered.   (Baxandall 1969: 68–69)

The description of this event, together with the claim as to its significance in introducing an era of 'radical dramaturgy', comes from Lee Baxandall's essay 'Spectacles and Scenarios: A Dramaturgy of Radical Activity', published in 1969. As his title says, Baxandall's essay is an attempt to model and analyse political actions as performances. Almost thirty years later, inspired by Baxandall's essay, and drawing on theoretical approaches developed in the time since, Baz Kershaw proposed a model of the dramaturgy that structured these events, a dramaturgy 'which stressed qualities such as multiplicity, discontinuity, abrupt eruptions of dramatic intensity, sudden shifts and changes of direction, tempo, focus'. He argues that there was not just an increased number of demonstrations and such in the sixties and seventies but that they were also, crucially, of a different kind. Whereas the events in Paris in 1968 could be related back to 'the tradition of modernist radical dramaturgy', with its more or less head-on confrontation of protestors and state, in the United States a new 'dramaturgy of protest' developed (though radical students themselves in the late sixties also thought they saw new dramaturgy in Italy and Germany). In Kershaw's view the new 'dramaturgy of protest' had 'all the polyphonous eloquence which Bakhtin had claimed for classic carnival, plus original forms of theatricalized spectacle that, true to Debord's recipes for symbolic revolution, fashioned new relations between the imaginary and the real.' As Kershaw sees it, the sources for this newly theatricalised spectacle came from various theatre groups. With the San Francisco Mime Troupe, which brought together Brecht and commedia dell'arte, Ronnie Davis developed a model of 'guerrilla theatre'. Bread and Puppet, drawing on both religious spectacle and Artaud, developed new sorts of often metaphoric imagery to be used in street protest. Living Theatre, looking for ways to undercut the grip of learnt behaviours and rational analysis, broke down divisions between audience and performance, turning spectators into participants (Kershaw 1997: 260, 262, 264). To these might be added one other source, which more concretely links the US dramaturgy back into new European practices. For an Art Workers' Coalition protest against the My Lai massacre in Vietnam masks were worn on the backs of heads. These were the idea of Irving Petlin, who had been politically engaged in France between 1959 and 1964. As Frascina argues, 'Petlin's political "apprenticeship" in France helped to formulate a sense of what he calls "primitive situational politics" which characterised the early activities of anti-Vietnam-War protests' (1999: 170). In this source of the new dramaturgy we see not so much an adaptation of traditional theatrical techniques but the anti-spectacle theorisations, and play, of the Situationists.

Kershaw's essay is not only an extremely useful piece of thinking but it has important implications for some of the assumptions that were later to be associated with one version of so-called performance theory. His idea of protest as 'an integral aspect of civil society' raises, he says, 'some difficult questions' for, in particular, the then-dominant version of performance theory in the United States. The reason is that his analysis 'relocates resistant power in a social arena that is not so easily recuperated by the dominant as the "marginal" identities that tend to be the subject of their analyses'. He then adds, somewhat pointedly: 'it may even problematize the influential notion in much critical discourse across a whole range of disciplines that the marginal is the chief repository of active organized insubordination' (Kershaw 1997: 274). But important as it is, Kershaw's essay is an analysis and theorisation done after the event. As he himself makes clear the aim was not simply to model the dramaturgy of the late sixties events but also to intervene in the readings of them that were settling into place (to which end he puts straight some of Schechner's casual generalisations). For our purposes, once again, the effort here is to track the emergence of new concepts as they happened, to see how the demonstrations were producing a new idea of performance. That said, we return to Baxandall.

In his description of the Pentagon event he says that 'Everywhere there pervaded a spirit of Epic Theatre (so many actions and performers, so much detached awareness of one's deeds even as one acted)' (Baxandall 1969: 69). This, though, was an evocation of one specific event. To model political activity more generally he needed language that did not take its reference point from theatre. This was necessary for reasons that will become clear if we follow his argument.

The essay is structured in such a way as to replace linear argument with conflict and diversity. The first half or so is written as if it were a speech from a right-wing perspective given as 'the Edmund Burke Memorial Lecture for 1969'. The second half is written as if by 'an activist who shall be known as "Rimbaud Vivant"'. Dispersed through the essay are descriptions of political events: Nuremburg 1936; Columbia University spring 1968; Grinnell College, Iowa 1969 ('Playboy Meets the Women's Liberation Front'); Paris May 1968; The Pentagon October 1967; Vallegrande, Bolivia, October 1967 (state photograph of the state-murdered Che Guevara). The right-wing lecturer begins by causing distress to his audience when he observes that 'the New Left – how consciously is not yet clear – has discovered the performance element of politics for its own ends.' This observation causes distress because it suggests that the New Left have discovered, and adopted for themselves, a traditional political weapon of the right. For, as the lecturer tells us, invoking Hobbes, performance has been crucial to the maintenance of a ruling order's power: 'reputation of power, is Power'. And, while the supremacy of the right 'on the terrain of social dramaticism' is currently being challenged, there is a crucial difference between the two political groups. Whereas the 'radicals' do no structured classes in or theorisation of performance, the right has 'uncounted management training schools and seminars'. It also has sociologists who are 'resources consultants on "social integration" through dramatistic interaction'. Among these sociologists he includes Erving Goffman, whose *Presentation of Self in Everyday Life* he commends in that it 'offers radicals no guidance whatsoever' (Baxandall 1969: 53, 55–56, 62). Sociology, we should note, was attacked by radical students as a discipline that simply assisted the consolidation of capitalism, the 'rise of sociology' being 'tied to the social demand for rationalized practice in the service of bourgeois ends' as the Nanterre students saw it in 1969 (Cockburn and Blackburn 1969: 373).

But if the right had all the techniques of mass persuasion, in the late sixties it could be said that the left had their art, their happenings and such. So Baxandall has his Burke lecturer ask whether art can free itself of 'our encapsulating spectacle', observing that it is only the very rare artist who manages to 'release himself from spectacle obsequiousness' (Baxandall 1969: 58). This raises a question that bugged other commentators and activists. As Jean-Jacques Lebel put it, while there are some 'anti-artists' who want to destroy the culture industry as a part of capitalism, there are also 'non-political Fluxus-type events, arty-farty happenings, and street shows ... which claim to be "unintentional" and not aimed at the destruction of the existing social structure'. He may have been thinking of the 'propaganda action' that George Macunias proposed for Fluxus in New York. This was to include not just 'Sabotage and disruption' but also 'Sale of Fluxus publications' (in Home 1991: 53). All such events, says Lebel, 'tend to be quickly absorbed into the art market, the "avant-garde" department of Madison Avenue' (Lebel 1969: 111–12). Against Lebel's position activists in the emergent form of guerrilla theatre argued that they had a genuinely radical function in exposing 'repressive tolerance' or disrupting the 'spectacle', depending on your terminology. Estrin suggests that guerrilla theatre could counter the dominant spectacle by providing a way 'to sensitize people to the ubiquitous, insidious, and obscene con job of America'. These 'acts of redemptive theatre' create 'new realities'. 'By acting as if certain things were true,' guerrilla theatre, he says, 'creates the conditions whereby they may *become* true' (Estrin 1969: 76).

Quite apart from that slightly romantic idealism, or possibly evidenced by it, it remained the case that guerrilla theatre was 'theatre' and therefore could be fitted into a readily available category. The extension of theatre into political activity, as guerrilla theatre or street pageant, follows a line of development that extends across the twentieth century, and indeed earlier. The 1920s saw the use of theatre techniques in agitational propaganda, pioneered in the early Soviet Union, but so too, in the seventeenth-century Commonwealth in Britain, theatre developed more agitational forms, as it did on into the eighteenth century. True it is that the 1960s' developments were not merely extensions of formal aesthetic techniques, though. As Ronnie Davis saw it the mark of real guerrilla theatre was in its organisational structure and the relations between members of the group. It is also the case that there was analysis of the particular theatrical strategies in terms of their political efficacy as required by a specific historical negotiation or conflict. Davis criticised the traditional agitprop mode as one that appeared to consist of seizing the ethical high ground and simply shouting at people, whereas his group, the San Francisco Mime Troupe, did such useful things as helping motorists cheat parking meters. This sort of critique emerges from the activity amongst theatre groups which Sainer describes as an attempt 'to understand the nature of events'. Writing in 1975 he thought that supposed political theatre had already settled down into a formulaic pattern, where groups thought it sufficiently political, and experimental, simply to manufacture 'ritual'. The best work, Sainer said, comes from that effort to understand the 'nature of events and sometimes to change circumstances' (1975: 42). It is the thinking about 'events', and how they work, which began to generate a different vocabulary of performance. The generation of this vocabulary is what is of more interest to us here than the local developments of new forms of theatre practice. This takes us back to Baxandall.

For Baxandall the importance of political actions is that they challenge available categories (and thus of course the structures that sponsor those categories), but in doing so they present problems of terminology. 'Dramatistic action' is a way of describing an event that is neither 'ordinary' behaviour nor theatre, but is somewhat sociological. In his title Baxandall refers to dramaturgy and his account of the Pentagon event invokes the form of epic theatre. Largely, though, he steers clear of comparing radical activity to theatre. The student action at Columbia University, which he offers as a 'paradigm instance of the dramaturgy of radical activity', can be regarded neither as spectacle nor as theatre, because each of these is part of dominant order, and indeed the project of the activity is to unmask the operation of spectacle. So he calls it 'radical scenarism' and 'counter-spectacle'. The event was part of a campaign based around issues which, he says, 'dramatized' the political complicity of the university system. Use of that word indicates the limits on the vocabulary. This may not be theatre, but it employs drama. So too for all that it is a counter-spectacle it is nevertheless spectacle.

Terminology alone then cannot necessarily define the distinctness of the radical activity. But when Baxandall talks of the university administration's 'policy of remote spectacle', which masks their ineptitude, we are closer to the real distinction. For while this sort of spectacle is 'scenaristic' it is also 'reinforcive' and 'cooptive'. By contrast the activity in 'radical activity' is not just 'a mere expenditure of energy in movement' but 'a unification of theory and sensuous conduct'. In short, if the dominant order's spectacle is enclosing and disciplinary, the anti-dominant counter-spectacle is full of energy and sensuousness. This contrast gets sharpened up into a binary pair of terms when Baxandall explains that the French Revolution could be seen as 'spectacle vs. scenarism' where, to use phraseology he takes from Plekhanov, while the spectacle worked to stifle them the citizens embraced a 'poetry of action'. In the same way, he says, Lenin 'deeply distrusted spectacle' but against that 'stressed scenario action' which manifested itself in insurrection, for, quoting Lenin, 'revolutions are festivals of the oppressed' (1969: 61–62, 66).

Behind this formulation of a liberatory 'scenarism' lie several influences. Strongest among them – 'the best prevision of universalized scenarism' – is Marx's commentary on Fourier's 'cabalism': 'Compare the tone of a formal social gathering, its moral, stilted, languishing jargon, with the tone of these same people united in a cabal: they will appear transformed to you, you will admire their terseness, their animation, the quick play of ideas, the alertness of action' (in Baxandall 1969: 70). Baxandall also refers here to Marcuse's *Essay on Liberation* and Huizinga's account of 'play'. But there is also another influence, historically very close, yet not specifically mentioned. This influence is felt in various places. In Lebel's account of the May 1968 events in Paris, his reference to 'arty-farty happenings' adopts a similar position to the situationist dismissal of experimental forms as yet more commodities spawned by the spectacle. It's that situationist sense of the imprisoning spectacle which lingers under Baxandall's argument, and it's there again in Estrin's notes on 'guerrilla theatre without actors' when he commends the use of spray paint for turning STOP signs into 'STOP WAR signs' (Estrin 1969: 77), a classic piece of *détournement*.

By engaging with the protests and 'radical activity' of the late sixties, Baxandall defines a kind of performed behaviour that was not only different from but also resistant to the aesthetic theatre of the culture industry. And, while similar sorts of non-theatrical performance had been defined elsewhere, Baxandall's argument emphasises an additional feature of it. The circumstances of the radical activity produced a logic whereby, precisely because this sort of performance was opposed to the cooptive spectacle of the dominant order, it necessarily would be the case that it was characterised by qualities that were the opposite of that spectacle. As seen in events at Columbia University or the Pentagon such non-theatrical performance was thus, almost by reason of its structural contrast, radical, sensuous and energetic.

One further point needs noting. Those who in the 1990s and onwards wrote about the emergence of performance make much of an intellectual lineage that includes, among others, Goffman. If we follow Baxandall's argument, we have to put to one side Goffman and social science as having any sort of influence on radical performance that was associated with protest and insurrection (we know what the Nanterre students thought of sociology). Instead the influence here comes, most immediately, from the language and ideas of the Situationists. And back behind them were Marx and Lenin. This lineage seems to have been discreetly airbrushed from the institutionalised forms of the study of performance.

Chapter 11

Happenings and everyday performance

At 1 pm on Sunday, May 16, 1965, something over a hundred people in dark clothes stood in silence at the entrance to Los Angeles's new County Art Museum. The people were artists and they were making a protest.

The Tower on Cieniga Boulevard

The event was one of a series over a weekend in the gallery quarter of Los Angeles. It led from here to a larger scale event that opened in late February 1966. This was a structure built at the junction of Sunset Boulevard and La Cieniga Boulevard in West Hollywood, the 'Artists Tower of Protest against the War in Vietnam'. The Tower consisted of a range of artworks contributed by numerous artists. Their aim was to create an outdoor event that lasted over time, so that it could not be ignored by the press, and was collectively composed, so that it would resist becoming another collectable art commodity.

The positioning of the Tower was very precise. La Cieniga Boulevard was full of art galleries and the crowds they drew constituted an image of the city's civil prowess and importance, seen on display in 'the weekly Monday night ritual of "La Cieniga art walk"'. Although some of the galleries had a close relationship with avant-garde art and oppositional politics, in general in southern California 'high culture was an important activity, process and pleasure for its participants and collectors, many of whom were in the military and science-based corporations and institutes' (Frascina 1999: 61, 26). High art and gallery culture were thus readily associated with a dominant, oppressive, order. The floodlit Tower on the hill above showed that it was not content with the Boulevard's spectacle.

Artists who were opposed to the oppressive order of those who had the money faced the problem of how to take cheap action which would cause maximum disruption. So they developed strategies 'to think of the ideas of the "space", the "theatre", the disposable and transitory life of the streets'. What they came up with was, among other things, the silent vigil in dark clothes at the entrance to a new gallery and the great collective Tower of Protest. Looking back three or so decades later, one of the organisers of that Tower, Irving Petlin, described it 'as an "event", a version of "situationist" street politics'. He had been in Paris in the late 1950s and 1960s, and had witnessed 'the "Manifesto of 121" signed by French intellectuals in 1960 advocating "insubordination" to France's colonial war in Algeria' (Frascina 1999: 25, 29, 57). The Tower may therefore be a coincidental piece of similar thinking or it may have had origins in European political activity, being claimed in hindsight by one of its makers as situationist politics.

Like the Situationists themselves what the artists were doing was to demonstrate a new way of inhabiting social and cultural space, in order both to interfere with assumptions about that space and to assert their own presence within it. In the circumstances of gallery culture, and its capacity to turn artwork into commodity, artists who are opposed to it have to make something which is not amenable to being commodified, something that will be neither sellable object nor the sort of practice that would find a market in institutions such as theatres. What they make is somewhere between political protest and artistic creation. It can be seen as parallel to, and indeed part of, the practices and thinking being developed by the counterculture in general and at the same time it shares interests and attitude with the explorations being conducted in the specific domain of arts practice. The thinking developed in relation to these artistic practices, like that developed by the wider counterculture, informs the persisting assumptions as to the defining characteristics of performance, its relationship to other arts and to social institutions, and its efficacy as a practice.

Various sorts of happening

In the sixties the artists' protest outside the County Museum might well have been called a 'happening'. This was a label which could be readily applied to any event that didn't fit into a recognisable category, from political demonstrations to invited events in New York lofts. Insofar as they were enacted practices which challenged categorisation happenings provoked and exemplified new ways of thinking about performance. The other main provocation to ideas about performance came, slightly later, from 'body art' or 'performance art'. These two sets of innovations – happenings and body art – shaped subsequent thinking about the concept of performance. We begin, therefore, with looking in more detail at happenings.

Most accounts of this well-documented term suggest it has a precise point of origin as an art form. This was in a course run by the composer John Cage at the New School for Social Research in New York in 1957. Back in 1952 at Black Mountain College he had collaborated with artists in different media (music, dance, visual art) to make a presentation in which a variety of pre-planned elements were juxtaposed in apparently random relationship. The elements happened between and around the audience which was in four blocks, so that it could see itself watching. The improvised nature of the dance allowed the spontaneous participation of an audience dog. As a composer Cage was interested in the effects of randomness and chance, and a number of those in Cage's class at New School, such as Al Hansen, Dick Higgins, Allan Kaprow and George Brecht, went on to make similar events. These came to be called 'happenings', though it may not have been the best name, from the title of Kaprow's *Eight Happenings in Six Parts* done in 1959.

In general terms happenings were important in developing a model of performance that seemed separated from all the practices associated with what was understood to be traditional theatre. That separation was demonstrated in their approach to performance, audience and spaces. It was also underlined in the discourse happenings developed about themselves. This discourse emphasised particular values such as authenticity. As Hunter and Bodor say, 'a need for authenticity of action is typically regarded as the fundamental property of work which signals the action performed as "real" rather than "acted".' Such authenticity 'corresponds to an integrity that hinges upon the singularity of a once-occurring moment' (Hunter and Bodor 2012: 87). Being singular and thus not reproducible was in turn a means of rejecting the commodity system and the communications infrastructure that sustained it. But as Sell points out (1998) that rejection was actually highly ambivalent. Happenings also tended to use, enjoy and even celebrate the new commodity culture. This ambivalence of approach was to be symptomatic of the form, as was its discourse. Quite apart from its function in promoting articles of faith and values, this discursive productivity, the form's willingness to talk about itself, was in its own way a significant feature, sometimes feeling like a necessary extension, of the performed work.

Here we need to pause. 'Happening' was eventually a term as widely used as 'performance' came to be later on. In Part I we encountered different sorts of scholars warning of the mistakes inherent in using the term 'performance' as if it is 'a single, coherent thing', 'cramming' divers practices into one genre. The same warning can be applied to 'happening', for there are different accounts of how and where happenings originate and these different accounts establish a slightly different concept of what they were doing as performance.

It is also the case, as Heddon warns (2012: 175), that stories of origin do ideological work, establishing their own arrangements of allies and enemies, norms and transgressions.

The supposed first happening event was Kaprow's in 1959, mentioned above. Kaprow was a painter. This is reflected both in his approach to happenings and in his version of where they originated. They evolved, he argued, from a strand of early 1950s visual art practice: 'action painting – Pollock's in particular – led not to more painting, but to *more action*' (in Sandford 1995: 220). In Jackson Pollock's method of work the physical disposition of his body in relation to the canvas was a key factor in shaping what eventually appeared on that canvas. The way the paint looked had to do with how it had been dripped or splattered, and each new addition of colour was an element within a logic that was as much physical as visual. That physicality was emphasised in Namuth and Falkenberg's film of Pollock at work in 1951, where the camera was positioned as it were underneath the canvas so that the prime focus of the viewer was on the action of the hand and mobility of the paint. In these sequences the painted object disappears from view, being replaced by the viewing subject in such a position as if they were on the receiving end of Pollock's physical activity. As Harold Rosenberg said of it in 1952, 'At a certain moment the canvas began to appear to one American painter after another as an arena in which to act – rather than as a space in which to reproduce, re-design, analyze or "express" an object, actual or imagined. What was to go on the canvas was not a picture but an event' (1962: 25). The painter's 'act' came to have equal status to what was painted, or as a contributor to *Art News* put it in 1959: 'When Pollock painted, his situation, his inner behavior as an artist, were certainly more complex than the painting, for he was living the process' (in Kirby 1995: 15–16). In this respect, as Wollen (1989) says, with his emphasis on the spontaneous and the vital Pollock recalls a group of artists we have met before, CoBrA.

In this story of the emergence of happenings process is foregrounded. The story tends to emphasise action as opposed to representation or analysis, with the physicality presented in such a way that, rather than offering a position of overview, it absorbs the viewer into its rhythms. Process is foregrounded, with the result that the notion of the artist's 'act' – indeed his 'performance' – is conceptualised as that which blurs the divisions between process and product.

A slightly different picture of happenings' operation and significance as performance is drawn by another member of Cage's class of 1957, Al Hansen. For Hansen happenings were to do with 'communication and education', which were politically important because re-education would take people beyond 'compartmentalized society' and would thus be one of the only ways in which the Vietnam war would be ended. But the radical function was carried out by a form which behaved less radically: 'Contrary to the public's conception, the majority of happenings are quite formal, are very carefully rehearsed, and do not invite audience participation at all. Audiences pay healthy amounts of money for admission.' The advertising of the events was, says Hansen, very similar to 'what one might call more normal, old-fashioned theater'. The difference from theatre is simply aesthetic in that happenings were put together 'in the manner of a collage'. This means that not only can happenings cope with accident better than, say, Broadway theatre, but also they deliberately encourage accident by leaving performers, once they get started, 'to go in whatever direction they felt like'. But Hansen is pretty cynical about the idea that this improvisatory quality brings openness or liberation. Difficult audience interventions need managing. And while there is 'something about games and play in happenings' there is also 'something about showing off'. In short happenings can be described as 'theater pieces in the manner of collage', where 'each action or situation or event that occurs within this framework is related in the same way as each part of an abstract expressionist painting' (1965: 1–24).

Hansen's positioning of happenings as theatre contrasts strongly with the account given by yet another class-member, Dick Higgins. While artists such as Kaprow came to happenings by meditating on 'the relationship of the spectator and the work', and gradually enveloping the spectator in collages which Kaprow called 'environments', Higgins was driven by a rejection of theatre as being old-fashioned and made for a previous society: 'others such as myself declared war on the script as a set of sequential events.' 'I began to work as if time and sequence could be utterly suspended, not by ignoring them . . . but by systematically replacing them as structural elements with change.' Thus, if there was no change in his pieces, the pieces would stop. In taking this approach Higgins was much more narrowly focused on aesthetics than was Hansen, and tended to assume that their aesthetics alone would guarantee a special new place for happenings: 'the Happening developed as an intermedium, an uncharted land that lies between collage, music and the theatre. It is not governed by rules; each work determines its own medium and form according to its needs.' So while Hansen sees happenings as theatre done as collage, Higgins sees them going beyond theatre and collage into 'uncharted territory'. But this difference between approaches was something of which he was also aware: 'Kaprow works with rituals, mass numbers of relatively anonymous participants, audiencelessness . . . Oldenburg uses the separate performer and audience functions' (1969: 23–24, 73; my elisions). For Higgins himself the key development above all associated with happenings was the new use of 'intermedia'.

Another contemporary, another story, another concept of performance: for experimental theatre-maker Michael Kirby happenings suggested a new way of doing acting. This characteristic feature begins with Cage's work as a composer. He was dissatisfied with traditional musical instruments, says Kirby, and therefore invented his own, for example a water gong, which was lowered into water while it was still vibrating. In a concert the effect of instruments such as this was to draw attention to the act of using the instrument: '*how* the sound is produced becomes as significant a part of the experience as the *quality* of the sound itself.' In these circumstances any instrument, anything made into an instrument, or indeed silence itself, may feature as part of a concert, but so too, crucially, the new visual interest, 'the emphasis upon performance', in turn 'draws attention to the performer himself'. But as against what performers are expected to do in a theatre 'the musician is not acting'. While actors traditionally seek to create character, the musician 'attempts to be no one other than himself, nor does he function in a place other than that which physically contains him and the audience'. This mode of performing Kirby calls 'unmatrixed', noting that 'Non matrixed performances are not uncommon'. He offers an example: 'Although the audience-performer relationship which is the basis of theatre exists in sporting events, for example, the athlete does not create character or place. Nor is such imaginary information a part of the halftime spectacle of a football game, religious or secular rituals, political conventions, or any other activities in "real life".' But his argument does not aim to 'change our view of these "common" events' and instead he confines his focus to the making of art by emphasising 'the profound possibilities and potentialities of nonmatrixed performing for the theatre' (Kirby 1995: 31).

This story of happenings not only develops a concept of a performing mode which is somewhere between art theatre and everyday life but also creates the concept of performance as a master category which embraces others. That concept of it was repeated a few years later by two other performance makers, Howell and Templeton: 'Performance art is an extension of all the specific properties of each particular art into the general arena of action in time and space. Performance is the term covering a multitude of activities ranging from sport to dance' (1977: 10). To think of sporting events, rituals and ceremonies as similar in arrangement to theatre, with the exception that they are not aiming to produce obvious fictions, and to think of them all as governed by a nameable practice – 'unmatrixed' performing – is to take the step that would see all of them as part of the same spectrum of activity, so to speak.

The idea of unmatrixed performing and its wider usages allows for a contrast with the practices and arrangements of the more narrowly specified aesthetic theatre, a contrast promoted by numerous happenings makers. Erickson notes that 'The specialization of acting was singled out for critique. Acting represents a twofold problem: the alienation of the actor from role – the perfection of dissimulative art in opposition to an authentically experienced life – and the resistance of a living spontaneity to a directed existence' (Erickson 1992: 41). The preparation of dissimulative art required craft training, so happenings makers who were opposed to dissimulative art encouraged, polemically promoted, a rejection of craft and training: 'Happenings should be unrehearsed and performed by nonprofessionals, once only' (Kaprow 2003: 63). Not only was the artist not expected to be a virtuoso but also, in the case for example of feminist dance, the performer needed explicitly to free herself from the corporeal discipline that turned the female body into spectacle. This rhetoric of antipathy to craft and training spread through political theatre and punk culture throughout the seventies, ranging so far and wide that by 2000 an otherwise sensible academic could say that the 'training requirements for students' forced theatre departments to 'cater to middle-brow taste', as if training itself automatically degraded aesthetic discrimination (Banes 2000: 230).

In part the rejection of craft was a way of claiming that the art of performance was not separate from everyday behaving. A similar merging of art and life could be achieved in the handling of the audience, whose position in relation to the show, whose notional separation, had been under question from at least Cage's 1952 piece. In happenings its relationship to the performed elements – whether people or lights or objects – is not clearly defined. It does not have a panoptic overview of the proceedings and is apparently as much subject to the operations of randomness as everything else. Sontag suggests 'This abusive involvement of the audience' is what gives the happening its 'dramatic' interest (Sontag 1966: 265). The audience was not simply physically involved. Its status and position were subject to commentary, if not abuse. Happenings makers in general, and Kaprow in particular, had much to say about the category of audience, with Kaprow in later works seeking to abolish the spectating role entirely: 'By willingly participating in a work, knowing the scenario and their own particular duties beforehand, people become a real and necessary part of the work. It cannot exist without them' (2003: 64). Audience has become 'participant'. In taking this step happenings declared their maximum distance not only from modes of art but also from social gatherings – the political hustings as much as the Shakespearean tragedy – in which the clearly demarcated positions and hierarchies for performers and audience are designed in advance and work to preserve a system of order, with its conventions of respect or belief or decorum.

Thus so far the performance mode inaugurated by happenings would seem to consist of the following features – blurring of process and product, apparent absence of controlling design, randomness and spontaneity of execution, the disavowal of fictional roles as against immediacy of response, the replacing of division between watchers and watched in favour of an as it were uniform participation.

But these features sit rather oddly alongside a political action, or as it could also well be called a 'happening', done by the Guerrilla Artists Action Group and the Art Workers' Coalition in New York following the My Lai massacre of Vietnamese civilians by US troops. The artists infiltrated the Museum of Modern Art (MOMA), smuggling in wreaths, flowers and copies of a poster showing Vietnamese corpses. At 1 pm they laid four wreaths underneath Picasso's painting commemorating the massacre at Guernica. A woman carrying a baby sat on the floor by the wreaths. A man read a ceremony for dead babies, collaging together extracts from the Bible and the *Life* magazine story about My Lai. The poster-photographs of corpses were juxtaposed with Picasso's image (Frascina 1999, Martin 2004).

This action, perhaps 'happening', followed a choreography of gestures, used a script and props, and was organised by a dramaturgy that moved from disparate infiltrations of the gallery to a precisely timed gathering at a specific place. The action around the painting seems set up to be observed by a separate audience. But however traditional these methods, they were designed for unsettling effect. They compelled a connection between the silent masterpiece on the gallery wall and the far-off reality of contemporary massacre. The museum's institutional distancing of high art from everyday news was attentuated. The silence of the gallery space was broken, the privileged place of the individual artist upstaged by group action and the painting forcibly supplemented by the dramaturgy into which it was cast. The whole action was shaped as a refusal of the rules imposed by the museum building, the physical decorum and silence. So too it established a stark contrast with the complicity of the collectable artwork. And while the performers were not creating characters they were not being random or casual either. The ethical authority of the piece seems to derive precisely from the fact that these are real people, a woman, Joyce Kozloff, holding a real baby (her eight-month-old son), agreeing to follow the discipline of rules, to be matrixed, in order to make their point.

What the MOMA event suggests is that happenings performance does not have a checklist of essential regular features. An event is developed in relation to a specific project in specific circumstances. Thus while Kaprow's first happening demonstrated in formal aesthetic terms how it was challenging conventions and breaking rules, it was harmoniously accommodated within gallery space (the Reuben Gallery) whereas the guerrilla action at MOMA observed more orthodox theatrical conventions and yet disrupted the gallery space. This is one reason we have to be careful about generalising on the basis of particular narratives. Another reason is that narratives are quite efficient devices for excluding information, without it being obvious that they have done so. My own narrative here, for example, has so far excluded any indication of the fact that happenings took place in Europe (while this exclusion has been deliberate, there are probably lots of places where my ignorance or prejudice has produced unwitting exclusions). In doing this it was following a dominant narrative which assumes that much of this sort of post-war artistic experiment began in the United States. But happenings not only took place in Europe; they also came from different origins, arguably started earlier, and weren't initially called 'happenings'.

Wolf Vostell's *Phänomene* of March 1965 took place in a Berlin car dump near the airport where, to the sound of jets flying above, participants painted themselves and cars, bound themselves to cars, and read news reports from the war in Vietnam while US flags floated in puddles. Two years later Vostell planned an event which included images of 'somebody burning himself in saigon – close combat – school for mannequins – child's doll – dead vietcong hooked up to a tank – bra ad – dummy with cameras – dummy with bomb' (in Berghaus 1995: 374). The 'bra ad', mannequins and camera recall Vostell's earlier work which grew out of his so-called dé-coll/age paintings: 'Torn posters were my first dé-coll/ages, & as I was demonstrating the dé-coll/age principle in action it became an event.' At such an event, in Paris 1958, participants walked down a street and read out bits of text found on torn posters. They were encouraged to discover more texts by ripping down layers of posters and to interpret the posters with gestures (in Berghaus 1995: 320–21). The focus on posters and later dé-coll/aged TV programmes and the commodities they sold indicate a political target larger than the Vietnam war: commodity exchange and the communications system which sustains it. In his attack on these targets, and in the method of the attack, which changes participants' relationships to a found everyday environment, Vostell recalls the analysis and techniques of Situationism.

If Vostell's work has similarities with the situationist position, Gustav Metzger's work in the United Kingdom in the early 1960s had a starting point in a different political engagement. It looked more like an individual artist's 'action', or something from Fluxus, than did Vostell's work. Metzger called it 'Auto-Destructive' art. In one demonstration of it he used a brush to paint acid onto a nylon surface: 'The effects of the acid made the nylon peel away and dissolve before his and his audience's very eyes' (in Hunter and Bodor 2012: 68). Here the art is about destroying objects rather than making them. As Metzger described it, 'Auto-destructive art is *material* that is undergoing a *process* of transformation in *time*. In designing a work the artist sees these three factors *as one*. The artist could be compared to a choreographer.' Its 'aesthetic of revulsion' connects auto-destructive art to theatre and happenings. But it also explicitly refused compliance with commodity production: 'I laid so much emphasis on the public nature of auto-destructive art . . . in order to direct the movement away from the dealers' system.' For these artistic experiments the immediate political context was Metzger's active involvement with the Campaign for Nuclear Disarmament together with influence from intellectual developments, such as quantum theory, but in general terms there was a sense of having to respond to 'a rapidly changing and on the whole deteriorating social situation' (Metzger 1965: 14, 16, 10, 3; my elision). As with the other artists Metzger was developing a form that sought to speak directly to the material social situation and its ideas. All, however, had their own take on the analysis and its articulation.

Engaging with everyday life

While the makers suggest a set of diverse narratives, there was at the same time a more overarching narrative that grouped all the work together. This it did not by looking at particular material circumstances, such as the working relations, the place of the event and its targets, but instead by focusing on form. This focus allowed it to reveal an historical continuity which reached well beyond the 1960s, back to the early years of the twentieth century, to the work of avant-garde movements such as Dada. The non-meaningful noises made in a happening can be seen as similar to the sound poetry, with its found phrases and noises, of Tristan Tzara. The challenges to assumed divisions between art and life could be seen as repetitions of the moment when Duchamp presented an everyday urinal as a work of art in 1917. Fluxus and happenings were thus characterised as 'neo-Dada'. But that historical connection effaces certain elements from the concept and practice of the performance done in the fifties and sixties. As Jasia Reichardt put it in 1960, 'The great difference between the gesture of auto-destructive art and Dada is that, whereas the exponents of Dada were mainly nihilistic in their intentions, those behind auto-destructive art are to demonstrate with a similar method – the idea of perpetual impermanence. It is really a protest. A protest against adjustment in an unjust society, a protest against standardization of values, against rigid canons of taste' (in Coutts-Smith 1970: 60). Duchamp's urinal was a mockery of the definition of art and Tzara's nonsense poetry aggressively staged artists' contempt for the decorums of their society. By contrast the performed art of the late fifties and sixties was not satisfied with nihilism and no longer assumed the embattled but heroic rightness of the artist. As the British artist Kenneth Coutts-Smith noted in 1970, the ideas of the impermanence of art and the anarchy of artists were far from new. What was new in the concept of performance in the sixties, he thought, was its interest in the malleability of subjectivity. Performance was, in part, an exploration of social adjustment.

This was the function Metzger claimed for his pieces: 'by providing a socially sanctioned outlet for destructive ideas and impulses, auto-destructive art can become a valuable instrument of mass psychotherapy, in societies where the suppression of aggressive drives is a major factor in the collapse of social balance' (1965: 6). Indeed throughout the 'whole area' of happenings, in Coutts-Smith's view, art was considered to be 'a social activity operating directly onto the environment in a programmed manner. More than the polemic, which merely advocated change, it is intended to be the instrument of change itself. The loosely plotted "total" theatre, the event constructed like a collage in various dimensions, provoking the audience into participation, frequently has a cathartic effect.' In observing that it 'picks up aspects of recent developments in psychiatry' he was referring to one branch of psychiatry in particular: 'there are certain "existentialist" psychologists such as Ronald Laing whose teaching and practice seem to bridge into the same root areas as Happenings, and whose works are widely read by artists' (Coutts-Smith 1970: 55–57).

Artists were reading other people besides Laing. Bruce Barber notes that Goffman's 'dramaturgical metaphor' was 'a major influence on Acconci's early work and writings' (1979: 192); Roland Miller, using a favoured sociological word, described performance as 'behaviour exaggerated or enhanced for effect' (in Hunter and Bodor 2012: 80). But even before Goffman's publication of his 'metaphor' the framing of everyday life as performance appeared alongside the new interests of ethnography. In September 1953 an exhibition opened at the Institute of Contemporary Arts in London called 'Parallel of Life and Art'. One of the organisers, the photographer Nigel Henderson, exhibited a photograph called *Chariot*, which showed a rusting hand-barrow, found on a street in London's East End and photographed where it stood, like a surrealist ready-made. Another exhibit was the film of Pollock painting. Just as the film invited a different view of what the act of painting is, by giving his image its title and then hanging it on a gallery wall Henderson's photograph proposed a different way of viewing the original object. The *Chariot* doesn't stop being a rusty hand-barrow, but the hand-barrow thus named is also cast in a new role. That role is not as fully developed as a theatrical role but neither is it completely ordinary life. When he and his wife moved into Bethnal Green, in London's 'East End', the middle-class Henderson said later that the sense of their alienation in a predominantly working-class environment 'intensified the feeling I had that I was watching live theatre . . . like an audience of one in a public lecture of All. My neighbours appeared to be living out their lives in response to some pre-determined script.' His wife Judith, meanwhile, was also watching a neighbouring family, as part of an ethnographic project. This project was very like the larger and better known Mass Observation, founded in 1937 (see Jeffery 1999), with the aim, well before Goffman, of establishing an 'anthropology of ourselves' based on very detailed information about the lives of 'ordinary people' (in Walsh 2001: 49, 53; my elision). In their introductory pamphlet (1937), Mass Observation authors presciently noted that: 'At the time that this pamphlet is being written, art and science are both turning towards the same field: the field of human behaviour which lies immediately before our eyes' (in Jeffery 1999). Fifteen years later, looking at the East End both as theatre and as found surrealist ready-mades, Nigel Henderson shared his excitement with the Smithsons, those two architects who influenced Lefebvre by pioneering planning that put at its centre not heroic monumentality but the street and its games.

While the Hendersons and their friends were not making performances as such, they exemplify the emergence of an interest in viewing life as performance, and how that viewing was part of changes in thinking about social interaction and organisation. Ten years later the framing of everyday life was done much more literally. In Mark Boyle's *Street* (performed in 1964) an audience sat inside a London shop and then, following the opening of the ceremonial curtains across its window, they found themselves looking out at the street. Very early the following year, in Berlin, Bazon Brock set up chairs on the Kurfürstendamm boulevard, sold tickets to pedestrians, and took them to seats from which, again, they could watch the street. The interest in the behaviour of the everyday here becomes a polemical dissolution of its assumed separation from art.

The general point, then, is that happenings-type work, along with other modes of artistic thinking, was coming out of cultures that were not necessarily referring themselves back to Dada and surrealism but were instead interested in contemporary ideas. In Nigel Henderson, of course, we see the persistence of surrealism with the more modern interests. So too, in 1968 Kostelanetz saw the Theatre of Mixed Means as deriving both from Futurism, Dada and surrealism and from 'modern tendencies': its form shared features in common with developments in 'the new physics – Quantum Mechanics and the Theory of Relativity' (1968: 10, 38). But it wasn't just new ideas that fed into the new art; it was also new politics. Coutts-Smith observed that 'The thinking behind Happening theory' takes in 'political elements from the New Left as one might expect it to do'. And, moving outside the New Left, '*Cobra* mounted some events in the late '40s, and during the '50s the *Situationist* and *Léttriste* movements also mounted early proto-Happenings' (1970: 56–57). Some artists were part of this political action, for example Metzger, who was not only a peace activist but knew the leading Provos well enough to entertain them when they visited Britain. For Jean-Jacques Lebel, an artist, a maker of happenings and, perhaps above all, a political activist the happening form itself exemplified the widespread shift in political attitudes: 'The Happening was the first artistic concretization in Europe of a new consciousness, sharpened by adversity. The structural transformation of human relationships is beginning to be methodically advocated.' But for Lebel the definition of the happening blurred into, or was a higher form of, the political demonstration: 'One of these days, an anti-racist and/or anti-war demonstration in New York will end as a Happening' (Lebel 1995: 272, 280). And the roles of maker and activist came together in May 1968: 'There is more honor in being a street guerrilla than being an artist – and it is more useful. The ideal, of course, is to be *both*, and in May there were millions of them on the streets of Paris creating and living the revolution' (in Berghaus 1995: 375).

But there were some who questioned the assumed values of this work. In 1963 the *Internationale Situationniste* journal noted the press reports of happenings in New York and argued that the form is 'a dadaist-style improvisation of gestures performed by a gathering of people within a closed-off space. Drugs, alcohol and eroticism are often involved. . . . This form of social encounter can be considered as a limiting case of the old artistic spectacle, a hash produced by throwing together all the old artistic leftovers.' Such an event 'can even be considered as an attempt to construct a situation in isolation, *on a foundation of poverty* (material poverty, poverty of encounters, poverty inherited from the artistic spectacle, poverty of the "philosophy" that has to considerably "ideologize" the reality of these events)' (in Knabb 1981: 109–10; my elision). This response could have been nurtured by the language of the press reports rather than the events themselves, since it's unclear what the Situationists actually saw. But that there was an issue about the commentary on happenings is made clear by Ronnie Davis (1988) who was specifically critical of academics who wrote about them as 'theatre'. The confusion may, however, have stemmed from happenings makers themselves. Kaprow said his events were 'essentially theater pieces, however unconventional' (although eighteen years later, in 1979, he said they were an example of a 'new art/life genre') (2003: 17, 195). Deeply built into happenings performance, therefore, was an ambivalence about their formal and institutional status. Given the persistence of this ambivalence, it is salutary to finish here with the situationist critique.

This critique underlines not only that there were very different practices going on but also that the characteristics of these practices didn't always work as it is claimed they work. On the basis of the situationist responses, Jon Erickson raises some questions about the efficacy of the sort of performance promoted in happenings. First, while happenings rejected language, Situationists emphasised the value of language in arguing with and opposing the seductions of the commodity. For them an ironic gesture did not amount to a critique and was thus easily assimilable by gallery culture. Second, while happenings may have been composed of '*decontextualised* elements of everyday life in urban society', Situationists said this sense of decontextualisation was already a feature of the society of the spectacle and that the real work was to recontextualise. Third, Situationists distrusted art and social movements that 'looked to the unconscious as a source of "authentic" existence, seeing them as an evasion of material exigencies' and in this respect the happening sustains the mythic hold on consciousness which prevents engagement with the real structures at work, much as does the spectacle itself. Fourth, happenings, wherever they took place, were regarded as art events, offering 'periodic carnival that did nothing to alter the structure of everyday existence' (Erickson 1992 50–52). To this we might add that, as art events, while they may have problematised the role of the actor, they consolidated the power and remit of that relatively new figure, the director-dramaturg, and the connected roles of creative producer and curator, sowing the seeds for new art-management infrastructures. This, together with their ambivalence about their status as theatre, facilitated their assimilation to the commodity system. Their art was inappropriate, it seemed, and their politics ineffective. As Baxandall saw it, in 1970, 'the development of political struggle and also the *dramaturgical character* of the struggle have perhaps been chiefly responsible for the eclipse of happenings' (1970: 149).

Finally it is worth giving separate emphasis to a remark of Debord's which is noted by Erickson under the point about language. Debord says that the destruction of language works 'to advertise reconciliation with the dominant state of affairs'. In this respect it does the spectacle's work for it, since the function of the spectacle is '*to make history forgotten within culture*' (Debord 1983: § 192). Where performance is defined in terms of a commitment to engage the present, opposing tradition and history, it is arguably doing the reverse of politically oppositional work. It is instead providing, as in all the other areas, a mechanism for reconciling people to life under the dominant order of the spectacle, and it does so effectively because it claims, or imagines, that it is doing exactly the opposite.

Chapter 12

Body art and feminism

Crucial to the shaping of the concept and operation of performance in happenings were the stories told about the origins and aspirations of the art form. As we have seen, happenings could be positioned as works derived from, say, opposition to dominant order or simply as experiments in new art or theatre practice. In the same way, but perhaps with even greater lasting effects, the other major art initiative of the period was positioned by its genealogies.

In 1973 the art critic and journalist David Bourdon, writing about Vito Acconci, said that he was a major figure in 'a new art movement known as *body art*' (in Battcock and Nickas 1984: 187). As Bruce Barber shows, the term had become increasingly popular in art journals over the preceding years, appearing first around 1971/1972, while happenings had all but faded out by about 1975/1976.

The new movement, like happenings, appeared in both the United States and Europe more or less simultaneously. Its most startling early manifestation was in the work of those who cut open other bodies or damaged their own. In Hermann Nitsch's celebrated *Blutorgie* 'he tore apart the cadaver of a freshly slain lamb [and] also gave a learned lecture on the "liberation of violent urges through catharsis"' (report from 1966 in Hunter and Bodor 2012: 71). In Chris Burden's performances between 1971 and 1975, among other things, 'he imprisoned himself in a locker, crawled nearly naked across broken glass in a city street, had a steel stud nailed into his sternum, had pins pushed into his stomach' (Loeffler 1980: 398). In an effort to categorise the new work the art magazine *Avalanche* published an essay in 1970 called 'Body Works', by which it meant works that 'present physical activities, ordinary bodily functions and other usual and unusual manifestations of physicality' (in Barber 1979: 192). Assumptions about what 'ordinary' and 'usual' might mean were, however, subject to challenge, and that challenge, driven by a very specific political imperative, made body works, quite as much as happenings, a potential site of contestation and new thinking.

It is autumn 1971 in California. A group of students is listening to Allan Kaprow. He suggests that a good exercise to prepare for doing a performance piece might be to sweep the floor. One of the students, Faith Wilding, interrupts to protest that half the country was already oppressed by the expectation that they would sweep floors, and goes on to say that Kaprow's comment was insensitive to the reality of women's lives (the story told in Sayre 1989: 92).

The assumptions about the world held by many men – and by those who believed those men's assumptions – were put under pressure from the late sixties onwards by the emergence of what became known as second-wave feminism (the first wave being in the early years of the century). In art and performance practices this had two main effects. First there were questions about the purpose of making the art. Sayre, from whom much of my informa-tion here is taken, quotes the dancer Yvonne Rainer criticising John Cage's assumption that 'the very life we're living ... is so excellent': 'What is John Cage's gift to some of us who make art?' Rainer asks.

> This: the relaying of conceptual precedents for methods of non-
> hierarchical, indeterminate organization which can be used with a
> critical intelligence, that is, selectively and productively, not, however, so
> we may awaken to this excellent life; on the contrary, so we may the more
> readily awaken to the ways in which we have been led to believe that this
> life is so excellent, just, and right (in Sayre 1989: 88–90).

Just as Situationists disturbed comfortable acceptance of the spectacle, feminist art critiqued received ideas about how life 'is', and especially did so by drawing attention to, and disturbing assumptions about, the activity and place of women in this shared world. That place was frequently relegated to the status of being looked at, and looked at in a way which assumes the woman is there to be entirely opened up to, and consumed by, the male. Rainer's own way of dealing with this was to return to sweeping the floor. In mapping out a new dance, on minimalist lines, she said, in 1966, that 'The display of technical virtuosity and the display of the dancer's specialized body no longer make any sense. Dancers have been driven to search for an alternative context that allows for a more matter-of-fact, more concrete, more banal quality of physical being in performance.' As against the technical display piece of classical ballet, with 'its involvement with connoisseurship, its introversion, narcissism, and self-congratulatoriness', the alternatives 'are obvious: stand, walk, run, eat, carry bricks' (in Battcock 1995: 267, 269). Rainer's choreogra-phy thus not only developed a mode of performance that demoted the emphasis on displayed craft, but contested expectations about the performer and, in doing so, problematised the relationship of performer and audience.

Another critique of this relationship revealed, somewhat literally, the depth at which it was rooted, and guarded there by taboo. In her films Carolee Schneeman offered herself to be looked at naked and having sex. But at the same time she herself, as Rebecca Schneider notes, was the film-maker, controlling the movement of the camera and the editing of the shots, so the looked-at woman was also the person arranging how the looking was done. The point was made with rather more immediacy in a live performance in which Schneeman read out a text about a male structuralist film-maker who had criticised one of her films for being full of 'personal clutter': 'he said we can be friends/ equally though we are not artists/ equally I said we cannot/ be friends equally and we/ cannot be artists equally/ he told me he had lived with/ a "sculptress" I asked does/ that make me a "filmakress?"/ Oh No he said we think of you/ as a dancer' (in Sayre 1989: 90). The text she was reading was written on a narrow strip which Schneeman slowly unravelled from her vagina. Taken together these elements question what on earth might be meant by the statement: 'we think of you/as a dancer'. She is both the body to be looked at and the agent of the performance; she is reading prepared script but the script comes from within her; her supposedly most secret 'feminine' part is the place from which emerges public critique. By breaking the decorum around display of that which is supposedly both very personal and yet always available to men, the performance not only closes off the assumed availability of the vagina, which is always already full of a critique of the male, but it also draws its very authority from its decision to be so confidently 'personal'.

Now although Schneeman's work could also be categorised as happenings, it distinguishes itself from that form in the way it foregrounds the artist-maker. The male structuralist film-maker drew on himself Schneeman's anger because he dismissed an artwork for being full of 'personal clutter ... persistence of feelings'. The second effect of feminism in the arts was to lay emphasis on the fact of women's feelings, not as clutter but as a central rationale for the work. For the marginalisation of women's feelings was part of a more general inability, or unwillingness, to notice the self-assertion of female identity, as Judy Chicago observed when she reflected on her one-woman show in Los Angeles in 1969: 'I wanted my being a woman to be visible in the work and had thus decided to change my name ... as a way of identifying myself as an independent woman.' But 'male reviewers refused to accept that my work was intimately connected to my femaleness.' As a consequence she understood that 'if the art community as it existed could not provide me with what I needed to realize myself, then I would have to commit myself to developing an alternative.' This alternative for Judy Chicago had to be performance in that it was a form that 'released a debilitating, unexpressed anger' (in Sayre 1989: 93–94; my elision).

The creation of art that unmistakably asserted the sex of its maker went hand in hand with the idea that art could, and should, state feelings directly. Against a prevailing culture of minimalism, of coolly abstracted work, some feminists were making art that was 'direct', not undecideable but definitely deliberate. For Martha Rosler, as a primarily visual artist, this was not just about the gender system but also about the commodity system: 'it was very important to de-aestheticize your relation to the work so that it didn't become formalized into an aesthetic commodity ... I want to make work where the content is so clear that you *know* you're violating it by fixing only on its formal properties.' And the pre-eminent medium for direct expression, in these terms, seemed to be performance. As Judy Chicago said, 'Because performance can be direct, because we were developing our performances from a primitive, gut level, we articulated feelings that had simply never been so openly expressed in artmaking.' The effect of such performance was that it gave 'the opportunity to make men feel themselves "other" and thereby force them to identify with us on a psychic level' (in Sayre 1989: 94–95; my elision).

One of the ways Chicago developed her 'alternative' to dominant practices was to develop a set of feminist educational programmes, at Fresno State in 1970–1971, Cal Arts and Womanspace. This meant that not only was she producing documents that reflected on her own work but also discussing and making work with students, one of whom was Faith Wilding. The making of shared work necessarily included the development of a vocabulary for talking about the work and its effects. The articulation of feelings that had not been expressed before was not simply about expression but about claiming the right to that expression, and thereby changing the assumption of authority. When the supposed clutter becomes the core text, assumptions about what is relevant and irrelevant, important and trivial, central and marginal get shifted. As a consequence of this men in the audience are now placed in the position of the 'other' and thus, the argument runs, in being forced to explore how they might then identify they need to question their received ideas about women and their images of women. In making a performance of their hitherto unexpressed anger women artists thus simultaneously had to think about the structures and relationships of that expression, and about the mechanisms of representation and identification that underpinned the anger.

This combination of performance practice with extended, and hard-thinking, discourse about it was itself significant but that significance was profoundly enhanced, and, crucially, sustained, by the political urgency that drove early feminism, by the decisive clarity of its intervention and perhaps above all by its rapidly growing mass support. Precisely because of the nature of its project, its particular political aims and necessary ideological critique, in its art practices feminism of the early seventies created both new work and new commentary, performance and theory that challenged the basis of existing ideas.

Chapter 13

The arrival of Performance Art and Live Art

The more surprising it is, then, that feminism does not appear in the index of one of the most influential accounts of the history of body or performance art, RoseLee Goldberg's *Performance: Live Art 1909 to the Present*. Just as the histories of happenings positioned them conceptually, so too it was for what became known by many as 'Performance', now with a capital P, or Live Art, also a capital affair.

Claiming a heritage

Next to nothing has done this positioning more influentially than Goldberg's *Performance*, which has been reprinted several times since its first publication in 1979, with additional material and a slightly reworked preface. When it appeared it was a pioneering attempt to marshal a great body of diverse material into one place, thereby offering a way of making sense of it, and it begins by announcing a watershed moment: 'Performance has only recently become accepted as a medium of artistic expression in its own right.' That acceptance has meant that what had been a 'hidden history' can now be comprehensively reviewed. In discovering the hidden history it becomes clear that 'artists have always turned to live performance as one means among many of expressing their ideas.' A characteristic of this expressive medium is that 'Live gestures have constantly been used as a weapon against the conventions of established art.' This claim ties in with the first chapter's topic, the Futurists and their calls to 'go out into the street, launch assaults from theatres'. But Goldberg is clear that this 'hidden history' begins well before Futurism and includes 'tribal ritual or medieval Passion plays, Leonardo da Vinci's experiments before invited audiences or his river pageants, Bernini's staged spectacles'. In the twentieth century, 'Performance manifestos, from the Futurists to the present, have been the expression of dissidents . . . Performance has been a way of appealing directly to a large public, as well as shocking audiences into reassessing their own notions of art and its relation to culture. For this reason its base has always been anarchic. Moreover, by its very nature, performance defies precise or easy definition beyond the single declaration that it is live art by artists' (1979: 6, 12; my elision).

While she quite properly admits the slipperiness of the term of which she is trying to write the modern history, this slipperiness is somewhat lubricated by the foreword. It is, for example, quite difficult to connect together tribal rituals, medieval passion plays and Dadaist cabaret. Although they all consist of live gestures the medieval passion play or the Renaissance spectacle was hardly declaring war on 'the conventions of established art'. Nor were they particularly anarchic. Indeed the job of tribal rituals and medieval passion plays was in large part to secure, and celebrate, orderliness. But this sort of quibbling misunderstands Goldberg's idea of performance. For to make any 'stricter definition' than declaring that performance is live art by artists 'would immediately negate the possibility of performance itself'. Not only does performance draw on a wide range of material but 'Each performer makes his or her own definition in the very process and manner of execution.' While it may be defined as anything anybody says it is, however, performance has certain consistent features. Performance manifestos establish 'a utopian vision for an all-inclusive art', its artists 'create work which takes life as its subject', and it is 'about the desire of many artists to take art out of the strict confines of museums and galleries' (1979: 6–7). So while it may be anything anybody says it is, it must never be exclusive, take death as its subject or extend its all-inclusiveness to working in galleries. Performance is, paradoxically, both weapon and all-inclusive, both designed and anarchic.

The paradox, or confusion, here indicates that what we are dealing with is the promotion of a set of ideological claims. These claims arguably have their roots not in the whole history of artist performance but in the rhetoric of the 1960s and 1970s, with its interest in everyday life and its rejection of the gallery system. The concerns of that particular era have an historical parallel found for them in the work of the twentieth-century avant-garde, that heroic minority of artists who told the world what they thought of it. Thus Goldberg's thesis, which is both selective and combative, could be said to operate more or less as a continuation of the projects of Futurism and Dada and the rest. In doing so, as Klein perceptively notes, it connects modern performance to the 'romantic ideas' associated with this avant-garde, thereby helping to create its appeal (Klein 2012: 12). Those romantic ideas include the ideological claims to all-inclusiveness, being a weapon, and the rest. But the really powerful ideological work done by Goldberg's story is to anchor the claims in transhistorical concepts. Thus the phrase 'artistic expression in its own right' seems to imply some sort of recognised autonomy, even though it is actually unclear as to what this right is and by what it is guaranteed. But even more ideologically effective is the suggestion that performance's all-inclusiveness, its flexibility of definition and its engagement with life all derive from its 'nature'. This is an ideologically successful move because on one hand it shows how performance draws all variants into itself, turning lack of definition into a defining quality and on the other hand it gathers up all this multiplicity into an entity that feels not constructed but organic, a 'nature' that will guarantee that performance will always be inclusive, concerned with life, anarchic and a weapon by its very essence as performance. This nature transcends history and specific practices, and its success is to be seen in its influence on writing about performance for decades to come.

The limits of art history

In claiming this 'nature' for performance Goldberg's account contrasts rather strikingly with the sorts of practices and thinking done by artists themselves. Interviewed in 1979 Terry Fox reflected on the supposed origins of contemporary performance work: 'The impetus might have been similar in Dada, but that was a war situation, an anarchistic situation, and it has nothing to do with this art form, which is an original way of trying to communicate. This art form has to do with the day in which it originated, the seventies, not the sixties' (in Battcock and Nickas 1984: 205). Fox's caution about what he called the 'art form' is echoed by Loeffler in 1980. Loeffler, much like Ronnie Davis, is cautious about synthetic narratives:

> During the 1970's California occupied a leading role in the development of performance as a contemporary expression of visual art. Interestingly, the term performance has continued to elude a specific definition and most of the artists who have produced performance-type works do not think of themselves as performance artists. Consequently, performance has sometimes served as a misused catch-all category.

He is agnostic about there being such a thing as a coherent 'nature' of performance, and notes that the work that was made 'is variously called actions, events, performances, pieces, things, or even happenings' (Loeffler 1980: viii). Anthony McCall, for example, called his fire events 'conditions'. Within this variety Goldberg's insistence that performance is seen as part of a history of (visual) art looks far too circumscribed. Loeffler notes that while in 'sculpture as action' 'the work only exists during the time utilized to demonstrate it, often through a non-theatrical, direct use of materials', by contrast, 'Other performance work is theatrical in the use of illusion and can convey a fictional or autobiographical narrative'. For Loeffler performances are plural in their activity, effects and functions, and as part of that plurality they are often in constant negotiation with such entities as theatre. But there is a more substantial point of difference from Goldberg. This is seen when Loeffler adds that 'the idea of performance can "frame" religious rituals and daily routine activity' (Loeffler 1980: viii). Here he seems to make direct connection, much as did Acconci, with the work of the social scientists and the folklorists. By contrast Goldberg's story of live art performance seeks both to position it firmly within the cultural domain of 'art', in terms of its origins and practices, and to discover for it a transhistorical 'nature'.

The contrast between sociological and art history accounts of performance, and their implications, was the subject of a long essay by Kenneth Coutts-Smith that appeared in 1979 immediately before Goldberg's and Loeffler's books were published (the essay was written in 1978). This argues that performance art is a practice 'quite distinct from "theatre" (in the sense of the dramatic stage) on the one hand and from the idea of performance in the more generalised meaning of public ritual, spectacle, ceremony, circus or cabaret, on the other'. There is, however, no consensus on how the distinctions can be made. Art criticism dodges the issue, subsuming performance art to already available categories such as Dada, without realising that the 'myths of the avant-garde' are 'no longer apposite due to an increasing *institutionalisation* of culture'. That attention to institutionalisation reveals what is really at stake in the link to Dada. For in Dada the 'performance' always amounted to 'an individual assertion of ego, the unilateral seizure of personal liberty'. In ideological terms, 'the individual rejects a history (that is to him necessarily meaningless) in the search for an instantaneous "gesture" that can transcend, not merely social and cultural conventions, but time itself, and thus all blocks to personal freedom'. Freedom here, Coutts-Smith argues, 'is not understood as the development of the personality, but as the cancelling out of all that which is alternative to the personality' (Coutts-Smith 1979: 219, 221).

While Fluxus, and to a certain extent happenings, could be seen to be trying to democratise art by claiming that anyone could be an artist if he '*creates himself anew through a sequence of "gestures"*', this was only rhetoric. The designation of such practices 'anti-art' or 'non-art', as Kaprow did, simply restricted them to the cultural sphere where their 'apparent *disavowal of culture* was ultimately nothing more than the *rejection of past established culture*' (Coutts-Smith 1979: 220).

Refusing the simplifications of art-history narrative, and indeed any notion of an essential 'nature' of performance, Coutts-Smith attempts to tell a history of happenings, performance art and body art that attends to changing historical circumstances and their ideological negotiation. Thus in attempting to specify performance art's distinction from theatre he lists a series of institutional differences. For example he notes that while theatre demands an audience performance art does not, and in that respect may be likened to a musical concert played by performers for their own pleasure. So too theatre's *audience*, which amounts to a 'ritual collective', differs from the relationship of the *spectator* to the happening, which is governed by 'gallery conventions'. This relationship is symptomatic of the happenings' lineage from visual art, and action painting in particular. The emergence of body art breaks with this lineage by altering the artist's approach to the artwork. While previously artists regarded the artwork as exterior to them, now they 'meld' with the work: 'Rather than the artist operating as an element in the art-work, the art-work now begins to become a component part of the artist.' Art history has, however, failed to notice, yet alone analyse, this 'major orientation' (Coutts-Smith 1979: 224–26).

It can be made sense of better by approaching from somewhere different. Coutts-Smith suggests that by moving away from a traditional 'product-orientated focus' it can be observed that 'the major characteristic' of performance art is '*not* the performed event, but the essential process of play-acting – *the assumption by the performer of roles*'. This centrality of 'role' in performance art is foregrounded by its focus on 'sexuality'. Coutts-Smith's proposed change of approach requires a shift away from thinking in terms of 'art-culture', itself becoming ossified in a more institutionalised society, to a 'social frame of reference': '*both critical response and the self-view of studio practice must now be couched in sociological terms*'. Hitherto critical practice had focused only on those artists whose work was amenable to its analysis, a group for which Coutts-Smith finds a word that is interesting in terms of my argument in Part I: they are 'susceptible to a neo-positivist approach'. By contrast his 'sociological' approach, which focuses on role, allows him to explain the effect of artists such as Beuys in whose process 'the merely egoic assumes the lineaments of collective myth.' By assuming a role and projecting it as 'personal myth' it '*enters me as spectator, and becomes part of me, the spectator*'. Similarly Schwarzkogler 'becomes a self-creation', enabling him to find a 'freedom' which differed from that of Dada-like egotism, being instead 'an assertion of complete control' over both 'a private bodily existence' and 'a public social existence, a relationship-in-the-world'. This specific form of engagement with the social is what distinguishes performance art from all that preceded it, for the individual artist is 'no longer conditioned or supported by the century-long tradition of the "bohemian" beaux-arts'. As such performance art marks the ending of the avant-garde (Coutts-Smith 1979: 229–35).

This narrative is powerfully different from, and richer than, that of Goldberg. It refuses to be a merely journalistic description of artistic events and departs from the ideology of art-history narrative. What is driving both its turn to a 'sociological' approach and its consciousness of the shaping effects of institutions is a political perspective that blends together the New Left and existentialism. As such its own intellectual history would appear to go back into the Situationists. It is this political lineage, and commitment, which insist on the specificity of performance art as a practice that cannot be assimilated either to a notion of the avant-garde or to a generalised sense of 'non-theatrical' practice, defining it instead on its own terms and effects.

Funding bodies

But the rot had already set in, spread by the processes of institutionalisation.

Those processes use exactly the devices that Coutts-Smith was arguing against: the establishment of false historical continuity together with generalisation on the basis of selection. These are shown in operation by Beth Hoffman's sharply observant analysis of the cultural status of the first British happening. This took place at the Edinburgh Festival International Drama Conference organised by the publisher John Calder in 1963. It is usually assumed to be a moment in which the force of new experimental performance challenged and disrupted the composure of the theatre 'establishment'. But Hoffman suggests it can be read differently, 'namely, as an attempt on Calder's behalf to situate modern drama and the new developments in visual art performance practice within a continuum'. A later publication by Calder (in 1967) contained an essay which lamented the mutual attacks by happenings and 'traditional' theatre. The reason these persisted, Hoffman suggests, is because the similarity between the two modes of practice exacerbates 'the desire to maintain distinction, autonomy and uniqueness, and thereby claim a kind of value, authority and political force' (Hoffman 2009: 97).

There was also a more specific force driving the need to make the distinction. This emerges in Graham Saunders's account of the UK Arts Council's early attempts to formulate 'performance art' as a fundable category. An early step, Saunders notes, was the formation of the Experimental Projects

Committee in 1969–1970 which included representation from Literature, Art and Music panels and thereby provided a structure that 'enabled the multi-disciplinary nature of much of this work to be taken into consideration'. This consideration was helped on its way by a report from Roland Miller in 1973 which defined 'a clear set of differences between theatre and performance', termed 'Declared' and 'Undeclared'. In the first, 'intention is expressed clearly through text, director, actors, technicians' while in the second 'even the performers are unsure of the outcome' of a combination of elements (Saunders 2012: 36, 41). In the same year Jeff Nuttall published a short pamphlet, 'The Situation regarding Performance Art', a document uncovered in Saunders's research. This maps the different kinds of work that, since the mid-sixties, were challenging traditional English theatre. Of these Nuttall applies the label of 'performance art' to two groups, both of whom owe a debt to Cage. One group, the 'mess-artists', have come out of action painting; the other group do 'simple, clear cut, minimal acts' which question the identity of their own work. Both do 'performance art' because 'what they do has *nothing to do with theatre at all*. Theatre is always compromised because it is orientated to the public from the start' (Nuttall 2012: 177). What this fierce binary does is to destroy the possibility of that interstitial space carefully protected in the artists' naming of what they were doing such that it was always neither one thing nor the other, neither Washington nor Moscow as the slogan used to have it.

The struggle for funding gives a material urgency to the promulgation of conceptual, and thereby fundable, distinctions between one art form and another. But in Hoffman's analysis the worrying at conceptual definitions of the 'experimental' in relation to the 'traditional' reaches further than the artists and their institutional positioning. After the adoption of 'performance art' as a funding category, in the years between 1987 and 1991 the Arts Council replaced the term with 'live art'. This put pressure on the need to define the form. Discussion about definition leaned heavily on Goldberg's narrative, which not only supplied a visual art genealogy but also characterised performance as that which breaks free of the dominant. This was picked up by Lois Keidan's 1991 National Arts and Media Strategy Discussion Document on Live Art, which defined live art as 'a rejection of single art form practice; a way of opening frontiers to any political, social or cultural agenda'. That definition was then formalised by the Live Art Development Agency, co-founded by Keidan in 1999, which asserts that live art is 'not a description of an artform or discipline' but instead is 'a framing device for a catalogue of approaches to the possibilities of liveness by artists who chose to work across, in between, and at the edges of more traditional artistic forms'. This language, Hoffman notes, was taken up by academic scholarship. She instances a couple of essays for the volume *Live: Art and Performance*, where Adrian Heathfield says that 'liminal temporality' is one of live art's 'most vital elements' and Andrew Quick opposes against, in Hoffman's words, 'the fixity, authoritarian practices of meaning-making and the reinforcement of social norms that constitute "the theatre"' 'the fluid, unpredictable, innovative and generative' practices of live art. As Hoffman says, in order to work these arguments 'rely on a troubling but familiar reification of "theatre" into its most conservative philosophical as well as formal terms' (Hoffman 2009: 101–03). And what they conceal is that live art has its own well-rehearsed script in which it is characterised, by its own decades-long tradition, in an entirely predictable way, as that which is innovative and unpredictable.

The script that characterises live art and its precursors was already settled into place by 1979. In that year Chantal Pontbriand described the new work as 'difficult to define, characterised by the multiplicity of tendencies and forms'. Instead of operating in 'a closed time and space' it substitutes for them 'multiplicity, simultaneity, totality in space and time'. The new work is 'associated with ritual, with technology, it is associated with being as much as doing, with the process more than the finished product. It unwinds in time, seeks out the ephemeral, captures life in a desperate effort to search in a different way for something to which the silent works of the museum no longer reply' (Pontbriand 1979: 9–11). The same year, in a new journal, Ian LeFrenais also described the characteristics of some new 'events': 'They are difficult to pin down [...] to separate from the sludge of spectacle [...] they consist of people doing odd things in front of others. They are performance. Anyone can do one but once money changes hands their value is under scrutiny' (in Klein 2012: 18).

LeFrenais and Pontbriand were not the only people thinking in print about performance in 1979. That year also marks the publication of Goldberg's account of *Performance*. Indeed, as Roms and Edwards note, 1979 'saw a remarkable rise in the number of publications devoted to the art form' (2012: 31). To the British ones that they list we can add Bronson and Gale's *Performance by Artists*, and from 1980 Loeffler's *Performance Anthology*. Ian LeFrenais's *Performance Magazine* was founded in 1979 as was *P.S. Primary Source*. So too the producers' organisation Artsadmin and the biannual showcase *Performance Art Platform* were initiated in 1979, and in Venice there was an exhibition called *The Art of Performance*. For many this seemed to be a watershed moment. Bonnie Marranca, looking back in 1995, contrasted the energy of the seventies' avant-garde with what she felt to be the contemporary dominance of theory and politicised art (1996: 161). For others by 1979 it was already all over. To Tom Marioni, interviewed in 1976, it seemed that 'performances have become academic. They've become part of the academy. And there isn't a need to do it anymore' (in Loeffler 1980: 377).

This was a powerful synthesis of elements in one historical moment. It fixed the discourse in print and expanded its mechanisms of distribution. Pontbriand marks the significance of this juncture in her use of the term 'performance'. In an earlier French-language version of her essay, in 1977, she had found it necessary to import the word from English, commenting 'Performance est un mot qui, appliqué au vocabulaire de l'art contemporain, peut poser quelque difficulté' (1979: 9). In English, of course, there was less difficulty because the word had already been institutionalised, by the Arts Council among others, with its new meaning. But the coming together of discourse and publication had the effect of more widely consolidating the assumed characteristics of 'performance'. This was done principally by detaching the work from its actual circumstances of making in order to give it a history that could appropriately foreground particular characteristics. As Jennie Klein perceptively remarks, part of the appeal of 'performance' 'has much to do with its ability to signify romantic ideas that were first associated with the historical avant-garde in the early twentieth century', including individual agency, 'psychic/spiritual transcendence' and revolutionary kickback against dominant culture. There were some, such as Terry Fox and Kenneth Coutts-Smith, who were highly critical of that narrative and the values it enshrined, but dissenting opinion was marginalised in the process of institutionalisation. Klein argues, very convincingly, that the success of this process, with its proliferating network of live art 'organizations, venues, promoters and funding schemes', was assisted by a rhetoric that 'proffers performance/live art as a site of congregation – conversion – for an imagined community of like-minded people united in their opposition to hegemonic, bourgeois values'. Historiography also did its work. Klein notes that Keidan strategically used Goldberg's narrative to position live art in a history going back to the avant-garde of Futurism. By the 1990s the avant-garde may have been 'radical' but it was radical in a way that made it canonical, and collectable, high art. Its characteristics were now safely distanced from the sometimes highly challenging purposes of the work's original creation. This was 'radical' as commodity.

The text in which Heathfield and Quick summarised the characteristics of live art, quoted by Hoffman above, included an essay by Goldberg linking contemporary live art back to the 1970s, leaping over institutional and social changes to reinforce what Klein calls a 'fiction of continuity' (2012: 12–13, 23).

Indeed it goes further back than the seventies, because Goldberg had already linked it to the avant-garde. Thus the ideological work of securing a single 'nature' for performance in 1979 bears its fruit in 2004. When Heathfield celebrated 'the impetus' in contemporary culture to 'the immediate, the immersive and the interactive: *a shift to the live*', he was not only repeating the received characteristics of 'performance' but also repeating the assumption that these were always, time after time, new. His essay, along with those by Quick and Goldberg, was part of a catalogue for an exhibition called *Live* at London's Tate Modern gallery in 2003. In this instance, one among many of course, we see the assumed characteristics of 'performance' settling into the arms of a rather large institution. And fitting very snugly there, for in 2014 Tate Modern was still discussing such things as 'Liveness', with the support of its sponsor BMW. By now the image of a high-spec car has presumably added to the qualities of immediacy, immersion and interactivity those of efficient fuel consumption, finger-tip controls and a luxury interior.

And that addition might also be seen as an appropriate legacy from 1979, the year which saw the Thatcher government come to power in Britain. This led not only to changes in funding for the arts but also, in conjunction with Reagan's United States, to the consolidation of the ideology that came to be called neo-liberalism.

Chapter 14

Dance party politics

Among the dissenting voices in 1979, the German artist Klaus Rinke refused to allow his work to be called 'performance'. The better word, he said, was 'Aktion' or 'Demonstration'. Not only was 'performance' a North American term, from the 'Happening era', but it also had inappropriate overtones of theatricality (in Bronson and Gale 1979: 195). Similarly his contemporary Franz Walther noted that 'Ever since the word "performance" was first applied to my work I've had difficulties with it, because for me it has too many theatrical associations. All sorts of words have been used, but I haven't found the one that's right.' He would prefer to use the word 'Handlung' or 'Aktion art', but this presents problems when translated into English, in that the word 'action' has, he thinks, 'something programmatic about it' because it seems to amount to 'a definition of content'. Therefore, he suggests, 'A better way to put it in English would be just "doing" – it's simply an activity' (in Bronson and Gale 1979: 195).

When Rinke and Walther objected to their work being called 'performance' it was because it was being put into the wrong category, assimilated to something it was not. Their battle over terminology was about maintaining ownership over the products of their own labour. What they were doing was something more than refusing to let their art become commodity. In circumstances where their work was named by others in a way the artists could not or would not recognise it was in a sense being taken out of their hands. They were becoming alienated from their own work. To insist on the work being named as one wants to name it oneself is to refuse alienation.

Rinke and Walther were not alone. A number of performed practices, whatever they were called, however consciously artistic or not, seem to share an impulse to resist alienation. This is what Stuart Hall thought he saw when he was looking at the hippie counterculture. In an attempt to explain their activities he put them in the larger historical context of 'post-industrial societies' where 'the technical-productive system has been enormously expanded and revolutionised – raised to such mature forms as to have transformed social consciousness itself.' That transformation of social consciousness produced conditions experienced as alienation. By way of response to it, says Hall, 'new modes of consciousness' are being produced, 'opening new possibilities for the superior reign of "culture" over "nature"'. The intention is to negate and transcend existing forms (Hall 1969: 185).

The production of such new modes of consciousness was the project of the Situationists, but let's note that they are not simply talking of 'consciousness' here:

> The really experimental direction of situationist activity consists in setting up, on the basis of more or less clearly recognized desires, a temporary field of activity favorable to these desires. This alone can lead to the further clarification of these primitive desires, and to the confused emergence of new desires whose material roots will be precisely the *new reality* engendered by the situationist constructions.   (in Knabb 1981: 43)

The project is driven by desires and allows new desires to emerge. It involves a liberation of that which has been suppressed. Its mode of operation is the setting up of 'a temporary field of activity', constructing a situation. The construction of situations is, as we know, a form of performance. Seen in these terms performance is a practice that produces new consciousness and allows the emergence of desires in order to produce an alternative to the dominant alienating social conditions. In short, constructing a situation transforms the constructor.

Behind this logic stands Marx's thinking about human labour and its estrangement. Labour can be estranged in three ways. First, for workers the product of their labour becomes an alien object, and this relationship can extend to seeing the 'sensuous external world' as 'an alien world inimically opposed' to them. Second, workers experience the act of production as hardship, suffering, an activity that belongs to someone else. The third estrangement has to do with 'Man' as 'a species-being', a notion taken from Hegel by which Marx means that the human being is conscious of existing in a practical and organic relationship with all of nature, all species human and other. As species-beings humans produce themselves both in the activity of production and in what they produce by it. Humans live by using and transforming the products of nature. When humans are estranged both from nature and from their own activity they are estranged from being species-beings, which then 'makes individual life in its abstract form the purpose of the life of the species'. As against such estranged activity 'the productive life is the life of the species. It is life-engendering life. The whole character of a species – its species-character – is contained in the character of its life activity; and free, conscious activity is man's species-character.' Marx adds, slightly later, that in productive labour the human 'duplicates himself not only, as in consciousness, intellectually, but also actively, in reality, and therefore he sees himself in a world he has created'. Thus estranged labour 'estranges from man his own body, as well as external nature and his spiritual aspect, his *human* aspect'. This also estranges one human being from another (1986: 40–43).

The construction of a 'temporary field of activity' is a form of labour that is not estranged. What it makes is not alien to the makers, their activity belongs to them and perhaps above all the activity undoes their estrangement from their own bodies and enables them to see themselves in a world they have themselves created. Henri Lefebvre has a similar view of what he called 'moments' that necessarily break routine. Humans have, he says

> specific needs which are not satisfied by those commercial and cultural
> infrastructures which are somewhat parsimoniously taken into account
> by planners. This refers to the need for creative activity, for the *oeuvre*
> (not only of products and consumable material goods), of the need for
> information, symbolism, the imaginary and play. Through these
> specified needs lives and survives a fundamental desire of which play,
> sexuality, physical activities such as sport, creative activity, art and
> knowledge are particular expressions and *moments*, which can more or
> less overcome the fragmentary division of tasks.   (1996: 147)

Alongside temporary fields of activity and 'moments' there appears another concept that was dear to both the Situationists and Lefebvre, play. But play on its own is not a guarantee of escape from alienation. Jorn summarised the issue in 1948: 'if play is continued among adults in accordance with their natural life-force, i.e., in retaining its creative spontaneity, then it is the *content* of ritual, its humanity and life, which remains the primary factor and the form changes uninterruptedly, therefore, with the living content. But if play lacks its vital purpose then ceremony fossilizes into an empty form which has no other purpose than its own formalism' (in Wollen 1989: 46).

In each case – the temporary field of activity, the 'moment', even creative play – we are envisaging a mode of deliberately constructed, consciously enacted, behaviour: a performance. But it is not any sort of performance. It exists in a conscious relationship to conditions of alienated consciousness and estranged labour; it is both analytic and empowering, and it releases desires in the self as part of re-confirming that self's species-being with others.

In looking at the hippie mode of life and activity, Hall also turned to Marx and found a word to describe what he thought he saw. The hippies, he said, 'have tended, in their non-ideological way, to "stand Marx on his head" (or rather, orthodox versions of Marxism': 'they give primacy in *praxis* to the place and role of "consciousness" in restructuring the environment.' This takes the form not of a theoretical argument but of 'an *enactment* based on certain empirical deductions'. Thus they 'begin to explore, live through and act out in fragmented, broken forms the outer limits/inner spaces of revolutionary and post-revolutionary *praxis*. They inhabit, embody and become, in Hegelian terms, "the negation of the negation"' (Hall 1969: 200). In *praxis* reflection and action are combined, and in actualising a plan or vision those involved actualise themselves, or in constructing their temporary field of activity they construct themselves. Within the specific context of the sixties the understanding of the non-estranged labour and praxis of the counterculture was in part shaped by an emphasis, stated most famously by Herbert Marcuse, on the need to liberate desires. Thus in the performance of the constructed situation new desires will emerge. And, as Hall saw it, the hippies, like the rest of the counterculture, envisaged a utopian future where men will have 'reappropriated sensuous activity as "their own essential powers" (as Marx once remarked)' (Hall 1969: 202). To reappropriate sensuous activity is to learn (again) to work with nature as a species-being.

Anti-institutional, countercultural and liberatory forms of performance thus seemed to offer ways of rediscovering non-alienated activity, providing a model for the sensuous practice which would overcome individualism and commoditisation. This understanding of it establishes a powerful addition to the assumed potency of performance. It could easily be seen, from the trouble it caused, that performance could disturb the world around it. But to see it as sensuous practice was to understand it as an activity that, by the action of people making it, transformed and liberated them.

These ideas still persist, rightly or wrongly, in a generalised sense. Where they persist specifically is in a set of performances that took place, and take place still, well outside Tate Modern or the club circuit or the university studios, performances that, even as the institutionalisations were happening, persisted somewhere out there in the streets and trees.

When for a brief time on July 13, 1996, a British motorway, the M41, was turned into a dance party there was among the banners one bearing a situationist slogan. It wasn't a one-off. Through the extraordinary phase of political actions of the very late eighties and early nineties in the United Kingdom, through the so-called DiY protest movement, in the parties that reclaimed streets from cars, in the burrows underground and houses in trees that resisted new road building, in the direct action against bulldozers and cranes, the Situationists were there. As the group 'Reclaim the Streets' saw it the street party functioned to 're-energise the possibility of radical change . . .

It is an expansive desire; for freedom, for creativity; to truly live' (in Jordan 1998: 141). In his account of street actions and the work of Reclaim the Streets John Jordan quotes Raoul Vaneigem: 'revolutionary moments are carnivals in which the individual life celebrates its unification with a regenerated society.' This is part of an explicit alignment of DiY protest with the situationist position which rejected the 'specialised sphere of old politics' as well as art: 'Its insistence on creativity and yet the invisibility of art or artists in its midst, singles it out as a historical turning point in the current of creative resistance' (Jordan 1998: 131, 140). He is not of course correct to say that this is a turning point in bringing together art and resistance, in that something very similar had been done before, but the desire to make that claim shows the pleasure and excitement of inhabiting, being part of, that which transforms the person as well as taking action against an oppressive dominant. McKay quotes Seel, 'Frontline ecowars!' 'The feeling of institutional disenfranchisement may well be complemented by a feeling of radical empowerment' (McKay 1998: 19).

The radical empowerment comes from direct action, which Jordan describes as 'literally embodying your feelings, performing your politics': 'The playfulness of direct action proposes an alternative reality but it also makes play real.' Jordan clearly has done his homework on concepts of performance and is using his essay to argue that direct action is a form of performance. In doing so his concept of performance can trace its roots all the way back to the Situationists and sixties' counterculture: 'Direct action takes the alienated, lonely body of technocratic culture and transforms it into a connected, communicative body embedded in society.' And in this context a familiar word turns up: 'Direct action is praxis, catharsis and image rolled into one' (Jordan 1998: 133–34).

It is only perhaps in special circumstances that performance functions as praxis, re-engaging its makers in sensuous practice. In the DiY protests that sensuous practice might have involved throwing your body against a bulldozer knocking down houses or balancing precariously in trees in the path of a new road. Sensuous practice is not luxury or indulgence. It is a form of full engagement of emotions and body in the constructing of situations, and it is thereby transforming. This often testing, although sensuous, potency is easy to lose sight of as we follow the concept of performance and its commentators into the classrooms of the academy.

Part III

Theorising performance

The concept of performance developed by sociologists, ethnographers and theatre scholars amounted, in general terms, to a form, or, rather, set of forms, of communicative behaviour. Neither presented nor received as theatrical, it is designed to have effects on its respondents. Although an apparently habitual part of everyday living, such behaviour is nevertheless constructed. This conceptual modelling identified new objects of study, often by framing them as performance, but its work was largely continuous with, and bound by, the evolving interests of specific academic disciplines and the dialogues between them. In the world around it meanwhile there were performed practices that polemically sought to question boundaries and continuities. They often refused to be categorised and labelled, and they posed challenges to institutions. Among the challenged institutions were the universities. The political and cultural conflicts of the late sixties and early seventies turned the universities into all too literal battlegrounds. Students and lecturers joined and organised campaigns around peace, democracy and social equality and, as part of this, they asked questions not only about the world outside but also within the classroom. Traditional disciplines fractured under the pressure of new ideas, one of the most spectacular examples being English in the United Kingdom. From the fracturing, new disciplines emerged, such as cultural studies and film studies and, somewhat later, Performance Studies and as those disciplines emerged they brought with them, well, new discipline.

Chapter 15

Performance, postmodernism and critical theory

A feeling of the new disciplinary shaping is suggested by the programme for the first few years of the Milwaukee Center for Twentieth Century Studies. Founded in that seminal year 1968 its activities gathered steam in the early seventies. Although there were seminars on subjects across the humanities, photography features frequently at the start. Then in 1973 there was a symposium on the 'Self-Reflective Artwork in Contemporary Literature and Art', followed later by a week of events on French women artists and thinkers. For 1975–1976 the theme was Film, with a symposium in November 1975. This, though, was the mid-seventies and discussions of art and ideas were never far away from economics: in September 1975 there was a conference on Public Taxing and the Humanities in Multi-Campus University Systems. Then in 1976–1977 the theme was Performance, with talks by Umberto Eco, Ionesco, Herbert Blau and Victor Turner, and a symposium in November 1976. The next year the theme was Technology and the Humanities.

The programming showed awareness of, and desire to respond to, emergent subjects and trends. That response was made by drawing on ways of thinking that seemed appropriate to the various innovations and that were, themselves, undergoing change. New theoretical models were building on and revising traditional psychoanalysis and Marxism, pushing structuralism into poststructuralism, rethinking historiography, circulating intensely around notions of ideology, discourse and the subject – all the various elements that came to be named, with a capital letter, Theory.

Like similar research centres elsewhere the Milwaukee Center was seeking to think about new materials in a new way. Its declared intention was to 'sift theories of contemporary culture', and this it formally commenced with its first publication, based on the November 1976 event, 'The International Symposium on Postmodern Performance'. The insertion of the word 'Postmodern' both aligns this sort of 'Performance' with an area of contemporary concern and marks it off from anything else which might be known as performance. What makes it so special in postmodernity, and a worthy subject for the Milwaukee Center's first publication, is that, according to the

Center's director, Michel Benamou, performance is 'the unifying mode of the arts in our time' (1977a: n.p.).

Performance, as a concept, can take on this role because of its range of application, which Benamou differentiates into three 'aspects': 'the dramatization of life by the media, the playfulness of art, and the emphasis on functioning in a technological environment' (Benamou 1977b: 4). These 'aspects' are more fully elaborated in the next essay, by Jerome Rothenberg, who observes that 'Sixty years after Dada, a whole range of artists have been making deliberate and increasing use of ritual models for performance.' With 'ritual' placed in the primary position, Rothenberg then lists the 'going assumptions as these relate to performance'. The first is 'a strong sense of continuity', seen in the linking up of avant-garde art with 'traditional' archaic or tribal performance. Such continuity reveals that there is no such notion as artistic 'progress'. This connects to the second assumption, about the 'breakdown of boundaries and genres', not just between art and non-art (say, music and noise), but between art and life, meaning that there is no hierarchy of media or privileging of 'advanced technology' over 'primitive devices'. Third, there is a move away from 'masterpieces' to obsolescence of art, leading to, fourth, 'a new sense of function in art', where value lies less in aesthetic content than in 'what it does'. The fifth assumption is that there is 'a stress on action and/or process', which 'includes the act of composition itself'. If the artist becomes the artwork, then, sixth, the audience becomes participant, or, indeed, the 'distinction between doer and viewer' fades. Finally, there is 'an increasing use of real time', and blurring of distinctions between this and 'theatrical time'. With these assumptions listed, Rothenberg concludes that 'the place, if not the stance, of the artist and poet is increasingly beyond culture' (Rothenberg 1977: 12–16). Which raises the question of where the artist, and indeed the audience, might be. This is a very different way of thinking than that which, more or less contemporaneously, wanted to understand performance as, precisely, something which was culturally located and spoke about that culture. In Rothenberg's phrase we hear the telltale sound of postmodernity facilitating its abstraction from material cultural, and historical, engagement.

Although Rothenberg finds these 'going assumptions' in all the arts, it is performance in particular that is given pride of place. The reason for this is that, in Benamou's words, performance is an artform that circulates around, is driven by, tensions between 'presentation and re-presentation, Being and absence, presence and play'. Of these it is the last which Benamou emphasises. Performance, in its seventies' avant-garde version, rejects domination by text and offers, as Rothenberg has it, real-time process and composition, a form of presence. Yet performance is also a form of play: 'Between these two oppo-sites, performance as presence, performance as play, we cannot, perhaps must not, decide' (Benamou 1977b: 3, 5).

Deciding is a thing definitely not to do. As part of the reaction against positivist modes of knowledge, postmodernism takes up a position based on the refusal to decide on, and instead looks for the play between, those issues and beliefs which had been so decisive in previous cultures. As Benamou says, speaking for the mind-set that Geertz described a few years later, 'We must extricate ourselves from strict positivistic causality, find play in the physical machinery which has replaced the divine order.' Art practices that offer process rather than product, that range across primitive and high art, that blur boundaries, that are governed by chance, all such practices work to create a sense of indeterminacy, and indeterminacy gestures towards a refusal of the certainties of faith and fact, the deceptive clarity of positivistic causality. It is because performance oscillates, more than other arts, between presence and play that it seems to be the 'unifying mode of the postmodern' (Benamou 1977b: 3–5, 1). With its very recent history of placing itself outside institu-tions, refusing categories and wilfully occupying interstitial spaces, perfor-mance seemed to be a prime example of practice that was undecidable. As such, it offered a template for other practices. Criticism, for example, 'no longer content to gesticulate in the margins of texts, also takes hold of a part of the stage, and plays'. And through the late seventies into the eighties, literary criticism, in the service of 'Theory', with its puns and typographic jokes, played, remorselessly played, played so much that the word lost its meaning. But performance, not just a model of practice, also works as unifying meta-phor: 'Postmodernity exists in a technological society in which machines perform' (Benamou 1977b: 4).

In saying this, Benamou, as literary critic, has himself allowed his critical writing to play, for he has discovered the English-language multiple meanings of 'perform'. What he actually means is that machines 'operate' or 'function', and his word-play wouldn't work in another language. This suggests how important language is in this conceptualisation of performance. Indeed it begins to position performance not as material practice but as an abstracted metaphor, a way of describing the supposed feeling of the postmodern. About this Benamou's co-editor, Charles Caramello, comes clean: 'Let us take the range of postmodern performance activities – non-matrixed theatre events, the new music, intermedia fiction, the various permutational, concrete, and sound poetries, experimental cinema and video – as analogical strivings toward the hypothetical *writerly text* that Barthes posits.' This text, Barthes says, is 'a perpetual present' '*ourselves writing*', before the 'infinite play of the world' is stopped by 'some singular system (Ideology, Genius, Criticism) which reduces the plurality of entrances, the opening of networks, the infinity of languages' (in Caramello 1977: 225).

When he speaks of them as 'strivings' Caramello is positioning performance and its practices not simply as a 'unifying mode' of the postmodern but also as something that works as analogy for, helps us to conceive of, the hypothetical entities modelled by theoretical discourse. What is going on here is that the concept of performance derived from the artistic practices of the sixties and early seventies meets and merges with the theoretical discourse that in the seventies took hold of university arts and humanities. A concept of performance that sees it as the archetypal progeny of postmodernism, shaped by and within it, is simultaneously a vehicle for stating, indeed embodying, the favoured concerns of postmodernism. When it is pushed towards this metaphorical function, 'performance' becomes dislocated from specific material practices. This in turn allows for the concept to be generalised, in a way that, say, social scientists, engaged with material practices, would have disallowed. Indeed the capacity of this new abstracted term to accommodate all other forms is exactly what is celebrated. And with that generalisation, and that celebration, something else is going on. Viewed as the unifying 'mode' of the postmodern 'performance' seems to begin to acquire for itself inherent characteristics, characteristics that only a few years later would congeal into something that could be called the 'nature' of performance.

Benamou and Caramello's volume, as a product of the Milwaukee Center, is a manifestation of what emerges from the mutual insemination of new Theory and contemporary practices, and in the coming years more and more departments were to take to their bosom a newly Theorised performance. What seems in general terms to be driving the merger of Theory and performance was the production, on one hand, of new sorts of artwork which called out for analysis, and, alongside them, the increased availability of models to use for such analysis. Thus in 1986, for example, Judith Hamera observed that the new performance work by such people as Laurie Anderson and Stelarc lacked critical treatment which could engage with it on its own terms, rather than using terms from theatre. What was needed, she said, was 'a postmodern criticism for a postmodern form' (Hamera 1986: 17). So to analyse a solo performance by James Grigsby she drew on theories of depth psychology and play. Other critics readily turned to models already developed in social sciences, favouring in particular ritual as well as play. The intellectual culture of postmodernism encouraged such cross-disciplinary borrowings, for these not only could engage with undecidable and playful texts but also established a space and function for playful criticism. And here is the other driver behind the merger of postmodern performance and Theory. As we have noted, performance was a useful analogy, a metaphor for a way of thinking and doing. It spread across disciplinary areas not, perhaps, so much because of its interest as a specific practice but because of its capacity to be a figure for new modes of postmodern criticism. Its amenability to fashionable Theory took performance outside drama and theatre departments, to spread across the academy. Until it was called back.

While the climate of postmodern thinking facilitated that cross-disciplinary expansion of modes of approach, opening up performance to be read as play or ritual or game, the later implementation of 'postmodern' as a generic category had the effect of setting limits to what might be understood as performance, and indeed returning it firmly to the domain of aesthetic practice. Thus while Benamou sees performance as having to do with the general dramatisation of life by media, conceptually operating as a means for characterising a variety of modes of cultural production, when Kaye writes about postmodernism and performance in 1994 'postmodern' performance has become simply an art category, and a compendious one at that. It includes Happenings, dance, the Wooster Group and Robert Wilson. Working under the rubric that postmodernism resists categories, Kaye crams into the category of performance a variety of events between which others made careful distinctions. Writing earlier than Kaye, Steven Connor in 1989 also mainly conceives of performance as an art category, this time stretched to include rock performance. The difference here, though, is that rather than showing how particular works might be said to be 'postmodern' (admittedly a difficult exercise with a concept that resists categorisation), Connor tries to define how the theoretical developments of the postmodern period change ideas as to what performance is, and thereby constitute a 'postmodern performance theory'. The problem, though, is that Connor draws many of his examples from experimental theatre and identifies the originating moment of many theories of postmodern theatre as Derrida's essays on the theatre of Artaud. Just as in Kaye's book, performance is bundled up with theatre, and both are contained by Connor within a single chapter that takes its place alongside others dealing with such topics as architecture, literature and TV and film. Performance here is presented as an art product, not a generally applicable metaphor or analogy. The overall way of seeing is instead provided here by Theory itself, a shift made apparent in Connor's comments on Schneeman's *Interior Scroll* (1975). Connor observes that this 'kind of theatre' is political and 'it is also in some sense subversive' but 'it is not easy to see how it exemplifies the elaborate apparatus of deconstruction and postmodern theory that is ranged behind it' (1992: 146). At this point Theory steps in to reveal that performance, that erstwhile unifying mode of the postmodern, has not come up to scratch in delivering the agenda of the postmodern.

Indeed however attractive performance was as an image of the postmodern the real master discourse was Theory, and for those dealing with performance in theatre departments it was Theory which was opening the new doors. This process seems to begin in the United States, as a sectorwide development, round about 1982. That year marked the beginning, as Philip Auslander has it, of 'the application of Theory to Theatre Studies in the North American academy', formally marked perhaps by the publication of an issue of *Modern Drama* with essays on performance by Josette Féral and Chantal Pontbriand. Then, as Auslander sees it, the major 'watershed event' that 'galvanized the field' came in 1984 with the two panels called 'Toward a New Poetics' at the conference of the American Theatre Association: 'these panels were designed to examine the implications for theatre of the new critical methodologies' (Auslander 1997: 5). Auslander followed this up himself with a college seminar on critical theory and performance and then, the following year, on a panel at the American Theatre Association conference in Toronto. In the specific area of feminist theory, Sue-Ellen Case published *Feminism and Theatre* in 1988, her anthology of essays *Performing Feminisms* in 1990, and a paper for the History/Theory/Revolution panel at the ATHE conference in 1992. This paper was then published in Reinelt and Roach's hugely influential anthology *Critical Theory and Performance* in 1994. By 2002 Féral revisited and reflected on her twenty-year-old essay now not in a drama journal but in a special issue of *SubStance*, a 'Theory' journal.

This highly selective narrative offers to illustrate a conscious drive to embrace what became called 'critical theory' as a mechanism for describing and analysing performance and theatre. What it doesn't show is how critical theory is also used to make separation between performance and theatre. This it does in much the same way as Benamou and Caramello construct performance as the 'unifying mode', the 'analogical strivings', for postmodernity and the writerly text. Possibly driven, as Pontbriand seemed to be in 1977, by the effort to explain a difficult new form, critical theory distinguishes performance from theatre on the basis of its ability to reach beyond the narrow artistic constraints of theatre, to become a vehicle for the hypotheses and concerns of Theory. This separation of performance from theatre was very differently motivated from those artists who needed to get themselves a separate funding stream for their non-categorised work. For the academic commentators like Pontbriand the motivation is to explain the new and, in doing so, perhaps themselves to be part of the staging of the new, by speaking its language and wearing its sign. The academic work of distinguishing the new form, performance, from the old, theatre, was thus facilitated, or brought into being by, the current languages of Theory. With this particular objective in place, what was created was an apparently discrete entity called 'performance theory'. As Reinelt saw it in 2002, it was the 'poststructuralist critique of the sign' which formed the 'philosophical backdrop' to performance theory's 'concern with performance processes and its deliberate rejection of totalized/completed meanings' (Reinelt 2002: 205). But as theatrical folk know, backdrops are painted to serve specific scenes. The poststructuralist critique of the sign may be one, cultural performance's engagement with the embodying of totalised meanings might be another. In other words, the performance theory articulated here has specific interests which result from, and service, a specific historical moment. We can see this working itself through in Féral's essay, 'Performance and Theatricality: The Subject Demystified' from 1982.

Féral says her demystificatory objective is to see what the 'new genre' can tell us about theatricality. Like RoseLee Goldberg she assumes a narrative that begins in the early twentieth-century avant-garde and on this basis identifies 'the essential foundations of all performance'. These are 'the manipulation to which performance subjects the performer's body', 'the manipulation of space' and 'the relation that performance institutes between the artist and the spectators, between the spectators and the work of art, and between the work of art and the artist' (1982: 171). Her ensuing commentaries on each of these 'foundations' evidence the preoccupations of contemporary Theory. Thus, performance shows 'a body in pieces, fragmented and yet one, a body perceived and rendered as a *place of desire*, displacement, and fluctuation, a body the performance conceives of as repressed and tries to free' (1982: 171). This is language that borrows from Theoretically reworked psychoanalysis, with Kristeva's commentary on Artaud being referenced. It positions performance as the mechanism which can reveal bodily repressions and make them known by spectators. The body, seen in this way, then is a model for the manipulation of space, 'which becomes existential to the point of ceasing to exist as a setting and place'. Space 'becomes the site of an exploration of the subject' and, in the context of gestures that are repeated, or duplicated by a camera, 'This is Derrida's *différance* made perceptible'. Performance is thus both 'the absence of meaning' and 'the death of the subject' (1982: 172–73). In terms of the artist's relation to his [*sic*] own performance, this is not that of actor to role. Instead the artist is 'a source of production and displacement', 'the point of passage for energy flows – gestural, vocal, libidinal, etc. – that traverse him without ever standing still in a fixed meaning or representation'

(1982: 174). These energy flows seem perhaps to recall Deleuze, to add to Derrida and Kristeva.

The same features tend to appear in each of the three 'foundations', namely displacement, lack of fixity, lack of meaning, desire, flow. In a similar fashion, as it were, Chantal Pontbriand, writing in the same journal issue, says that 'Performance appears much more as disarticulation of the whole than as signifying totality.' Again there is the attribution of displacement, fragmentation, lack of meaning, together with a psychoanalytic inflection to the argument. Just as Féral says performance will reveal that which is repressed so Pontbriand says 'performance lifts the barrier for us to the experience of the unconscious'. So too, like Féral, Pontbriand takes evidence for her claims from the work of Richard Foreman. But that comes with an awkward proviso. Foreman, she says, 'admits that for him the text is all-important, and in this sense he contradicts all performance theory which seeks to abandon the text in order to investigate the very materiality of things' (Pontbriand 1982: 156, 158, 160). And there's the rub.

Just as 'performance theory', or should we say 'performance Theory', hoves into view, with its articulation of defining characteristics and foundational features, it starts to wobble, albeit, I suppose, in an appropriately undecidable way. You will probably have noticed that Féral's first 'foundation' of performance, manipulation of the body, doesn't appear at all in Rothenberg's list of 'assumptions' about performance. For Féral it is perhaps primary because of her disposition towards using a psychoanalytic model. Rothenberg's last 'assumption' about 'real time', on the other hand, chimes with Pontbriand's observation that 'essentially what interests us in contemporary art is this criterion of temporality, this coming into being: the characteristic presence of performance could be called presentness. It is this quality of "presentness" that distinguishes "classical presence" from "postmodern presence".' This distinctive presence of performance, as opposed to that of theatre, is necessarily brought about by 'technical mediation' (Pontbriand 1982: 155–56). Thus far the argument might be said to be similar to that of Benamou, except that here presence is not in that definingly undecidable tension with play.

If assembling agreed characteristics of performance can be a generally slippery business, certain points here stand firm. Performance is modern, in that it moves with technology. But it's also modern in a deeper sense. It's the mode where current preoccupations of Theory can find themselves manifested. And a proper concept of 'performance', we gather, will subscribe to these preoccupations, and presumably an improper one won't. Her 'definition of performance', says Pontbriand, 'excludes any mystifying acts, any shamanizing performance' (1982: 157), a drawing of the line with which in one stroke Nitsch and all that anti-repressive body art – the very foundations of the mode as other people might think of it – are cut, if cut be the word, from Pontbriand's concept of performance. With this diligently guarded boundary we find ourselves quite a long way from Barthes's blissfully open writerly text.

The Theoretical alignments here are clearly giving shape to a very particular definition of performance, albeit one often offered, by the adherents to a postmodernised performance, as a general definition. Alongside them there is another shaping force at work here. It makes itself felt in the emphases on 'presentness'. What's going on is neatly unpacked for us by Philip Auslander. He notes that both Féral and Pontbriand take as their point of departure Michael Fried's essay on 'Art and Objecthood' from 1967. Here Fried argues that minimalist art is debilitated because it depends on the presence of a spectator in order to be fulfilled as an aesthetic object. It is not self-sufficient in its own right. This dependence on the spectator is the defining condition of theatre, which also is a time-based art. For Fried modernist art should transcend temporality, through 'presentness' (Fried 1995: 146), just as it achieves independence from spectators. Art that does neither of these is corroded by 'theatricality'. As Auslander argues it, Féral and Pontbriand are engaged on a similar exercise to Fried. While for him art needed to assert presentness against theatricality, and defend the 'integrity of modernism against an emerging postmodernism', for them 'performance needed to defeat representation and assert presentness in order to establish its specificity as a medium (that is, to distinguish itself from theatre) and to differentiate an emerging postmodernism from an existing modernism' (1997: 56).

The effect of the Fried argument is thus one more of the forces positioning the concept of performance that is developed here. Performance is seen as the expressive form of the new, the privileged exemplar of the postmodern and a practice which enacts fairly precisely the interests of Theory. Added to these a new assumption comes into being. While Benamou and Caramello may have viewed performance as part of a metaphor or analogy, Féral tells us she is discussing the 'essential' foundations of performance, just as Goldberg, before her, said she was describing the 'nature' of performance. It is slightly odd, given the poststructuralist tendencies of Theory, to find any Theorist sub-scribing to what looks like an inclination towards something rather similar to essentialism. It is even odder in that Féral, like Pontbriand, only considers performance in relation to artworks. While performance as behaviour might have led into the territory of that which can be thought of as natural, performance as art is entirely in the domain of the wilfully constructed. Which makes it a very strange move to look for and define its nature or essence. But that move happens quite often in work that aims to describe a theory of performance, and it occurs in very surprising places. Take, for example, Sue-Ellen Case's nicely perceptive essay on the naked body in performance. She does a properly sharp, feet-on-the-ground, reading of the heterosexist assumptions circulating in Richard Schechner's production *Dionysus in 69*. Then she says: 'The unexamined re-enactment of normative gender roles and heterosexuality found in the experiments with theatricality bars them from being regarded as consonant with theories of performance.' Given that many practices from John Cage up to the arrival of feminist performance, and perhaps beyond, could be said to contain 'unexamined re-enactment of normative gender roles', to say that none of this work is consonant with theories of performance is to produce yet another exclusionary boundary, and one which makes Pontbriand's look positively meek in its statement. It also raises the question as to what the makers of normative stuff thought they were theorising if it wasn't performance. What gets the essay into this odd moment is an argument founded on a binary which pits 'the aggressive strength of modernism' against performance's 'theory of representation', with a privileged site for the conflict being around gender and sex: 'the contestation of normative gender and sexual practices formed the inception of the notions of performance and performativity' (Case 2002: 190–91).

Just as performance practices were, and are, shaped by the specific cultural and political battle-lines with which they engaged, so too the theory of those performance practices is shaped by specific material factors. In the midst of a general and abstract formulation, when a line seems to be arbitrarily drawn, when there is a moment of essentialism, this is what confides in us that the formulation comes from a particular position, with particular interests being at stake. And so, many would say, it should be. In Case's example, her early engagement with critical theory was tied up with her feminism, and it is this perhaps that leads to her incorrect remark about the 'inception of the notions of performance'. Feminist critical theory produced models and vocabulary for the new thinking that was necessary to challenge a male-dominated academy. Case tells us something of what she was up against in her 'Introduction' to *Performing Feminisms*. The book was composed of articles taken from *Theatre Journal*, edited by Case and Timothy Murray. Their project there was 'to publish the feminist critique in theatre studies and even more broadly, to publish critical theory in theatre studies. Both projects were contested by the parent organization (ATHE)' (Case 1990: 1). In this sort of academic world the break point from the old and the dominant was facilitated by and declared as an alliance of critical theory and feminism.

This line of conflict has an interesting effect. In Féral's narrative, performance was traced back to the avant-garde of surrealism. She was interested in artworks that were aligned with, that's to say spoke the opinions of, the poststructuralist critique of Enlightenment thinking, with its emphasis on the fragmented body as a riposte to Enlightenment notions of the whole coherent subject. As Peter Dews says, from the 1970s poststructuralist thought 'had been the vehicle for generic radical sentiment, with an emphasis on the "liberatory" breaking-down of academic compartmentalizations, and on the fictionalizing release of an expressive subjectivity' (Dews 1989: 33–34). Performance, as filtered through poststructuralist theory, was on the side of the new, as against theatricality. Case's battle-line is somewhere different, namely between old and new ways of disciplinary thinking, less with an interest in the breaking down of compartmentalisations than in challenging the male dominance which persisted through both broken compartmentalisations and their re-assembly. The supposed potent essence of performance could be available to men as well as women. In that respect performance's lack of political discrimination could end up aligning it still with the masculine dominant. Against this a more genuine force for the new was presented by the practice which took it as its business to make discriminations, Theoretical discourse, particularly in the form of its specifically political manifestation and purpose in feminist theory. That feminist theory could show its own liberating capabilities by engaging with a range of topics from the representation of lesbianism through to the texts of early-modern plays. Here performance, as a separable practice with an avant-garde lineage, slides out of view. There is no political or theoretical need to insist on a division between performance and theatre. While as a particular practice performance with its avant-garde nature could be seen to be compromised in its role as agent of the new, what instead could inaugurate the new was a new way of thinking and analysing, a method of revealing the assumed hierarchies and unpicking that which was deemed to be natural. Bringing with it an agenda for feminist and gay liberation the real agent of the new was critical theory.

And this is where it is placed in Reinelt and Roach's anthology of 1992, *Critical Theory and Performance*. 'There has been a theory explosion', they say, and point to two major consequences of it: 'First, it has enlarged the conception of performance in ways not envisioned in the traditional study of drama and therefore reduced some of the separation of specialites [*sic*] between theater history, theory/criticism, and theater practice' and, second, it has 'returned the humanities to philosophy', meaning that humanities subjects have 'returned to a fundamental examination of the underlying assumptions' both of methodology and objects of inquiry. Their book consequently ranges across major critical theories and combines essays on the 'extraliterary' with ones that offer new readings of canonical texts. It acknowledges, and draws energy from, 'the divisions created by the diverse institutional sites of research in the field', which include 'departments of theater, Performance Studies communications, literature, media studies, and anthropology' (Reinelt and Roach 1992: 4, 3). What brings these departments and objects of enquiry together is the unifying circumstance of post-modernism, which has had an impact, as has had 'the pluralistic eclecticism it inspires – on critical theories of performance as well as on performers themselves. Performance research and practice both have found in postmo-dernity a positive stimulus to creative work' (Reinelt and Roach 1992: 1). While for Michel Benamou in 1977 'performance' was the 'unifying mode' of postmodernism, for Reinelt and Roach postmodernism seems to be the unifying mode of 'performance scholarship'.

In that phrase, and in the book as a whole, just as with Case there is no gesture towards, indeed no apparatus for, the separation out of a discrete category called 'performance'. The book demonstrates what critical theory can do for performance; it doesn't show what performance can do for critical thinking. The journey to this point began with Benamou in 1977 identifying performance not as a specific practice, with its own craft and institutions, but as a mode, a mode which could even be adopted by such non-fictional textual production as criticism. This mode was 'unifying', in that it was common to all practices in, and exemplified the characteristics of, postmodernism. The work done by 'postmodern' performance was perhaps less as a practice than as a way of thinking. It offered an analogy, a frame for analysis, a way of doing things that identified postmodernism. It became 'performance theory' in its own right. In 1992 Reinelt and Roach's book has performance no longer set in opposition to theatre but as one of a range of practices, some experimental, some canonical, some new, some old, some art, some theatre. Here there is little sense of a 'performance theory' based in its presumed distinction from other practices. Instead it is critical theory that is the unifying mode across a range of disciplines and makes sense of performance for a postmodern context. The book's title is *Critical Theory and Performance* not *Performance Theory and Criticism*. Performance is no longer the mode that unites a range of postmodern activities; performance is a range of activities, including theatre, united by postmodern critical theory. As such performance once again slides out of view as a discrete practice, and no longer seems to do anything particularly different from theatre. The social science notion of performance starts to evaporate. But help was at hand.

Chapter 16

What Performance Studies is: version 1
New York and Northwestern

In the same year as Reinelt and Roach's book, at the annual conference of the USA's Association for Theatre in Higher Education (ATHE) at Atlanta, the relationship of performance and theatre was brought under new discipline. A member of the New York University Graduate Department of Performance Studies, Richard Schechner, suggested from the podium that theatre departments should change their focus and their names. The business of offering training 'for the orthodox theatre' was, he said, neither economically nor academically 'acceptable': 'The new paradigm' is 'performance', not theatre. Theatre departments should become 'performance departments'. By studying performance rather than theatre these departments could engage with a wider range of material, 'a broad spectrum', that included 'entertainments, arts, rituals, politics, economics, and person-to-person interactions' (in Dolan 1995: 30).

The variety of performance study

This speech was not entirely welcomed. For those in other departments already deeply thinking about the definition of the subject area, the call to arms by the man at the podium may well have seemed somewhat impertinent. Some assumed it was less about academic innovation but was instead more of a bid to claim institutional territory. For as we know the academic debates around performance and theatre had been going on in different places for at least a decade, and change of various sorts was well under way. Some of it was being driven by the work we have already noted, namely the engagement with new theoretical models and political positions such as feminism (Auslander 1997, Case 1992, Dolan 1995). A second force for change came from some of the constituent members of the National Communication Association (NCA), previously known, prior to 1997, as the National Association of Academic Teachers of Public Speaking. Within this association its

Interpretation Division provided a forum for 'teachers and scholars of performance-based literary study who worked outside the institutional boundaries of "English" and "theatre"'. This work is often referred to as 'oral interpretation', a combination of rhetoric and textual analysis. In 1991 the Interpretation Division changed its name to the Performance Studies Division, thereby, as Edwards notes, 'cultivating what appears to be the first national association of Performance Studies scholars out of its deep roots in literary study, speech arts, and elocutionary training'. By contrast, Edwards says, 'Performance Studies international', formally inaugurated in 1995 in New York (though actually this was not PSi itself), came from very different institutional roots (Edwards 2006: 144; see also Dailey 1998, Jackson 2004, Jackson 2006, Pelias and Van Oosting 1987, Shields 1998, Stucky 1998). And then, third, there was that New York initiative.

These various points of origin for disciplinary change, and their subsequent developments, have been well documented, in part to ensure that the different territorial claims are heard. As we noted in Part II, the stories of origin of 'performance' or 'live' art did ideological work in the interests of establishing, and getting funding for, the new forms. Such stories function in a similar way in the case of Performance Studies. But in this case the points of origin are even more stridently various. As such the 'new discipline' has to be seen as a set of parallel initiatives, where Performance Studies is properly a plural noun denoting several different programmes of performance study. The exploration of these differences, regularly niggled as it is by a persistent worrying at the identity of the discipline, has prompted much, so much scholarly prose. One of Performance Studies' favourite topics for enquiry has been the definition of Performance Studies. It is not, however, that disciplinary self-interest, so to speak, which concerns us here. Instead our focus is on what Performance Studies means, in its various ways, by 'performance'. Here the territorial claims and narratives of origin are relevant insofar as they construct, and deploy, a concept of performance. For instance, that address at ATHE in 1992, needing to draw a clear boundary in order to establish the territory of the new discipline, proposed that theatre was associated with the orthodox, the old, and the narrow, thereby associating performance with all that was the opposite. It became quite important to Performance Studies that performance was opposed to things.

The concept of performance that Schechner nailed to the mast in 1992 took its shape from his own institutional positioning and history. The ways that institutional positioning shapes concepts are demonstrated by Shannon Jackson in her essay 'Rhetoric in Ruins', which tracks the development of the Performance Studies pedagogy associated with oral interpretation within the US university system. To frame her account she begins with the ideological crisis around the definition of the university and its function as an institution, which saw the old idea of the 'University of Culture' being put under threat by a more 'techno-bureaucratic' university model, with its valorisation of supposedly 'scientific' models and goals. Thus, within the institutional history of communications studies, the increasing trend towards 'scientizing' put pressure on the commitment to the study of literature. Placed in contrast to 'techno-bureaucratic definitions of knowledge' the teaching of literature within oral interpretation 'functioned as the last bastion of a University of Culture'. But whereas oral interpretation had a 'delegitimated relation' to as it were proper literature departments, this was not the same sort of delegitimated relationship as 'drama' professors had to the institution of literature. These different sorts of institutional negotiations and tensions then produced different emphases within what is thought of as Performance Studies. By contrast with what she calls 'rhetorical Performance Studies', that's to say that which originates through the NCA and oral interpretation, Jackson suggests that the Performance Studies more associated with the East of the United States, and specifically New York, had its attention fixed on theatre, rather than literature, as the 'high cultural' site from which it was trying to break (Jackson 2012: 76–77). This might seem to express itself in the high value placed on modes of performing which displayed their difference from the formal conventions of traditional theatre, such as in the 'experimental' theatre made by Richard Schechner and his colleague Michael Kirby. In this particular institutional context the clearest point of rupture was marked by those practices that seemed furthest distant from theatre, namely the 'entertainments' and 'rituals' that Schechner felt everybody should now study.

This relationship between point of origin and concept of performance gives its shape to Schechner's *Performance Studies: An Introduction*, published first in 2001, and now in its third edition. From 1979 Schechner had taught a course at New York University on 'performance theory' which drew on work done by the various social sciences in which he had been interested since at least the mid-seventies. The ideas he developed in various publications since that time are brought together and re-stated in the *Introduction*, which is in effect a Summation. It is also, as Schechner candidly admits, very much a story of one institution, New York Performance Studies.

The Schechner view

Although it admits to being the story of just one institution, this admission is soon effaced as the book lays out what Performance Studies is in general. It derives authority for its views from the status of its author, who has been claimed, not least by himself, as a founder of the field. The story according to Schechner runs like this. Performance Studies began in the mid-1950s with Bateson and Austin, then Goffman's *Presentation* in 1959, Lord's *Singer of Tales* in 1960, Callois's *Man, Play, and Games* in 1961, Schechner's 'Approaches to Theory/Criticism' in 1966, then Hymes, Turner, Singer and others. This is a fairly disparate collection of work, and the dates of first publication are not always correct, so it's pretty dodgy as a linear genealogy. More secure to grasp is a particular personal encounter. In 1977 Schechner was invited to a conference by the cultural anthropologist Victor Turner, and the two began working together. Their explorations, together with the work already done by their predecessors, led to a concept of performance which included not only theatre, ritual, sports, ceremonies and such but also every-day behaviour such as cooking, socialising, 'just living'. Indeed, as Peggy Phelan understood it, this was performance conceived on the model of universal language. She says that when she began teaching at New York University in 1985 'the story that surrounded me' was that

> the field was born out of the fecund collaborations between Richard
> Schechner and Victor Turner. In bringing theatre and anthropology
> together, both men saw the extraordinarily deep questions these
> perspectives on cultural expression raised. If the diversity of human
> culture continually showed a persistent theatricality, could performance
> be a universal expression of human signification, akin to language?
> (Phelan 1998: 3)

But Performance Studies, as Schechner tells it, didn't just emerge from intellectual explorations. It was in part a response to the world around it. That world was experiencing a dissatisfaction with the status quo, an explo-sion of knowledge and a new way of disseminating via the Internet. 'The world no longer appeared as a book to be read but as a performance to participate in' and the New York department came into being to 'deal with these swiftly changing circumstances' (Schechner 2001: 21, 25). Performance Studies was thus a synthesis of a range of academic work across two decades as well as an articulation of the spirit of the times. It was inclusive, exploratory and always plugged into the present. Or rather, more accurately, plugged into the future since, in 1980, it seemed with uncanny prescience already to be aware of the efficacy of the Internet.

Under the heading 'What Makes Performance Studies Special', Schechner defines 'performances' as 'actions' and says that 'Performance Studies takes actions very seriously.' It does this in four ways. First, 'behavior' is its principal object of study, so that, while Performance Studies scholars may use the 'archive' (photographs, books, etc.), their 'dedicated focus' is the 'repertory', which Schechner defines as 'what people do in the activity of their doing it'. Second, a major part of Performance Studies is the making of art, so that 'the relationship between studying performance and doing performance is integral.' Third, the favoured method of doing fieldwork is 'participant observation', which has been adapted from anthropology. This method 'positions the Performance Studies fieldworker at a Brechtian distance allowing for criticism, irony, and personal commentary, as well as sympathetic observation'. Such a positioning in relation to both the self and objects of study prompts 'the recognition that social circumstances – including knowledge itself – are not fixed, but subject to the "rehearsal process" of testing and revising'. Thus the fourth approach to action: 'Performance Studies is actively involved in social practices and advocacies.' This means that those who do Performance Studies tend not to be ideologically neutral and take the position that 'There is no such thing as neutral or unbiased' (Schechner 2001: 1–2). In short, it studies behaviour, makes art, views given circumstances as relative and takes sides.

Schechner himself has a stalwart record of taking sides, from supporting students protesting against the state in the late sixties through to his sustained critique of globalisation and the 'new world order'. He is characteristically insistent, therefore, that the Performance Studies approach needs to be intercultural. This recognises that 'cultures are always interacting' and that differences between them are 'so profound that no theory of performance is universal'. Such an insistence is necessary because globalisation produces major inequalities of power and resources between societies and yet, at the same time, promotes cultural homogeneity, often based in the commodities sold by dominant global corporations. 'Cultural sameness and seamless communications' enable this dominance. Against such sameness, (New York) Performance Studies takes the innovatory step of refusing to organise its 'wide array of subjects' into 'a unitary system'. It knows that knowledge cannot be 'reduced to coherence', and it has a characteristic appetite for 'encountering, even inventing, new kinds of performing while insisting that cultural knowledge can never be complete'. In short, 'If Performance Studies were an art, it would be avant-garde' (Schechner

2001: 2–3). But while it may not be an art it does seem, on this account, to be a political project.

The whole project has variety and multiplicity at its core. The performance it studies is to be viewed as a 'broad spectrum' of activities that includes ritual, play, sport, aesthetic performing arts and everyday life performances. This definition of 'performance' is a major break point: 'Before Performance Studies western thinkers believed they knew exactly what was and was not "performance".' To study this 'broad spectrum' the emergent discipline draws on 'a wide variety of disciplines', but, as Schechner's quotation from Barbara Kirshenblatt-Gimblett notes, its mode of study is deliberately inclusive: 'Performance studies starts from the premise that its objects of study are not to be divided and parcelled out, medium by medium.' In this it takes its lead from 'the historical avant-garde and contemporary art, which have long questioned the boundaries between modalities and gone about blurring them' (Schechner 2001: 3).

In dealing with this range of material, (New York) Performance Studies does not study artefacts of art or culture as such, Schechner tells us, but, instead, 'texts, architecture, visual arts' and such 'are studied "as" performance'. That's to say 'they are regarded as practices, events, and behaviors'. So in dealing with a painting Performance Studies does not 'read' it but inquires about its 'behavior', namely 'the ways it interacts with those who view it, thus evoking different reactions and meanings; and how it changes meaning over time and in different contexts' (Schechner 2001: 2). 'Behavior', when defined this way, is really of course the behaviour of those who look at and study the painting, rather than the painting itself – much as we might enjoy the image of the *Mona Lisa* smiling at one person and scowling at another, as her eyes follow you round the room. But defining behaviour that way, or any way, takes us to the heart of the concept of performance – and its difficulties. 'Performances', Schechner says, 'are made of "twice-behaved behaviors"'. By way of glossing the last phrase he says: 'Every action, no matter how small or encompassing, consists of twice-behaved behaviors.' With a shift of terminology, but not meaning, this idea is repeated a few pages later: 'all behavior is restored behavior', and the special quality of 'restored behavior' is that 'Because it is marked, framed, and separate, restored behaviour can be worked on, stored and recalled, played with, made into something else, transmitted, and transferred.' On the other hand, it also requires the attention of specialists: 'Its meanings need to be decoded by those in the know.' By this stage all that I confidently know is that I am not in the know. The questions are piling up. If all actions, all behaviour, are twice-behaved or restored behaviour, what is 'restored behavior' separate from? And how is it 'framed'? And why are specialists needed to decode it? And if performance is twice-behaved behaviour, and twice-behaved behaviour is behaviour, then performance is behaviour. Ah, but it's not. 'There are limits to what "is" performance' (2001: 23, 28, 30). But if performance is behaviour it seems to me unclear what these limits are.

It makes me feel a little better to know that I am not the only one who is confused. Back in 1996 Bert States did a more thorough job than mine in trying to sort out Schechner's muddles around behaviour and his attempts to draw the line that distinguishes between what is or is not performance. For example States notes that in one essay Schechner says that performances 'are always actually performed', which appears to exclude rehearsal, but five years later he says that the 'whole performance sequence', including workshops and rehearsals, is 'identical to what I call "restored behavior"' ... Ritual process is performance'. From here States begins to explore what might or might not be included as performance, observing that the 'most obvious' difference between himself and Schechner is that he has a 'wider conception of behavior'. That said, 'Schechner's notion of restored behavior seems to me an almost unassailable criterion for performance, even if one wishes (as I do) to extend the range of behavior that gets restored. Put simply: something is always restored in performance, even if the restoration comes through a simple framing device.' At this point he begins to hammer in the nail that closes the coffin good and proper. 'My main problem with the principle of restored behavior concerns the term *twice-behaved* ... The notion of twice-behaved behavior dialectically posits the notion of once-behaved behavior.' To illustrate he quotes Schechner reporting on Goffman's work, and observes that Schechner seems 'slightly uneasy with Goffman's appropriation of the word performance and its possible relation to his own definition of performance'. While Goffman's 'performances' 'don't restore anything' Schechner 'is assuming that to the extent that ordinary life is *like* performance, it must therefore be like art, meaning (I suspect) theatre art', which is to miss the basic fact that 'theatre is patterned on life, rather than life on theatre'. This very neatly flushes out the persistent, if hidden, presence of aesthetic practice which frames, and delimits, much of Schechner's thinking. But the real twist is to come.

The 'twice-behaved behaviors of theatre', says States, 'are normatively based on behavior in ordinary life that is itself *already twice-behaved*.' By way of example, 'we may safely assume that Hamlet's behavior – or more correctly, "Hamletic" behavior – was already "twice-behaved" before

Shakespeare and Burbage created Hamlet, and the characterization would have been meaningless unless it was based on behavior the audience recognized.' Tucked in here, though States doesn't reference it, is the notion of iteration and citation as the enabling machinery for any individual human expression, but more of that later. But States doesn't need that to conclude, perfectly correctly I think, that 'the term "single behaved behavior" refers to something that doesn't exist in human experience, or at least in the experience that theatre, in its turn, strives to restore' (1996: 14–19).

The essays on which States was commenting were written, obviously, before 1996. With the texts available to him he was uncertain as to precisely what Schechner might classify as performance. For example according to the terms set out in Schechner's original essay called 'Restoration of Behavior' from 1985 films might not be included, and as we have already noted States thought there was some difficulty around inclusion of Goffman's 'performances'. But what also becomes clear is that the original, more cautious and specific, essay gets loosened up as time goes by. The status of rehearsal as performance changes over five years. By the time the *Introduction* to Performance Studies was written the original formulation had been loosened up so far as to be generous, indeed grandiose, in its inclusivity. It seems a curiously unstoppable process. For rather than States's argument prompting a rethinking back in 1996, with some more precision about terminology being introduced, the inclusion of more and more stuff under the heading of performance simply presses ahead in a mechanical process of acquisition. Which then leads to the grand, but fatuous, pronouncements of the *Introduction*.

Here it is having another shot at defining twice-behaved behaviour, this time under the rubric of ritual and play: 'twice-behaved behaviour is generated by interactions between ritual and play. In fact, one definition of performance may be: Ritualized behaviour conditioned/permeated by play.' This seems appropriate enough given that 'Ritual and play both lead people into a "second reality", separate from ordinary life.' But twice-behaved behaviour is defined as behaviour, so behaviour may be said to be generated by ritual and play, so performance is behaviour, again, and how, therefore, is it 'separate' from 'ordinary life'? And if ritual gets us unstuck, so does play: 'Playing – doing something that is "not for real" – is, like ritual, at the heart of performance'; 'restored behaviour has a quality of not being entirely "real" or "serious"' (2001: 45, 79). Performance is restored behaviour, restored behaviour is behaviour, behaviour is not entirely real. But by what means might we know? Presumably this is where we need the opinions of those in the know.

And the opinions of those in the know would say that they wouldn't start from there. Take, for example, the very social science that is so much fêted as being a core element of what defines (New York) Performance Studies. Back in 1975 Dell Hymes warned about the use of 'performance' as a 'wastebasket' term: 'Performance is not merely behavior, but neither is it the same as all of culture (or conduct, or communication)' (Hymes 1975: 13). A few years later, in 1979, in developing a 'performative' approach to the study of ritual, S.J. Tambiah was clear that ordinary communication could and should be distinguished from 'constructed' communication. In support of his argument for insisting on the specificity of practices he quoted Lévi-Strauss's distinction between game and ritual. Now although Schechner made much of Lévi-Strauss in a couple of essays from the late sixties, he opted to ignore the great anthropologist's careful distinctions when he lined up games and ritual in parallel with one another. The anthropologist with whom Schechner later collaborated, Victor Turner, also insisted on precise distinctions, warning that 'social drama' was 'heavily dependent on the cultural values and rules by which human conduct, as distinct from behaviour, was assessed' (Turner 1984: 20) (see pp. 43–44). Again 'behaviour' is being delimited as a category. Similar delimitations are recommended in relation to other words which have been used as catch-alls, such as ritual. Recall Bell's words from Part I (p. 52): 'the greatest challenge to current performance theory lies in its tendency to flirt with universalism, that is, to substitute performance for older notions of ritual in order to create a new general model of action' (1998: 218). Rather than attending to the precision of distinctions, such as those between behaviour and conduct, ritual and performance, made by those fêted social sciences, Schechner's argument tends to work towards generalising diagrams and overviews which usually have the effect of forcing subtly different activities into imposed equivalence. His collaborator Turner noted this, albeit very gently. Describing Schechner's recent development, in 1977, of his binary model of 'efficacy/entertainment' to include everything as performance, Turner notes that: 'Schechner's "performance" is a fairly precise labelling of the items in the modern potpourri of liminoid genres – but it indicates by its very breadth and tolerance of discrepant forms that a level of public reflexivity has been reached totally congruent with the advanced stages of a given social form – western capitalist liberal democracy.' He then adds a 'personal footnote', which is where the critique really sharpens:

> I see the liminoid as an advance in the history of human freedom. For this reason I relish the separation of an audience from performers and the liberation of scripts from cosmology and theology. The concept of

individuality has been hard-won, and to surrender it to a new totalizing
process of reliminalization is a dejecting thought.   (Turner 1977: 54)

The theoretical precision was not confined to social scientists. It could also
be found in the newly theorised theatre studies of the late seventies and early
eighties. One of those who attended the Milwaukee Conference in 1976 was
Herbert Blau, and in an essay from 1982 we can see him adopting poststructuralist models for thinking about theatre practice. In seeking to define the
'Universals of Performance' he notes 'the current discourse on performance
which, now refusing, now accepting, more or less obscures the ontological gap
between the actuality of everyday life and the actuality of a performance'.
Performance, he says, has some basic features, such as the management of
time, and perhaps above all the 'consciousness of performance'. It is these
characteristics which forced Richard Schechner to back off from his experiments with 'unmediated activity' and formulate the concept of 'restoration of
behavior' (Blau 1982/1983: 141, 143). Quite apart from the prescience of
Blau's comments, given the way that thinking about performance was to
develop, what is strikingly evident in the essay is the theoretical rigour of
'theatre studies' scholarship. This, recall, was precisely the discipline which,
ten years later, Schechner incited his colleagues to reject. As we have already
noted, though, this call for rejection had the effect, if not the motivation, of
clearing the field. The new kid on the block had to kill the old father, before
sitting in his chair.

Thus, by ignoring those nice theoretical distinctions, refusing to divide and
parcel out, the calculated vagueness of Schechner's definition of performance
allows it to acquire and accommodate not just theatre studies but almost every
human activity. This capacity for accommodation overrides minor quibbles.
While its claims to be both inclusive and yet 'avant-garde' are, as Bottoms
(2011) notes, strictly speaking self-contradictory, they work to cover all bases.
The cumulative effect is institutionally beneficial in that, in promoting its
mission of finding performance everywhere, (New York) Performance
Studies works like a centripetal machine, drawing bodies, of every sort, into
its orbit, with itself always at the centre. Indeed it's merely the word at the
centre that guarantees that the more or less heavenly bodies whirling around
have anything in common at all. As Simon Goldhill puts it, 'for all the claims
of Performance Studies to be a discipline, it remains a bricolage, loosely
collected around a central term' (1999: 15). But this universalising embrace,
this whirling mass, brings exactly the problems of which Bell warns: 'This
tendency toward universalism and essentialism spawns many of the smaller
problems afflicting performance analyses, such as the tendency to assume that

performance is a single, coherent thing, sufficiently the same everywhere, that to approach something as "performance" implies a general formula for explaining it' (1998: 218).

The Conquergood view

By contrast with this concept and its mission, a different point of origin comes up with something different. Schechner's academic background was in theatre studies, from where he encountered various social sciences. At Northwestern University Dwight Conquergood had a literary background and his disciplinary base was in oral interpretation, whence he encountered ethnography. Along with the rest of the discipline of oral interpretation Conquergood's department had formally named what it was doing 'Performance Studies' in 1991. As chair of that department he addressed both the NCA's annual Otis J. Aggertt Festival and the First Annual Performance Studies Conference at New York in 1995.

His lecture, for both, reviews various concepts of performance and culture developed by cultural anthropologists and, specifically, folklorists. As we know from Part I, by the end of the seventies folklore studies was using the word 'performance' and had developed a subtle understanding of its operation. It was perhaps the most substantial body of thinking about the concept of performance. In relation to this existing intellectual tradition a newly arrived subject that also studied performance had to discover its place and indeed significance. Conquergood's lecture, delivered from a position of institutional authority, and with its origins in oral interpretation and ethnography, undertook to mark out the territory for what he saw as the new Performance Studies.

He did this by first telling his audience what was wrong with the folklorists, focusing in particular on Dell Hymes and Richard Bauman. After summarising their definitions of performance, Conquergood commented on the significance of their view of 'tradition': 'Both Hymes and Bauman construe the performer as a conservative exemplar of audience expectations and tradition.' This means that 'their view ultimately enlists performance in the service of stabilizing status quo norms and expectations.' By contrast with that which is 'stabilizing', the performance paradigm as conceived by Conquergood puts 'mobility, action, and agency back into play' (1998: 31). This paradigm had already been described in Conquergood's 1991 'Rethinking Ethnography' as part of his exposition of the meaning of 'performance-centred' research. He notes that ethnography has adopted a 'performance-inflected vocabulary' which he attributes to the 'renewed appreciation for boundaries, border-crossings, process, improvisation, contingency, multiplex identities, and the embodied nature of field work practice'. Turner in particular was 'drawn to the conceptual lens of performance because it focussed on humankind alive, the creative, playful, provisional, imaginative, articulate expressions of ordinary people'. Turner's 'performance-sensitive' research exemplifies the characteristics of the 'performance paradigm'. This privileges

> particular, participatory, dynamic, intimate, precarious, embodied experience grounded in historical process, contingency, and ideology. Another way of saying it is that performance-centred research takes as both its subject matter and method the experiencing body situated in time, place, and history. The performance paradigm insists on face-to-face encounters instead of abstractions and reductions.

From here he suggests that by rethinking the world 'as performance', as opposed to the 'world as text', five 'intersecting planes of analyses' can be identified: performance and cultural process, performance and ethnographic praxis, performance and hermeneutics, performance and scholarly representation, the politics of performance (1991: 187, 190).

Defined in this way the performance paradigm is positioned in the 1995 lecture as the opposite of the 'textual paradigm' the 'defining agenda' of which is 'to pin down meaning', to privilege what is said rather than the saying of it, valuing the product not the process. To conceive of the 'culture of a people' as 'an ensemble of texts', as Geertz does, is not only to marginalise the performance practices of a culture in which people played and danced and acted but it is also to do a disservice to non-literate disenfranchised peoples (Conquergood 1998: 31–32, 28). By positioning performance on the side of tradition and stability Hymes and Bauman are thus denying the transgressive nature of performance and making it behave like 'text'.

Except that is not what Hymes and Bauman say. Hymes, recall (see p. 35), said that verbal communication was one among a number of channels that also included drumming, singing and whistling; Bauman suggested that the text could itself be situated, and thereby changed, within the context of performance. To these might be added Kirshenblatt-Gimblett, by then chair of the department hosting the lecture, whose analysis of parable weaves together performances and texts of various sorts – the parable, its document, and the interview with the teller – all in a process without fixed product. But the work of seeing off Hymes and Bauman clears the space for the anthropologist who had already shown his engagement with Performance Studies, and had already been celebrated by Conquergood in 1992 as a 'pivotal figure'

(1992: 84), Victor Turner. He had collaborated with Schechner in the seventies, and Schechner had promoted his writings after his death. So too Conquergood celebrates the richness of his ideas about social drama, cultural performance, liminality, and *homo performans*. By these means Turner helped to shape ideas through 'his constructional theory of performance, epigrammatically stated as "making, not faking"' (1998: 31). Conquergood's generous celebration also simultaneously detaches Turner from other ethnographers. For example it's difficult to see how a performance conceived as taking on accountability to an audience, as Bauman describes it, is in the domain of the 'fake'. It's also difficult to see how Turner's model of liminality (see pp. 44–45), founded on the processes of a society trying to sustain its own stable status quo, could be so different from the traditions about which Hymes wrote.

The problem with Conquergood's argument is not that it ignores what Hymes and Bauman were saying, but it gets it back to front. So too, in an earlier essay, he had misconceived the history. In 1989 he greeted anthropology's engagement with performance as a 'breaking sub-discipline', which is shifting from a study of 'cultural performance' to a study of 'culture as performance' (1989: 82). By 1989, the 'sub-discipline' was surely already well broken, having formulated its ideas a good decade before. So too the study of culture as performance had also been well developed in the mid- to late-seventies by cultural studies (see pp. 10–15). This tendency to locate itself within the breaking news, to see itself as always at the very cusp of the newest now, is characteristic of much of Performance Studies discourse. But there is more going on here. Conquergood's arguments are part of a process which detaches performance from the grip of the social scientists and reshapes the concept. That reshaping finds for itself a rhetorical trope, and like most rhetoric its job is to persuade its listeners. The rhetorical trope found by Conquergood is the simple opposition between performance and 'text'. We might note the possible origins of this in Conquergood's own career trajectory, in that the vexed, or indeed harmonious, relations between performance and text are much more part of the territory of oral interpretation than of sociology or anthropology.

For Conquergood there is a stark opposition: while performance is 'a rallying point for scholars who want to privilege action, agency, and transformation' the academy is almost totally dominated by 'textualism'. This textualism is even creeping into the thinking about performance. So 'we need to recuperate from performance some oppositional force, some resistance to the textual fundamentalism of the academy.' This is necessary because 'performance-sensitive ways of knowing hold forth the promise of contributing to an epistemological pluralism' and, second, 'performance is a more conceptually astute and inclusionary way of thinking about many subaltern cultural practices.' In claiming performance's greater appropriateness to thinking about subalterns Conquergood is producing another version of Schechner's link between experimental theatre and the feelings of rural people (Schechner 1988: 39–40). But while Schechner argues that by embracing anthropology, Conquergood, for all his romancing of anthropology, is actually here trying to knock out of the frame a particular anthropologist, Clifford Geertz. His method straightforwardly involves a misreading of Geertz. In his 'Notes on the Balinese Cockfight' from 1972 Geertz clearly says that in referring to culture as 'an assemblage of texts' the notion of text is extended 'beyond written material. And even beyond verbal'. Its advantage was that it could produce readings of subaltern practices that were not otherwise available: 'to treat the cockfight as a text is to bring out a feature of it ... that treating it as a rite or a pastime, the two most obvious alternatives, would tend to obscure: its use of emotion for cognitive ends'. Rather than performance being the frame for reading, here it is text, and as a frame it can bring out some very deep insights: a Balinese can learn from a cockfight 'what his culture's ethos and his private sensibility ... look like when spelled out externally in a collective text' (1972: 26–27; my elisions). But this extended sense of text and its productivity in dealing with performed practices, even 'subaltern' ones – if indeed Balinese are subalterns – could not be allowed within the binary Conquergood wants, needs, to flog. Driven by the requirement that performance, and performance alone, be credited with inclusiveness and the rest, Conquergood's binary is summarised thus: 'a textual paradigm privileges distance, detachment, and disclosure as ways of knowing' while ' a performance paradigm insists upon immediacy, involvement, and intimacy as modes of understanding' (1998: 25–26). We'll note in passing that although performance is 'inclusionary' it isn't too keen on ethnographers who say the wrong things, or performance scholars who value text. Conquergood's own alliteration is not, here, presumably a textual device.

As part of the assault on textuality, Conquergood has a go at Derrida. Later in his essay, however, he invokes a model of performance that is transgressive precisely because it is 'poststructuralist': 'Instead of construing performance as *transcendence*, a higher plane that one breaks into, I prefer to think of it as *transgression*, that force which crashes and breaks through sedimented meanings and normative traditions and plunges us back into the vortices of political struggle.' Heroically, and sympathetically, political as this concept of poststructuralism is, it is rather different from Derrida's. Conquergood's transgressive poststructuralist performance has a form of agency that works by breaking through 'sedimented' meanings. This version of poststructuralism as bulldozer is founded in a model of agency that possesses the qualities of creativity and immediacy and energy and can apparently free itself of the network of reference and difference by which language establishes meaning. Conquergood's purpose, as we know, is 'to recuperate from performance some oppositional force', in its own right as it were, and in the course of the essay performance shifts from being a 'paradigm', a way of thinking, to something which has its own force. Weirdly, although he doesn't want to think of it, he says, as 'transcendence', this is an imagining of performance where it's not a practice done by people, in always negotiated circumstances, but something which has its own immanent force – perhaps an essence or nature.

In getting to this point the argument produces a notion of performance working like expressive speech. But, as Conquergood will presumably have known, Derrida had already demonstrated, and Blau and others had repeated, that the concept of this freely expressive speech is an illusion since it cannot operate as language without relation to the overarching system of reference and difference. But Derrida's argument has to be overridden by the superior force of the binary which keeps in place the opposition between mobility and stasis, empathy and refusal of empathy, being nice and being horrid. For this binary that sets up text – or 'textuality' – as the main enemy is one of the foundational orthodoxies of Conquergood's Performance Studies. But it's established on very fragile ground, not to say sediment.

Although his argument may position it as the enemy, Conquergood, with his origins in literary study and oral interpretation, has a somewhat ambivalent relationship with textuality. A writer who can produce this sentence, 'Oppressed people everywhere must watch their backs, cover their tracks, hide their feelings, and veil their meanings,' is a writer who is quite handy with textual devices (whether he is right in the suggestion that oppressed people should hide their feelings is perhaps at this point an incidental matter). And it is only textual devices that allow this sort of scenario: 'the asymmetrical power relations secure both the anthropologist's privilege to intrude and the people's acquiescence (although one can imagine what they would say about the anthropologist's manners and motives when they are outside his reading gaze)' (1998: 29–30). The syntax of the verbal construction is the mechanism for conjuring up a fantasised ability to get into what the observed people really think. And the same mechanism ensures that this penetration is not itself regarded as intrusion. But these are minor points. What's also sitting in that verbal construction is the binary of 'anthropologist' and 'people', and behind that binary is text versus performance, and behind that is stasis and conservatism versus movement and transgression. The whole lecture reiterates and reproduces a binarised way of thinking. That binary, with its twin poles fixed firmly in opposed relation one to another, is a pretty inflexible structure and certainly far from mobile, let alone playful. As a way of organising the argument it is a formulaic textual device placed in a very powerful position. Conquergood is thus right about the potency of text. His problem is that he is the one deploying the devices of that text.

Chapter 17

What Performance Studies is: version 2
Oral interpretation

While Conquergood's mapping of the issues may have derived from his own particular combination of oral interpretation and ethnography, the basic characteristics which he attributes to performance are shared pretty widely among those who come to the subject from oral interpretation.

There is a crucial difference, however. Conquergood's engagement with anthropology more or less put him in the same territory as Richard Schechner, with his enthusiasm for social sciences. Both men lionised Victor Turner. So although Conquergood's department was based in the discipline of oral interpretation he deviated from the disciplinary norm. And that norm insisted on some rather different emphases. An early statement of these comes from Conquergood's senior colleague at Northwestern, Wallace Bacon. Bacon was the great driving force behind oral interpretation's change to Performance Studies, indeed the magisterial authority of Wikipedia itself pronounces him the founder of Performance Studies. Somewhat more soberly, Strine, Long and Hopkins suggest that Bacon was one of three authors who provided 'the conceptual framework for text-centered studies that draw on performance-related insights to supplement the textual analysis of literary scholarship'. Alongside Bacon, Don Geiger made a 'theoretical integration of American New Criticism and principles of dramatism' and Thomas Sloan argued for 'the interrelationships among oral performance, rhetoric, and literary criticism', both in the mid-1960s (Strine, Long and Hopkins 1990: 182). For all three performance is deeply connected with, bound into the analysis and effects of, text. In Bacon's words oral interpretation teaches 'the art of performing texts – not simply the art of performing'. If some versions of Performance Studies were to pride themselves on their disciplinary inclusivity or lack of definition, Bacon does the reverse and insists on specificity: 'we are not, in essence, anthropologists, nor folklorists, nor sociologists, nor political scientists'. For him 'Our center is the interaction between readers and texts.' This interaction provided the transformative power of the educational project, in that it 'enriches, extends, clarifies, and (yes) alters the interior and even the exterior lives of students through the power of texts'. It also provides its ethical centre: the performance of texts develops 'that sense of the other so crucial to any concept of education as a humanizing, liberalizing experience' (1984: 84).

Instituting the inclusive classroom

Here in miniature are the aims and values that were to be so often reiterated in the work of all those who came to Performance Studies via oral interpretation. They were indeed a defining part of the Performance Studies that oral interpretation announced, and conceptually brought into being, in 1987. This was done in an essay by Ronald Pelias and James VanOosting which they called 'A Paradigm for Performance Studies'. They start by clarifying the origins of this paradigm: 'From within speech communication, Performance Studies derives from the interpretation of literature.' Then in their description of the 'central concepts' of Performance Studies we hear an elaboration of Bacon's insistencies. For instance, at base 'Performance Studies takes as its root orientations an inclusionary impulse toward performers and audiences and a noncanonical attitude toward texts.' Performance Studies 'calls into question the privilege of academic authority by including all members of a speech community as potential artists'. Its practitioners 'eschew artistic imperialism in favor of aesthetic communalism'. In its research methods and pedagogy it 'takes participation as its working procedure. Its mode of inquiry demands physical, sensuous involvement in a performance event.' Alongside this heavy prioritisation of its claims to an ethical method, both of research and pedagogy, the new paradigm is also celebrated for its intellectual inclusiveness. It does not distinguish between canonical texts, non-canonical texts and the oral tradition. But its inclusive capacity also enables it to embrace and improve on other disciplines: 'Performance Studies envisions theatrical events in more contexts than the traditional proscenium or arena.' By taking on board the insights of anthropologists and folklorists Performance Studies 'allows for broader conceptions of the theatrical event'. But again it improves on what it embraces, in that it 'allows for ethnographic insights unavailable to the nonperforming anthropologist'. This new, and powerful, inclusivity was realised, brought into being, by the simple act of declaring Performance Studies as a paradigm: 'the new name alone opens doors. While positioned squarely within the field of speech communication, Performance Studies suggests clear links to theatre, ethnography and folklore, popular culture, and contemporary literary criticism' (Pelias and VanOosting 1987: 219, 221–25, 228). So successful was this door opening that Schechner repeated the same trick five years later in his neck of the woods.

There's one other feature of Pelias and VanOosting's Performance Studies besides its ethical purposes and inclusivity. Performance is claimed to be personally empowering. Following in particular feminism, the performer is now defined as social activist, driven of course by the ethical imperatives and deeper insights that come from communalism. So too the audience is empowered, in that 'equal status is given to each audience member's perceptions' (1987: 227), an effect which presumably, in certain circumstances, could reduce all perceptions to their lowest common denominator. But that seems less important than the enactment of the democratic imperative and, with it, the demonstration of performance's capacity to empower. Subsuming into itself both the ethical commitments and the democratic inclusivity, the affirmation of personal agency that is enabled by performance was to become one of the most important features of this version of Performance Studies. It's this vision of potency that twenty years later was discursively institutionalised, indeed canonically fixed, in textbooks for students.

One example of such, chosen because of its wide dissemination, is D. Soyini Madison and Judith Hamera's *Sage Handbook of Performance Studies* (2006). Their introduction takes us through the by-now classic position as outlined by Pelias and VanOosting. Performance is rooted in elocution, which produces 'a public performance where audience and speaker were changing and changed by the urgent issues of the time'. The art of public speaking develops into the discipline of interpretation studies, which itself then affirms the beneficial effects of a reading process which enables the reader 'to enter beyond the self and reach respectfully into another's world'. It's an account of speaking and reading that enables them to assert that experience is the 'very source of performance'. By contrast with the narrower operation of theatricality, performance has efficacy, an efficacy that moves on one step from Turner's not faking but making to become a mode not just of making but of being. It is 'a generative force and a critical dynamic within human behavior and social processes'. Indeed, 'For many of us performance has evolved into ways of comprehending how human beings fundamentally make culture, affect power, and reinvent their ways of being in the world.' The understanding of performance has raised many questions: 'when we understand performance beyond theatrics and recognize it as fundamental and inherent to life and culture we are confronted with the ambiguities of different spaces and places that are foreign, contentious, and often under siege' (2006: xii–xv). In a way which had become familiar as a consequence of the multiple origins of Performance Studies, the concept of performance developed a characteristic feature of being different things at once. Performance is both 'contested' as a 'concept' and yet 'fundamental and inherent to life', both there to be argued with and yet organically immanent. One wonders at what level, and by what means, contestation happens in this situation. But such a quibble is over-ridden by the larger drive to see performance not only as something more real and more expansive than theatre, but also as something more socially engaged and useful. Yet again it takes us out of ourselves and out of our familiar places, not to new sensual domains as the old counterculture might have wished, but to places that are 'contentious' and indeed 'under siege'.

These characteristics don't culturally begin with the discipline of oral interpretation, but reach out beyond university discussions of the mid-eighties. Performance is said to be opposed to theatre on the grounds that it is not 'mere entertainment' but a 'generative force', and that force takes its propo-nents and practitioners into 'contentious' places. Once upon a time, say with an artists' action against the Museum of Modern Art, it may really have taken them to places 'under siege'. And it's in that once-upon-a-time place, the late 1960s and early 1970s, that these characteristics of performance get estab-lished, through actual activities against institutions in a discursive world where people were just beginning to establish the language for defining performance. It was also, at the end of this time, into the early eighties, that performance had constructed for it a 'nature', an essence, which in the more urgent language of the institutionalised subject's textbook becomes a 'force'. In other words, and somewhat obviously, the historical roots of the generation that were discussing performance in the 1990s lie back in the 1970s. But history moves on, and, while the language of several versions of Performance Studies seems to repeat and recycle language that began in the anti-institu-tional counterculture of the sixties and seventies, now it is firmly attached to the mission of delineating a new institutional entity.

Managing the contested concept

There is one further version of performance that is created by the processes of institutionalisation. This is not created by any one particular position but is instead a result of the palpable contrast between different positions all speak-ing of apparently the same thing. In that seminal institutional moment, 1995, Conquergood, writing about 'Performance Studies in Motion', observed that 'Performance Studies is a border discipline, an interdiscipline, that cultivates the capacity to move between structures.' It 'privileges threshold-crossing, shape-shifting, and boundary-violating figures'. In these circumstances 'Any attempt to define and stabilise performance will be bound up in disagreement, and this disagreement is itself part of its meaning' (1995: 137–38). Within this argument the 'performance' of Performance Studies gains the important conceptual characteristic which we have already met: it is a 'contested' concept. The importance of this idea is seen when Madison and Hamera begin their introduction to *The Sage Handbook of Performance Studies* precisely where Marvin Carlson began *Performance: A critical introduction* (1996). 'Performance', they say, 'is often referred to as a "contested concept" because as a concept, method, event, and practice it is variously envisioned and employed' (2006: xi). Their source for this observation, and Carlson's, is an essay published in 1990 by Strine, Long and Hopkins, who take the model of 'contested concept' from a 1964 book by the philosopher W.B. Gaillie. This defines 'art' and 'democracy' as instances of an 'essentially contested concept', meaning, as Strine, Long and Hopkins put it, that 'its very existence is bound up in disagreement about what it is, and that the disagreement over the essence is itself part of the essence.' (As an aside: a cynic might observe that where there is disagreement as to whether something is performance or not, then by definition it is one; and that it might be a touch alarming if the same logic were applied to that which is eatable or fireproof.) On these terms, performance can join art and democracy as a 'contested concept' since, as Strine and her colleagues note, performance scholars habitually 'expect disagreement not only about the qualities that make a performance "good" or "bad" in certain contexts, but also about what activities and behaviors appropriately constitute performance and not something else'. What is less regularly noted is that the contested concept is only one of three ways that Strine, Long and Hopkins suggest for approaching performance. The other two are performance as 'text', using Barthes's distinction between work and text, and performance as metaphor and metonymy. It is also the case that, contested though it might have been, Strine, Long and Hopkins' concepts of performance are actually quite narrowly delimited. The essay admits no sense of the rich ideas of speech communication and text already developed by folklore and cultural studies. Symptomatically, their taxonomy of 'eight representative sites of performance' has almost all such sites based in artworks or indeed formal aesthetic texts, with the sole exception of 'participatory ritual' as noted by Conquergood and other ethnographers (Strine, Long and Hopkins 1990: 183–88). Given that the essay is so explicitly located in, and indeed delimited by, the discipline of oral interpretation, the idea of contestation of the concept of performance doesn't seem to go very deep.

But that didn't stop it being picked up, in preference, say, to the concept of 'text', and given a new life of its own. For the claim to contestedness is in part attractive, and potent, because it seems to have a sort of ethical force. It is this contestedness that, the argument goes, inclines performance to be multidisciplinary in its applications and operation. In contrast to a world fixed by disciplinary distinctions and constraints, performance blurs boundaries. Its identity as a 'border' discipline has the effect of aligning performance, as Conquergood sees it, with those on the margins. For being contested and on the border and unfixed is to be anti-hierarchical. Performance's radical and ethical power as a concept may thus be said to derive from the fact that it has no agreed definition as a concept. Being a subject with no clear ownership, it is potentially available to all, like syphilis.

This is a matter for celebration by some performance pedagogues. Stucky and Wimmer note that pedagogy uses 'Techniques of embodiment' and 'experiential learning'. They also note a 'family resemblance between pedagogy and ethnography', and, further, 'A sense of play, experimentation, exploration, and humor' suffusing the pedagogy. Presumably some of the experiential learning has to set limits to the operation of humour, but that is a matter for the teachers. Of interest to us is this diversity of concept, and what Stucky and Wimmer do with it. Not content with simply celebrating diversity and multidisciplinarity they find for it a parallel, if not a precedent: 'Embodiment, ethnography, and play can also be seen as threads in the larger movement within Performance Studies utilizing such techniques to question the politics of representation through a compilation of pedagogical strategies ... This movement resonates with much recent work in education informed by cultural studies' (2002: 4–5; my elision). Cultural studies had already established its disciplinary presence before Performance Studies appeared, so it offers a useful model for the way a multidiscipline can function institutionally as a discipline, that's to say it offers a recognisable category within which the discipline's diverse embrace may snugly fit.

By following the logic of their argument Stucky and Wimmer end up speaking what many would regard as heresy. Both Conquergood and Schechner separately attacked cultural studies, for example, Conquergood being somewhat critical of it in his 1998 essay and Schechner, the following year, telling the Aberystwyth Performance Studies conference to abjure cultural studies. This reminds us that not only is multidisciplinarity not particularly unique but also that some multidisciplines are more properly multidisciplinary than others. In other words the idea of the 'contested concept', with the liberal extensiveness of its disciplinary promiscuity, is kept in check by the requirements of the – er – discipline. Performance's multidisciplinarity offers a point of contrast with other disciplines, all conceived as narrow if not self-interested. In its relationship to them Performance

Studies appears as the only one that has the capacity to absorb the others. It is a claim to a state of liberalism, tolerance and diversity, which also provides the rationale for suggesting that the projects of anthropology, cultural studies, literary studies and theatre studies all have necessarily to be taken over and, as we shall see, brought to their true destiny by Performance Studies.

Chapter 18

How Performance Studies emerged

While Performance Studies may claim itself as a multi- or interdiscipline, a dominant strand of it tells a widely disseminated story of its own emergence within which the commitment to multidisciplinarity does not seem to extend very far. This version of the Performance Studies emergence story repeatedly insists on particular key features and keeps silent about other possible variants.

Canonisation

This can be seen in the earliest, and by now canonical, rendering of the story, as told by Marvin Carlson in *Performance: A critical introduction*, which appeared in 1996, the year after the First Performance Studies conference. That closeness is not coincidental. The newly institutionalised discipline makes itself felt through the book. Indeed it shapes the understanding of performance, as we shall see.

Carlson's book begins with the general, and laudable, aim of drawing a map, in simple terms, of the various different understandings of the word 'performance'. Within these, the crucial difference, as Carlson sees it, is between an understanding of performance as 'the display of skills' as against a display, not of particular skills, but 'of a recognised and clearly coded pattern of behavior'. To these he adds a third usage of the term where the emphasis is on how far an activity succeeds 'in light of some standard of achievement that may not itself be precisely articulated'. This third usage is the one encountered when someone is said to perform well in class or when a product performs well in heavy mud, for example. In this usage a synonym in English might be the word 'achieve' or 'work' – and if you are not speaking English you could be using an entirely different word that might bear no perceivable connection to the word you use for the first two uses. This accretion of homonyms is quite common in English-language texts about performance, and McKenzie's general theory in *Perform or Else* (2001) seems to depend on them.

Having laid out these possible usages of the English-language word 'perform', Carlson rightly says that it would be futile to look for an 'overarching semantic field to cover these seemingly disparate usages' (Carlson 1996: 4–5). And it would be particularly futile, we might note, because the field would turn into separate little horticultural lots as soon as you moved beyond English. It only appears to be a project in the first place if you happen to be an English speaker. It is sensible, then, that Carlson restricts himself, in the first part of the book, to the task of providing 'a general intellectual background and context for the modern idea of performance'. This task, itself not unchallenging in its breadth, begins somewhere very specific. As he tells us at the opening of his first chapter, 'The term "performance", as it is encountered, for example, in departments or programmes of Performance Studies in the United States today, is heavily indebted to terminology and theoretical strategies developed during the 1960s and 1970s, in the social sciences, and particularly in anthropology and sociology.' This statement cues the introduction of the four authors who have been 'Especially important in making connections across the boundaries of traditional theatre studies, anthropology, and sociology': Richard Schechner, Victor Turner, Dwight Conquergood and Erving Goffman. The key text describing these interconnections, for those coming from theatre studies, he claims, was the 1973 issue of *The Drama Review* on 'Theatre and the Social Sciences', edited by Richard Schechner (Carlson 1996: 7, 13).

From here Carlson then takes his readers through a set of loosely social scientific accounts, showing how they employ or discuss the term 'performance'. This is a quick summary review, chronologically arranged, gathering together such authors as Dell Hymes, Milton Singer, Kenneth Burke, Richard Bauman, Gregory Bateson, Eugenio Barba, Arnold van Gennep and, of course, Turner himself, to arrive at a climactic point: 'No theatre theorist has been more instrumental in developing modern performance theory nor in exploring the relationships between practical and theoretical work in theatre research and in social science research than Richard Schechner' (Carlson 1996: 21). From here the Schechner-Turner interaction is described, before moving on to the topic of 'play' with Huizinga and Caillois.

This is a great conglomeration of names and ideas, not all of them necessarily in harmony with each other. But that, perhaps, is Carlson's point. 'Performance' as he defines it is an explosion of multiplicity and diversity of positions. This becomes clear in a much later essay, from 2011, where the sprawling survey of the 1996 book gets summarised into a readily graspable proposition, behind which a familiar binary greets us. In an effort to demonstrate the key difference between theatre studies and

Performance Studies, Carlson proposes that when theatre studies began to engage with the range of names and ideas he describes it necessarily became more complex and lost its simple identity as theatre studies. At this point it became replaced by 'its more wide-ranging and relevant offspring', Performance Studies (Carlson 2011: 18). The logic of this assumption as to how disciplines work is a little dodgy in that, say, physics managed to encounter quantum theory without stopping being physics. That the argument takes this shape may, however, be less to do with the nature of academic disciplines than with the man Carlson places at the centre. In Carlson's account the career of Richard Schechner demonstrates a clear break from theatre theorist to main inventor of Performance Studies. By being tied into the person of an individual academic the story of the emergence of this multiple and diversified subject area, together with its concept of performance, becomes neatly simplified, placed under a leader, and thus, so to speak, disciplined.

And as proper disciplinary subjects others not only told the same story but normalised it. Erin Striff's *Performance Studies* from 2003 says 'most scholars agree' the subject was 'initially popularised at New York University and Northwestern University', before quoting Schechner's 1992 call to arms (2003: 3). Harding and Rosenthal, who edited the book of which Carlson's essay is a part, assert on the first page that 'an increasingly complex understanding of theatrical practice has encouraged the kind of retheorizing of performance as a concept that has given rise to Performance Studies as a distinct area of cultural inquiry' (2011b: 1). This development, they calmly observe, mirrors, by some enchanting coincidence, the exact shape of Richard Schechner's career. The subject with a contested concept at its heart willingly, it seems, embraces scriptural orthodoxy in recounting its own narrative. Nearly thirty years after Carlson first told it, the story gets told again in 2014 by Henry Bial, who worked on *Performance Studies* with Schechner. It was necessary to retell it, says Bial, because Performance Studies is very good at reinventing itself. Underlying the reinventions, however, there is, he says, a straightforwardly simple starting point. This was – naturally – the moment when Schechner engaged with the work of the anthropologist Victor Turner. That meeting has such discursive force within the annals of (New York) Performance Studies that even someone as otherwise sceptical as Jon McKenzie makes it central to his own account of the history of Performance Studies. He notes the 'passageways between theater and anthropology are the ones most often cited as generative of the paradigm', leading, through the sixties and seventies to 'powerful and influential models of cultural performance'. In this mutual exchange 'The work of Victor Turner was especially influential ... in particular his concepts of social drama and liminal rites of passage' (2001: 35–36; my elision).

While McKenzie obviously wants to foreground liminality in order to argue that performance scholars use it to characterise their own practice, in doing so he draws a veil over all the other models, bundling them up together into a catch-all term, 'cultural performance'. In fact the models of performance were not all derived from a dialogue between theatre and anthropology, but McKenzie's narrative doesn't need us to know that. Nor does Bial's, where the 'most influential' of the 'foundational' texts have been narrowed down to three, those by Goffman, Austin and Turner. Told this way the story has two effects. First, while Schechner claims that his account of Performance Studies is specifically an account of the work done in New York, Carlson and Bial tend to suggest that the whole, multi-institution, subject area is instituted by what Schechner does, so too for McKenzie 'the' paradigm, singular, of Performance Studies is the one that features Turner. Second, this story implies a teleology for the social science work on the concept of performance. It is not seen as leading to a richer interactionist sociology, or cultural studies, or a remodelled ethnography but instead heads inevitably towards, has its destined fulfilment in, the work of Schechner's Performance Studies.

The fetishisation of (New York) Performance Studies and its founder requires a hypothesis that can't, however, be substantiated. When Carlson argues that its contact with social science necessarily made theatre studies more complex and thus transformed it into something different, this is not completely accurate. He notes that Schechner's 1973 list of connections between performance theory and social sciences has similarities with Georges Gurvitch's prospectus for a sociology of theatre, but he doesn't mention that Gurvitch's ideas were picked up by Jean Duvignaud, whose ideas in turn were picked up by Elizabeth Burns, who not only developed a theory about the pervasive social presence of theatricality but also ensured the dissemination in English of extracts from such as Gurvitch and Duvignaud in an anthology designed to serve the reading lists of the United Kingdom's fast-expanding interest in teaching this sort of approach to theatre studies. For example in Goldsmiths College, London, in the mid-seventies, 'during the course of three years, the student will "trespass" on other subject-areas, whether that of English, history, music, art, geography, philosophy or sociology, as a source both of dramatic material and as the "stuff" of which drama is made. Thus drama as a subject-area on the curriculum has its own identity, but an identity which encompasses and relates to other subjects. Over the last few years, elements of the above which were implicit in the structuring of courses have now become more explicit' (Gottlieb and Jones 1976: 115). In turn this approach developed a practice it called 'applied theatre' which was specifically interested in performance in non-theatrical settings. And all this went on in departments which carried on calling themselves Drama or Theatre.

Always already theatre

But Carlson didn't necessarily need to know about what was happening in Europe. His hypothesis could have been tested much nearer home, from the work of Richard Schechner himself. In the essay from 1966 which he himself lists as a foundational text for Performance Studies, 'Approaches to Theory/ Criticism', Schechner proposes a new approach to analysing scripted drama (see p. 26). This was very unusual for its time in the way it stepped aside from the mainstream assumptions about the modes of analysis suitable for scripted plays, these being either driven by character analysis or, via New Criticism, focused on detailed exploration of the verbal text. For example, more or less contemporary with the essay a scholar in the subject area of speech communication was working on the assimilation of New Criticism to the study of performance (see p. 167). Schechner suggested that the assumed origin of drama, ritual practice, be repositioned simply as one of a set of 'activities' related to theatre, of which 'The others are play, games, and sports (special kinds of games).' This suggestion echoed the views of other contemporary experimental theatre-makers such as Kaprow and Kirby (see p. 107). Schechner went further and placed these activities in 'horizontal' interrelationship to reveal how each autonomous form shares characteristics with the others. These characteristics consist of: 'a special ordering of time', 'a special value attached to objects', 'non-productivity', 'rules': 'Special rules exist, are formulated, and persist because these activities are something *apart from everyday life*.' The characteristics can then be tabulated in charts which allow for a schematic comparison of differing activities in relation to commonly shared elements. In 1966, in the context of obsessive attention to the special qualities of aesthetic text, the charts are a forceful rhetorical mechanism for disprivileging aesthetic work and equalising it with other social activities. In Jackson's terms the charts and diagrams may be said to enact a 'scientizing' stance, precisely as a way of breaking with 'drama'. Thus while social sciences might have insisted on detailed distinctions, the specific disciplinary context of theatre studies meant that it was politically more important to insist on shared characteristics. That necessary and beneficial 1966 tactic of drawing diverse materials into equivalence is the same one that subsequently produces all those dodgy, and finally vacuous, generalisations.

In proposing its new approach to aesthetic drama, 'Approaches' suggested the insufficiency of a focus simply on 'text' and denied any special status to aesthetic activity, and in doing so identified a set of performed activities that was larger than the merely theatrical. The analysis of this larger set became known as 'Performance Studies', and it necessarily contained within itself, as a constituent element alongside ritual and games, the study of theatre. But that's not quite what the essay said in 1966. It only got closer to saying it that way when it was reprinted, for the second time, in 1988, as the first chapter to the second edition of Schechner's book *Performance Theory*. The first reprint appeared in a collection of *Essays on the Theatre* in 1969 and was actually substantially different. It had a new opening section, of about twenty-five pages, about theatre and an appropriate mode of criticism, specifically 'structural criticism', with a lengthy account of Lévi-Strauss (discussed by Emigh 2011). The later part of the essay repeats the diagrams and the idea that 'The external structure of theater is in many ways homologous to play, games and sports, and ritual' (1969: 71). The word 'homologous' came from another structural critic, Goldmann. When the essay came to be printed a third time the interest in structural criticism in relation to theatre had lost its urgency, with its inclusion in *Performance Theory* being explained thus by Schechner: 'I've balanced necessary revisions with my wish to preserve the trajectory of my thinking about performance over the more than twenty years these essays span (1966–1987).' (1988: ix) Among the 'necessary revisions' are some very detailed tinkerings with the text of the 1966 essay. The effect of these overall is to construct it into an essay about 'performance' as opposed to an essay about theatre.

Rather than list every change (and they can be seen simply by juxtaposing the two versions, from 1966 and 1988), some general observations may be made. Apart from mere updatings, there is greater frequency of the word 'performance'. In 1966 descriptions of games, sport and play tended to refer to them as 'activities'. In 1988 these are more often called 'performance' or 'performative' activities. Thus 'During the activity' becomes 'during the performance' (1966: 30/1988: 9). A footnote explaining the focus of his essay has, in 1966, 'I thought it best to center my definition of performance around certain acknowledged qualities of theatre, the most staple being the audience' (1966: 27). In 1988 this becomes 'live theatre' and 'audience and performer interaction'. Where the 1966 essay says 'Origin theories, I think, are irrelevant to understanding theatre. Nor would I wish to exclude ritual altogether' (p. 26), this last sentence in 1988 is expanded by the words 'from the study of the performative genres' (p. 6). That phrase points up a set of slight shifts in the scholarly apparatus, among which comes the insertion into the narrative of a familiar figure. Into a footnote on Artaud and ritual is dropped a whole new sentence: 'The ritual process – as worked out by Victor Turner and others – applies more to the workshop-rehearsal process than to dramatic literature' (1988: 29). Turner is not mentioned at all in the 1966 essay. By 1988, of course, Turner had become a key name in the formation of Schechner's version of Performance Studies.

The regular insertion of the word 'performance' is accompanied by a firming up of what it is not. In the phrase 'traditional theatre', the adjective is replaced by 'orthodox'. This is cemented into a binary in the otherwise interesting footnote on audiences: 1966 has 'Happenings, and clearly defined sectors of our theatre – such as Off-Off-Broadway – are more surely solidarity occasions' (p. 34); 1988 has 'Experimental performances are more expressive of social solidarity than orthodox theatre' (p. 32). The word 'theatre' gets shifted out of association with 'happenings'. There is either experiment – as in 'performances' – or orthodoxy, as in 'theatre'. Thus the 'Conclusions' of 1966 anticipates that 'a unified set of approaches will be developed that can handle *all* theatrical phenomena, classical and modern, textual and non-textual, dramatic and theatrical' (p. 53) while 1988 anticipates that 'a unified set of approaches will be developed that can handle *all* performance phenomena, classical and modern, textual and non-textual, dramatic, theatrical, playful, ritual' (p. 28). That concluding emphasis is part of a process of revision that engineers the essay into a different place from where it started. In 1966 it was an essay written from within theatre studies by an author aware of all the latest developments, and Schechner has never been not thus aware. He himself was making 'experimental' theatre, and happenings were everywhere in the sixties' media. Between them happenings and Fluxus events had foregrounded non-productivity, special uses of time and objects, and the use of rules. Rule-bound activity had come into theoretical fashion not only from Goffman but also in games theory, which Schechner encountered being used in analysis of performance in an article by Philip McCoy, submitted to the journal *Tulane Drama Review*, of which Schechner was editor, but never it seems published. Beyond the specifics of games theory the whole thrust of the 'Approaches' argument is very much in line with the ideas of happenings makers as to theatre's relationship with cognate activities such as ritual, sport and game (see pp. 106–7).

In 1988 those cognate activities are given a term derived from the anthropologists, 'performative genres'. Back in 1966 they were part of the discourse of experimental theatre-makers. And that is where Schechner's essay comes from. Had it not been tinkered with it would have been one of those examples, at the forefront of its time, of the ways in which theatre studies was evolving. After the tinkering, with the argument remaining *precisely the same* it now becomes a foundation text for Performance Studies. What is effectively a rebranding exercise obliterates any sense of an evolving theatre studies, confining it to 'orthodoxy' and stasis. This then leaves Performance Studies as the acknowledged sole proprietor of an approach that promotes the 'broad', and always thoroughly inclusively broadening, spectrum.

The limits on inclusivity

Schechner's rebranding of theatre studies as Performance Studies is symptomatic of an institutional broadening that was at the same time a delimitation of concept. (New York) Performance Studies was, as we know, very effective in drawing almost everything into an undifferentiated category of performance. Or, rather, it was effective at ignoring those concepts which were not amenable to its purposes. They silently disappear from narratives. Carlson could have defended himself, perhaps properly, against the charge that he was apparently ignorant of European theatre studies' engagement with social science because, early on, he says plainly that he is writing about 'performance' as found in departments in the United States. But actually the concept he is dealing with is somewhat more limited than this. I suspect that in 1996 the majority of the programmes in the United States that called themselves Performance Studies were those based in communication and oral interpretation, because they had already collectively agreed on a name change. Their concept of performance was, as we have seen, not derived from social science, with the notable exception of Conquergood, but was instead founded on text-based work linking into literary analysis and elocution. Carlson's assumption that social science was key to the invention of Performance Studies is thus a little too simplified, and omits a different version. Nor is this corrected in the revised version of his book, issued in 2004, even though in 1998 Sheron Dailey, coming from oral interpretation, explicitly identified two routes into Performance Studies, and even though, by 2001, Schechner himself had woven oral interpretation into the narrative.

If, for a moment, one were to expand one's perspective, however tentatively, just for one moment, beyond the United States, then yet other basic foundational concepts of Performance Studies come into view. For instance Gay McAuley notes 'Performance Studies was introduced at the University of Sydney in 1988 as an interdepartmental course' (2012: 38). This was preceded by about a decade of teaching that involved academics working in relationship with professional theatre practitioners. Given this basis the Sydney concept of performance was not set in opposition to aesthetic performance and its skills (Maxwell 2006, McAuley 2012). In another institutional model entirely, Sybylle Peters tells how 'the interdisciplinary discourse that defines performance research in Germany preceded the efforts to institutionalize something like disciplinary Performance Studies'. It was thus a multidisciplinary research project which received public funding, from 1994 onwards, in order to study 'theatricality' and within that define key terms such as 'performance'. This project and its successor were chaired by Erika Fischer-Lichte, who developed a hypothesis which suggested that what is shared by modern art in general is a 'performative turn' and on the basis of this 'examples of performance art', says Peters, 'are regarded as resulting from a general sense of staging that has spread through all forms of art'. She rightly notes that this analysis works with 'stage performance as a template', and that with this assumption buried in it the argument 'implicitly claims that theatre studies has a certain competence to deal with developments in other forms of art' (Peters 2012: 155). Here the concept of performance is diametrically opposed to where Schechner had it. For him performance was the large category that contains, among many other things, theatre. For Peters theatre is the large category that contains performance.

The existence of Performance Studies in Australia and its critique in Germany did not seem high in the consciousness of those writing about the emergence of Performance Studies in the United States. Indeed the experience of a young British academic visitor to the 1995 inaugural conference was that the institutional focus and consciousness of this border discipline, this contested concept, were tightly delimited not even to the United States as a whole but to a small part of it. To Jools Gilson-Ellis it seemed the entire conversation was about two places: 'I kept hearing a quiet litany: Performance Studies at NYU and Northwestern, Performance Studies at NYU and Northwestern. As if these were the only places engaged in this kind of work' (1995: 176). Thus even as it was energetically and joyously establishing itself as a discipline Performance Studies at that moment also showed itself, to use Janelle Reinelt's phrase, somewhat parochial. Of course, there have since then been many discussions, much urgent and serious critique, about the extent to which Performance Studies was, to use Jill Dolan's word, an imperialist project. And there have been many interesting questions about what Performance Studies might be, what it can mean, in a range of cultures and academic systems across the world. The organisation 'Performance Studies international' takes very seriously that emphatically lower-case adjective in its name.

Allegations of parochialism and imperialism may no longer be, may never have been, appropriate. But they were anyway never quite sufficient. There is more to be said, and this has to do less with ethics and politics than with economics. The claim made by the dominant narrative about Performance Studies can be seen as functioning, in effect, as a monopoly claim on a commodity. Just as someone, especially a French someone, might claim that the only proper pinot noir wine is that which is made from grapes grown in the limestone soils of the Côte d'Or in Burgundy, so the dominant narrative seems to claim that it is only the Performance Studies cultivated by Schechner and Turner and fermented at New York University which constitutes the proper Performance Studies, or at the very least the only one worth repeating the story about. In economic terms the ownership of a monopoly brings returns. As such the business of establishing and holding monopolies is a key feature of the capitalist economy. But some monopolies need not necessarily be deliberate in origin. Stratford-upon-Avon was of interest as the fortuitously unique birthplace of a legendary dramatist long before the marketing juggernaut trundled into action. Presumably the dominant Performance Studies narrative also makes its monopoly claim by accident. But the returns on that claim, in terms of, say, graduate fees, will look as much like deliberate money as anything entering the till of a tourist shop.

It is not our business here, however, to pursue the economic history of Performance Studies. While the definitions and stories of Performance Studies may indeed have an economic function, our job is to concentrate on the concepts of performance that circulate within them. And what we find in the geographical and institutional diversification that is revealed by the challenges to monopoly is a very simple, and I'm afraid rather banal, point. The definition of the concept of 'performance' in Performance Studies changes according to where you are standing. Does it include conservatoire or professional theatre practice or not? Does it emerge out of social science or oral interpretation? Is it a subset of theatre studies? But of course it is all these and more, because it is a 'contested' concept. This means that 'performance' is what you say it is. And what you say it is depends on who you are and where you are speaking. Performance Studies is thus so to speak – as it were – a performative phenomenon.

Chapter 19

Gender performativity

A few years before Schechner told his colleagues to abandon old-fashioned theatre studies a new concept had appeared on the scene. This concept was to be adopted by Performance Studies and would become a major reference point for the efficacy of performance, even though it had arrived via theatre and indeed text. The impetus behind its formulation was derived from that source of so much political and theoretical innovation in the period, feminism and its distinct point of arrival was an essay in *Theatre Journal*, edited by Sue-Ellen Case and Timothy Murray. The essay, which appeared in 1988, was called 'Performative Acts and Gender Constitution', written by Judith Butler.

Back in 1988 that first word of Butler's title had less resonance in drama and theatre scholarship than it might have done in anthropology or linguistic philosophy, but that very soon changed. In 1990 the essay was reprinted in Case's anthology *Performing Feminisms*, and from here it was picked up by many theatre academics. Jill Dolan, for example, used it in her contribution to Reinelt and Roach's book in 1992. By the early years of the new century, 'performativity' had become the seemingly regular, if not obligatory, partner to 'performance'. But, although this now seems a perfectly natural pairing, like some of the most enduring relationships it began with arguments. Somewhat more alarmingly – at least as far as my metaphor is concerned – in the evolution of this relationship one of the partners appeared to lose their identity.

'Performativity' had made its significant arrival into academic discourse in the mid-1950s in a series of lectures on linguistic philosophy by J.L. Austin. In the years that followed, it was the subject of hilariously acrimonious philosophical dispute between Jacques Derrida and John Searle, but this had next to nothing to do with performance as hitherto understood. An exception was Tambiah's suggestion in 1979 that Austin's performativity might be employed as a way of thinking about ritual practice. In 'A Performative Approach to Ritual' Tambiah suggested three ways in which ritual could be thought of as performative: 'in the Austinian sense of performative wherein saying is also doing something as a conventional act; in the quite different sense of a staged performance that uses multiple media by which the participants experience the event intensively; and in the third sense of indexical values ... being attached to and inferred by actors during the performance' (1979; 119, my elision). But it was Butler's essay in 1988 that made the connection to a recognisable theatrical performance. From here she went on to develop her ideas into the hugely influential book *Gender Trouble*, which came out in 1990, and then she offered a corrective to them in 1993. The working out of the argument around performativity thus makes both the link to, and then the severance from, performance. It's a knotty story which could be titled *Performance Trouble*.

In the 1988 essay Butler draws on 'theatrical, anthropological, and philosophical discourses, but mainly phenomenology' to argue that gender 'must be understood as the mundane way in which bodily gestures, movements, and enactments of various kinds constitute the illusion of an abiding gendered self'. In the word 'enactments' there is an analogy with theatrical activity, whereby gender 'instituted through acts' constitutes identity 'which the mundane social audience, including the actors themselves, come to believe'. While she will later return to this set of theatrical relations, Butler first puts in place a concept of the body derived from phenomenology. She cites Merleau-Ponty's proposition that the body is 'a set of possibilities to be continually realized', where the 'possibilities' have to do both with the body's appearance not being predetermined and its 'concrete expression' availing itself of a set of specific historical possibilities. In this model, which is based on the taking up of possibilities, there is a sense of agency. Thus the body 'is a materiality that bears meaning, if nothing else, and the manner of this bearing is fundamentally dramatic. By dramatic I mean only that the body is not merely matter but a continual and incessant *materializing* of possibilities. One is not simply a body, but, in some very key sense, one does one's body' (1988: 519–21).

What modifies the sense of individual agency here – the doing of one's body by oneself – is the model of theatre, where theatre acts are shared and 'collective'. So just as for feminist theory the personal is expected to be the political so too the theatrical view of acts moves us beyond the individual:

> He act that gender is, the act that embodied agents *are* inasmuch as they
> dramatically and actively embody and, indeed, *wear* certain
> significations, is clearly not one's act alone. Surely, there are nuanced and
> individual ways of *doing* one's gender, but *that* one does it, and that one
> does it *in accord with* certain sanctions and proscriptions, is clearly not a
> fully individual matter.

The concept of theatre in here, even for 1988, is pretty traditional; indeed for Butler's argument necessarily so:

> Gender is an act which has been rehearsed, much as a script survives the particular actors who make use of it, but which requires individual actors in order to be actualized and reproduced as reality once again. The complex components that go into an act must be distinguished in order to understand the kind of acting in concert and acting in accord which acting one's gender invariably is.

From here Butler explores the ways in which gender may be said to be an act, and she draws on the propositions, first put by Goffman, about social dramas and social roles (see pp. 3–7). She notes Victor Turner's comments on the 'social drama' which requires a performance to be reported, and hence made publically effective, and she reviews notions of everyday performance. This part of the argument is thoroughly grounded in the social science thinking that began in the fifties. From it Butler proposes that 'If the "reality" of gender is constituted by the performance itself, then there is no recourse to an essential and unrealized "sex" or "gender" which gender performances ostensibly express.' In short, 'Gender reality is performative, which means, quite simply, that it is real only to the extent that it is performed' (1988: 525–27).

Here that relatively new word 'performative' seems to have very little connection with its usage by Austin, who categorised some utterances 'performative' in order to define them as utterances which make things happen (I promise you won't forget this bit). In the context of Butler's theatrical analogy, 'performative' has to do with performing as acting: 'As performance which is performative, gender is an "act", broadly construed, which constructs the social fiction of its own psychological interiority' (1988: 528). Gender works like the naturalist actor and compels belief. But the fiction doesn't begin with the actors. They merely speak the script written for them. The script has to be spoken to work, and by speaking it the actors keep the power of the script in place, in all senses. Into this argument there is tucked, but not openly acknowledged, an idea propounded by Derrida in his argument with Searle, published in various French and English versions between 1971 and 1982. Taking Austin's distinction of a 'normal' performative utterance as against the abnormal, the 'hollow or void' utterances of the theatre or poetry, Derrida asks if both sorts do not actually depend on citationality 'without which there would not even be a "successful" performative?' He elaborates the question: 'Could a performative utterance succeed if its formulation did not repeat a "coded" or iterable utterance, or in other words, if the formula I pronounce in order to open a meeting, launch a ship or a marriage were not identifiable as *conforming* with an iterable model, if it were not then identifiable in some way as a "citation"?' (1988: 18). Far from the individual being the sole source of the utterance, therefore, the language spoken by the individual is already in circulation before the individual steps onto the stage as it were. Indeed if, to use Derrida's word, a 'mark' is to be iterable, then it has to work in one circumstance after another, and can't be said to belong in any particular circumstance. Thus a performative cannot be assumed to be governed by the intention of the speaker, because, if it's iterable, it must work independently of any particular speaker. This argument compares closely with the way Butler uses the metaphor of theatrical script which precedes the actors: as she says, 'The distinction between expression and performativeness is quite crucial' (1988: 528).

That distinction was more heavily underlined when the essay was modified and reassembled in *Gender Trouble* (1990). Early on in the book Butler returns to the notion of 'doing' one's body, now specifically as the 'doing' of gender. She argues that the appearance in the individual of 'an abiding substance or gendered self' is produced by 'the regulation of attributes along culturally established lines of coherence'. This means that 'within the inherited discourse of the metaphysics of substance, gender proves to be performative – that is, constituting the identity it is purported to be. In this sense, gender is always a doing, though not a doing by a subject who might be said to pre-exist the deed' (Butler 1990: 24–25). That relationship between the subject and performativity is of course central to the 1988 essay, but in reusing that essay in *Gender Trouble* Butler prefaces it with a more emphatic statement of its central implications. She states very clearly that 'the effect of an internal core or substance' is produced by 'acts, gestures, and desire': 'Such acts, gestures, enactments, generally construed, are *performative* in the sense that the essence or identity that they otherwise purport to express are *fabrications* manufactured and sustained through corporeal signs and other discursive means.' This identity is not the source of those acts, much as a theatrical character is not the source of the script, but here the point is made without recourse to that analogy:

> In the place of an original identification which serves as a determining cause, gender identity might be reconceived as a personal/cultural history of received meanings subject to a set of imitative practices which refer laterally to other imitations and which, jointly, construct the illusion of a primary and interior gendered self or parody the mechanism of that construction.   (Butler 1990: 136, 138)

That last phrase is designed to recall Butler's brief account of drag. As a parodically imitative practice it has the effect that it *'implicitly reveals the imitative structure of gender itself'* (Butler's emphasis). This produces the liberating pleasure of watching a drag performance: 'In the place of the law of heterosexual coherence, we see sex and gender denaturalized by means of a performance which avows their distinctness and dramatizes the cultural mechanism of their fabricated unity' (Butler 1990: 137–38).

While this example illustrates that things can go usefully awry within the otherwise gloomily inevitable processes of citation and imitation, it also lands Butler somewhere other than her argument wants to be. For in the person of the drag artist it installs by the backdoor as it were the image of a subject who seems not so much to be fabricated as in control of manufacturing the fabrication. And with that comes the idea that in constructing the illusion of a gendered self the drag performance does the same work as performativity. This reduces performativity from citation of a general discourse, received and re-transmitted across history, to a localised instance of a particular performance.

Many readers thus thought that performance was indeed a form of performativity, an interpretation assisted by publication of the essay in *Theatre Journal* and then *Performing Feminisms*. So Butler clarified her position in *Bodies That Matter* (1993). She acknowledged that she created the confusion by 'citing drag as an example of performativity' which some took to be 'exemplary' of performativity, but 'If drag is performative, that does not mean that all performativity is to be understood as drag.' Further, 'The practice by which gendering occurs, the embodying of norms, is a compulsory practice, a forcible production, but not for that reason fully determining.' The emphasis is on the unavoidable determination, even though it may be locally incomplete. And it is this larger sense of performativity as compulsory practice which keeps it distinct from performance:

> performance as bounded 'act' is distinguished from performativity insofar as the latter consists in a reiteration of norms which precede, constrain, and exceed the performer and in that sense cannot be taken as the fabrication of the performer's 'will' or 'choice'; further, what is 'performed' works to conceal, if not to disavow, what remains opaque, unconscious, unperformable. The reduction of performativity to performance would be a mistake.   (Butler 1993: 230–31, 234)

Butler's argument here has features in common with a slightly earlier modelling of the relationship between the speaking subject and discourse. It is worth quoting here because it makes explicit some of the political implications that are potentially buried in discussions of performativity. In *The Subject of Tragedy* (1985) Catherine Belsey proposes this relation of subject and discourse: 'To be a subject is to have access to signifying practice, to identify with the "I" of utterance and the "I" who speaks. The subject is held in place in a specific discourse, a specific knowledge, by the meanings available there. In so far as signifying practice always precedes the individual, is always learned, the subject is a subjected being, an effect of the meanings it seems to possess.' Yet the ruling assumptions of the modern period take a reverse position, suggesting that 'the subject is the free, unconstrained author of meaning and action, the origin of history. Unified, knowing and autonomous, the human being seeks a political system which guarantees freedom of choice.' This set of beliefs about the individual and society is what Belsey calls 'liberal humanism' (1985: 5, 8). In a sense, then, Butler's basic proposition would have been familiar to the theoretical positions of contemporary British literary criticism, and in particular 'cultural materialism', a mode of analysis developed out of the work of Raymond Williams and very influential in the late seventies and early eighties. Butler's work has different emphases, and a more precise, and gender-specific, inflection, but it was not, at this point, a long way different. The problem for Butler, though, was that the passing invocation of performance cracked a door open that could never after be fully closed. Where performance is introduced as analogy or frame for reading it often transmutes itself into its related form, performance as practice.

Thus Butler's recommendation that 'performance' and 'performativity' be kept well apart did not have much effect. Although Austin's discussion of performatives in language dismissed theatre as a special case, cultural anthropology had begun talking about 'performative genres' – ceremony, ritual and the rest – since at least the late seventies, where the term clearly denotes genres that do a form of performed activity rather than genres that limit themselves to the enunciation of performatives. The slippage between performance and performativity is also of course helped by the fact that the words sound similar, like nature and naturism perhaps. So when Butler drew on an analogy with theatre in order to demonstrate how gender was done by declaring gender, even though she effaces any sense of an intentional performing agent, the analogy allowed for a blurring between the terms. Her argument is, as Loxley says, 'marked by the double history of performativity that is evident in performance theory' (2007: 141), where the word straddles both Austin's usage and that adopted by ethnologists of 'performative' genres. This blurring then gave rise to all sorts of fantasies about 'doing' gender, within a context where performativity shook itself free of the Derridean constraints on the subject's freedom.

Chapter 20

Performance and performativity

The process of shaking free can be seen at work in, for example, Elin Diamond's *Performance and Cultural Politics*. Diamond's introduction to this collection of essays is a commendable intervention in two respects. First, by connecting performance analysis to cultural commentary, she seeks to expand its range of usefulness and social effect. Second, she highlights the embattled position of US cultural studies and, by linking the disciplines, brings the power of the growing one to the assistance of the weaker. To argue the case for the link between them she reviews the relationship of performance and performativity. This review is almost obligatory since, as she wittily remarks, 'performance discourse and its new theoretical partner, "performativity", are dominating critical discussion almost to the point of stupefaction'. The performativity she describes is less Austin's than Derrida's, where 'the "I" has no interior secure ego or core identity.' But at the same time there is a need to counterbalance the shift in emphasis in Butler's notion of performativity that resulted from her correction of the misreadings of *Gender Trouble*. As Diamond sees it, in *Bodies* 'performativity moves closer to Derridean citationality, operating within a matrix of discursive norms and further from deliberate performances that *enact* those norms in particular sites with particular effects.' This critique of the more Derridean performativity is necessary if one wants to maintain the claim that performance can have social efficacy: 'in the sense that I do my performance in public, for spectators who are interpreting and/or performing with me, there are real effects, meanings solicited or imposed that produce relations in the real. Can performance make a difference?' (1996: 2, 5).

Driven by a perfectly understandable desire to retain material efficacy for performance, as something that can actually make a difference in the world, Diamond offers a rethinking of the model of performativity outlined in *Bodies*:

> Performance, as I have tried to suggest, is precisely the site in which concealed or dissimulated conventions might be investigated. Where

190

performativity materializes as performance in that risky and dangerous negotiation between a doing . . . and a thing done . . . between someone's body and the conventions of embodiment, we have access to cultural meanings and critique. Performativity, I would suggest, must be rooted in the materiality and historical density of performance.   (1996: 5; my elision)

The notion of a performativity that 'materializes as performance' or, in her earlier phrase, 'comes to rest on *a* performance' is a long way from Butler's argument that performativity is a repetition not a singular 'act', a very long way from it – actually the precise opposite.

This change is necessary in order to support the commendable purpose of Diamond's volume which aims to demonstrate how performance analysis can develop tools of cultural critique which are sharp enough and tough enough to make a difference. 'Performativity' is what will open the door for performance analysis to address 'questions of embodiment, of social relations, of ideological interpellation, of emotional and political effects'. Thus conceived performativity offers a new critical paradigm which performance can then use to radical effect: 'In performance, and in the developing field of Performance Studies . . . signifying (meaning-ful) acts may enable new subject positions and new perspectives to emerge, even as the performative present contests the conventions and assumptions of oppressive cultural habits' (1996: 5–6; my elision).

Viewed from the position outlined by Butler, the 'performative present' means the reverse of what Diamond wants it to mean. It means the present that reiterates, re-cites, the learnt moves, the cultural script, that precede it. Far from enabling the contesting of conventions, per se, it is more likely to be constituting them. By contrast Diamond's binary opposition of contestatory performance against oppressive culture contains an ideological invocation of voluntarist, if not individualist, action against a dominant structure: in a nutshell, my performance here and now that sets art against habit. The proper and necessary argument with Butler's diffidence around agency ends up by swinging to the other extreme and absorbs her version of performativity into the definition and remit of performance, it 'must' be 'rooted' in it. But it doesn't need to be. It is just as possible to conceive of a dialectical relationship between performance and performativity where each retains its own distinctive meaning and force. In this model there is the agency materialised, yes, in the physical doing of something in the presence of others while at the same time knowing, yes, that what one's doing is already at some level locked into, and thus recirculating, various uninspected norms and values.

This more judicious dialectical model of the relationship of performance and performativity is set out by W.B. Worthen. In a very astute essay from 1998, 'Drama, Performativity, and Performance', he begins with a commentary on Parker and Sedgwick's introduction to their edited volume called *Performativity and Performance* (1995). In order to show a convergence between Performance Studies and literary studies, Parker and Sedgwick had returned to Austin's discussion of performativity. In that discussion he said 'performative utterance will, for example, be *in a peculiar way* hollow or void if said by an actor on the stage' (in Parker and Sedgwick 1995: 3). Using Derrida's critique of this statement Parker and Sedgwick argue that everyday utterances are no less hollow, no more authentic, than what is said on the stage. Performatives work because they can be reiterated, whether off the stage or on it. To demonstrate they analyse Austin's example of the words 'I do' in the marriage ceremony, showing, very astutely, that the words, rather than making anything happen by themselves, create their impact because they quote a whole history and mode of ceremonial performance. A particular marriage ceremony and the individual utterances of 'I do' succeed because they cite previous performances.

Worthen picks up this analysis in order to show how it can be used to re-think the relations of aesthetic performance and text. As he sees it Parker and Sedgwick can't do this (or perhaps were not interested in doing it) because they use and reproduce an old-fashioned idea of realist if not proscenium theatre, assuming that 'theatrical performance' is merely the reiteration of dramatic text. By contrast, he suggests, a new way of thinking of 'dramatic performance' is already contained in Parker and Sedgwick's analysis of the marriage ceremony, which can provide a 'searching model' of the general relationship between texts and performances. This model suggests that 'It is not the text that prescribes the meanings of the performance: it is the construction of the text within the specific apparatus of the ceremony that creates performative force. The performance is not a citation of the text.' What is cited instead are the historical and cultural arrangements around institutional heterosexuality, the assumed relations between individual performers and the network of all such similar practices. From here Worthen moves, via Butler, to dramatic performances: 'Does stage performance operate citationally, less as an uttering or iterating of a text than as an iterating of the conventions of the performance, which accumulate *"the force of authority through the repetition or citation of a prior and authoritative set of practices"* (51)? As a citational practice, dramatic performance – like all other performances – is engaged not so much in citing texts as in reiterating its own regimes'. Far from the text being dominant the 'citational practices of the stage' include 'acting styles, directorial conventions, scenography'. All these could be said to be citing, and in radically challenging experiments resignifying perhaps, the 'social and behavioral practices that operate outside the theater and that constitute contemporary social life' (1998: 97–98).

If this logic works for both social ceremony and for theatrical performance it also works for modes of aesthetic performance which reject theatre. Listing such performers as Spalding Gray, Karen Finley, Anne Deavere Smith and Annie Sprinkle, Worthen comments that 'In all these cases, performance is performative in Butler's terms, working as a "ritualized practice" that "*draws on and covers over* the constitutive conventions by which it is mobilized" (*Excitable Speech* 51).' This is surely completely correct, although ironically we could also have got here by taking literally Butler's metaphors of theatre. What it comes up with can begin to be suggested by Annie Sprinkle's *Post Porn Modernism* in which, in Rebecca Schneider's account, dressed as a 'conventional' prostitute she chats to the audience, shows them a hand-drawn diagram to explain female genital parts, inserts a speculum and invites spectators to view her cervix, and ends the show with 'ritual' masturbation. Our analysis might observe that the show works by reiterating the assumption that the performer needs to be in a special separated place, as the given to be looked at, in control of the border between performer and spectator; it links with other works in assuming that entertainment lies, as it were, in skilful handling of props and verbal delivery, even as manufactured casualness; and while citing these conventions of theatre it also cites the ancient anti-theatrical idea that a staging will always only be able to quote, and thereby invalidate, authentic human relations, predicated on nothing other than a simulacrum of intimacy and trust.

Worthen's argument could be extended at this point to suggest that observation of citational activity need not confine itself to performances but could also work for analysis of writings about performance. We have already encountered a number of these, with their various assumptions about the central characteristics of performance. To these might be added Peggy Phelan's *Unmarked* (1993) which asserts that 'Performance implicates the real through the presence of living bodies', 'resists the balanced circulations of finance', 'refuses this system of exchange and resists the circulatory economy fundamental to it' (1993: 148–49). These assertions repeat the rhetoric of the sixties and early seventies, but by 1993 quite a lot of performance had taken place in galleries, had developed funding systems for itself, and, if you include Laurie Anderson or even Robert Wilson, had become global commodity. It's also odd, in 1993, still to be assuming that the mere presence of a living body is an unproblematic guarantee of the real, as if that member of cabin crew who smiles so generously really takes pleasure in your company. Irrespective, it seems, of historical developments, many of the post-eighties' accounts of performance produce a reiteration of the norms of 'radical' art practice, reciting the learnt history of expected characteristics. And insofar as they also imply that these characteristics have to do with the very 'nature' of performance then what their writing performs is a concealment of the processes of reiteration. In a way very similar to the citation of gender the citation of performance works with binaries– performance versus theatre, performance versus commerce – which rhetorically construct the 'nature' of performance, as inherently live, present, radical.

The application of Butlerian performativity as a method of analysis has extended well beyond art practices, however. In 2000 Gregson and Rose set out the ways in which the study of cultural geography could benefit from models of performance and performativity. These examples include the practices required in service sector workplaces and the performance of sexualities in public spaces. For Gregson and Rose performance and performativity are two separate models, with performativity being clearly identified with Butler's position in *Gender Trouble* and *Bodies That Matter*. Butler, they say, 'understands discourse as multiple and contradictory but always productive; it has specific effects, and this is where its power lies. Discourse ... disciplines its subjects even as it produces them.' This 'antifoundationalism provides a crucial critical tool for denaturalising social categories.' Nevertheless they observe a tendency in their subject area to move away from this implication of Butler's work:

> it seems to us that ... regardless of whether Butler is being cited or not, a certain consensus around performance is emerging in geography, one which is in many ways – notably in its conceptualisation of agency, subjectivity, and their effects – closer to Goffman than to Butler. The sense of anterior agents; the separation of performer and performance; the sense of performances occupying pregiven kinds of spaces; and a notion of a (constraining) script: all recur in geographers' discussions of performance.   (2000: 436–38; my elisions)

To which we might add that a similar consensus seems also to have emerged among so-called performance scholars.

The slippage from Butler to Goffman is in large part permitted by the instability of the concept of 'performativity' itself. As we have seen, it has been used both of performed activity, such as ritual, and of linguistic efficacy. In the case of linguistic philosophy Austin's original formulation was reconstructed by Derrida, whose work was then used by Butler. But Austin's original formulation is still operating unscarred. This can be seen in the case of so-called performative writing. Madison and Hamera say that 'performative writing' is a particular way in which performance scholars create performances. It's not quite clear, however, what 'performative' writing materially performs. When Eve Sedgwick taught a course on 'performative' writing her students were asked to produce text that would do something, have an effect, in the real world, such as painting on a public bench the misogynist insults made by the men who sat there. It may be harder to see what a piece of 'performative' writing that describes in published prose the personal feelings of the author actually performs. Of course it could be said to be breaking silence and making the world aware, willy-nilly, of the author's feelings. It could also be said to perform the assumption that it was publishable material. But it seems, conceptually, a slightly strange extension of the commitment to performance in that scholars who align themselves with a form that has historically had vexatious relations with written text have such a strong interest in generating yet more written text, and where the celebration of the evanescence of performance doesn't seem to extend to abjuring the permanence of published text.

These problems are but a part of the general sliding between Austin and Butler and back again, part of the great 'lexical abyss' created by the terminology of performance and performativity. This description is from the geographer Rob Sullivan in a book that adopts Austinian speech-act theory for the purposes of cultural geography. In his overview of the intellectual context he notes that there is no continuity between Austin's theory and the work of Turner and Schechner, and that usage of both 'performance theory' and 'performativity' led to ambiguity because 'no clear-cut referent is tethered to these terms'. This situation creates 'a somewhat opaque theoretical nexus for performativity, simultaneously referring to too much and yet not enough'. By way of example he instances Peggy Phelan's *Unmarked*, where she says 'Performance's life is in the present'. As Sullivan rightly observes, what she is really referring to here are 'literal performances or what used to be called happenings', and he quotes her view that 'Performance cannot be saved, recorded, documented, or otherwise participate in the circulation of representations *of* representations'. Phelan's language, we might note in passing, is a further instance of performance scholarship of the nineties continuing to re-cite, to be disciplined by, indeed voluntarily to inhabit, the discourse of performance experiments of the sixties, although now in a much changed historical and institutional context. The consequence for performance theorising, in the form Phelan attempts it, is made clear by Sullivan: 'Phelan's conception of the performance is one subsumed in a purity usually associated with regimes of strict asceticism' – performance 'in its own right' as Goldberg might have said. Sullivan continues: 'the citational reiteration necessary to the performative speech act must exist in a regime of discourse circulating precisely in a domain dependent on the dissemination of representations of representations. No wonder there's conflation and confusion with that wobbly term "performance"' (2011: 31–32).

While Phelan's book shows unwitting confusion with respect to the relationship of performance and performativity, just under ten years later there was an explicit attempt to conflate the terms. In 2002 Josette Féral revisited her twenty-year-old 'demystification' of the relationship between performance and theatre. In 1982, she says, she 'presented performativity and theatricality in opposing terms', a way of seeing it that resulted from her interest at the time in 'performance art and all forms of performance outside the theatre'. This oppositional relationship, and the essay in general, she notes, appealed specifically to an American audience. By contrast a second essay, from 1988, 'reflects a more European way of seeing theatricality, more inscribed in theatre as such, rather than performance'. That European view of theatricality shaped the original (French) title, 'Theatricality: On the Specificity of Theatrical Language'. This, she says, 'does not refer to performativity, but it is clear that "theatricality" as defined in this context includes performativity' (2002: 4–5).

There's some fancy footwork going on here. The 1982 essay doesn't mention the word 'performativity': its central comparison is between the two 'modes', performance and theatre (as opposed to 'theatricality'). Then we are asked to accept that in the title of the 1988 essay theatricality simply includes performativity. But there is, says Féral, no contradiction between these positions, for we need to understand that any 'spectacle . . . is an interplay of both performativity and theatricality' (my elision), noting that she said this in 1982. Indeed she did and it's one of the best moments in the essay:

> Theatricality can therefore be seen as composed of two different parts: one highlights performance and is made up of the *realities of the imaginary*; and the other highlights the theatrical and is made up of *specific symbolic structures*. The former originates with the subject and allows his flows of desire to speak; the latter inscribes the subject in the law and in theatrical codes, which is to say, in the symbolic. Theatricality arises from the play between these two realities.   (1982: 178)

Note there is no mention of the word 'performativity'. This is about the physical and emotional work of the acting, happening in front of us for real, panting and sweating, in relation to the scripted and representational elements of what is shown. Reduced to simple terms Féral is saying theatricality always consists of the combination of labour, here and now, and, in its widest sense, 'text'. This is surely right. But here's the fancy footwork: 'performativity' is retrospectively applied as a gloss on what could just as well be called 'performing'.

This is but the beginning. That 1982 formulation quoted above talks of 'performance' rather than 'performing'. It's a problematic usage here because, as she says in 2002, the essay begins with an interest in 'performance art and all forms of performance outside the theatre'. In one place 'performance' designates an art form separable from theatre; in another place it means 'performing' and as such is wholly assimilable to theatre, as she says it is in the title of the 1988 essay. Looking back in 2002 she then somewhat unsurprisingly observes: 'Today I am convinced that the opposition between performativity and theatricality is purely rhetorical, and that both are necessarily enmeshed within the performance' (2002: 5). 'Performance' here means any performed event. When she says performativity is necessarily included within any performed event, 'performativity' means the doing of performance, performing.

It is the assimilation of performativity to the activity of performing that prepares the ground for the process by which everything can with apparent legitimacy be called 'performance'. That drive to universalise is most marked among those who see themselves as scholars of performance. By contrast those who consciously use performance models for other ends tend to resist universalising. To explore the causes behind this difference would require a different project, though in simplistic terms it's tempting enough to assume that for those using performance models merely as a tool it is important to insist on the precision and efficacy of the tool, whereas for those whose identity is institutionally defined by their role as proponents of performance there may well be a need to assert the universal importance, nay grandeur, of the, so to speak, subject. As I say, the real cause, as opposed to my banality, needs demonstrating but it remains the case that, writing a couple of years before Féral, the geographers Thrift and Dewsbury are very clear about the dangers of universalised models of performance: 'A concept which allows such latitude of interpretation is not always easy to work with: it can become a kind of dump, a site which simply signals what is or what is not of interest' (2000: 419).

This sort of thing had been said, as we know, by various scholars of sociology, ethnography, religious studies for at least the previous twenty-five years. So too some working within the field of performance have also criticised this drift to universalism. Resisting Schechner's 'territorial imperative' in 1992, Auslander, for example, said that it was not clear to him 'that the performance paradigm has the kind of universal applicability some would claim for it', implying that the universalist discourse is a function of the institutional imperative (1995: 179). All of the anti-universalists saw, correctly, that, if 'performance' becomes a catch-all term, a crammed genre, a kind of dump, then, however grand it may sound, it loses its analytical functionality. What does it actually mean to say that everything is performed? And is this different from saying that everything is constructed or everything is connected? While the universalised claim may not have much scholarly practicality, it nevertheless has a persistence. This persistence possibly derives from its capacious ideological productivity.

Chapter 21

The relations between performance, theatre and text

One of the neatest and best-known descriptions of the ideology promoted by a universalised performance is that of Jon McKenzie in *Perform or Else*. He traces the emergence of the so-called paradigm of performance alongside the institutional expansion and consolidation of Performance Studies. From this perspective the arguments as to whether Performance Studies is a discipline or not, the debates about terminology and the promotion of the idea of the 'contested' concept, all of this he suggests results from 'a tension between two desires: the desire to create cultural performance as a field of study, one with institutional and professional legitimacy, and the desire to avoid recreating the norms of the academy, norms that are themselves tied to extra-institutional forces'. Thus what gets defined is a coherent discipline that has as its distinctive feature the fact that it questions and upsets coherence. This ideological duality is nowhere better illustrated than in the consistent, discipline-wide, use of the concept of liminality as a theoretical model. It is employed for two purposes: 'to define the efficacy of performance and of our own research'. Thus it has 'helped us to *construct* objects of inquiry by guiding the selection of activities to be studied, their formal analysis, and their political evaluation.' To make his polemical point McKenzie conjures up an apparent paradox: 'the persistent use of this concept within the field *has made liminality into something of a norm*' (2001: 48, 50).

As a formulation the 'liminal norm' neatly describes what McKenzie sees as the dominant characteristics of Performance Studies thinking. The fore-grounding of liminality in this thinking has in turn helped keep in place the disciplinary distinctiveness and stability of Performance Studies. But it can only be ideologically effective in this function if, first, the meaning of liminality is restricted to a generalised sense of in-betweenness, of being outside norms, and, second, if performance is assumed to have some sort of essence or nature which means that it not only exists in, but establishes a state of, liminal in-betweenness, irrespective of its actual institutional positioning. Both these features turn up in Marvin Carlson's definition of 'performance', which McKenzie quotes: it 'is a specific event with its liminoid nature foregrounded, almost invariably clearly separated from the rest of life' (in McKenzie 2001: 49). Defined this way, performance drags into its own orbit the scholars of performance, who themselves fortuitously come to inhabit a non-normative liminality. The same doesn't seem to be necessarily true of scholars of sexual perversion or degenerative diseases, however. Acquainted with, and positioned by, liminality, scholars of Performance Studies are, so the ideological claim has it, more explicitly open to the marginalised and excluded, to diversity and queerness (and its queer variant, unqueerness). There is, says Pelias, a 'disciplinary imperative of giving voice to the disenfranchised' (1998: 17). A concept of performance as non-normative activity thus allows for and promotes a vision of democratic inclusiveness, which in turn underwrites, and ethically consolidates, the institutional distinctiveness of Performance Studies.

By way of having us think afresh about the ideological work done by the liminal norm McKenzie reminds us that in Turner's observations the liminal rites of tribal societies most often function to reinforce the structural stability of those societies. In other words they generally have a normative function. It was, however, the rare moments when liminality undercut norms, creating transgression and schism, that came to be emphasised by performance scholars, influenced by the context of 'social unrest' in the sixties and early seventies. Thus liminality came to be predominantly associated with transgression in Performance Studies. But that association itself turns into a norm that not only governs the mode of thinking and values of performance scholars but also 'has shaped Performance Studies' image of itself, the self-representation of the paradigm in relation to both the academy and society at large'. Alongside this function of the liminal norm there is a second one. It 'suggests that any given conceptual model, even one constructed and deployed to theorize transgression or resistance, is necessarily limited in terms of both its formal and its functional aspects'. This suggestion prompts us to be careful in the work of developing general models for thinking about performance, encouraging us 'to fold generalization back on itself in order to avoid reducing performance to any one model' (McKenzie 2001: 51–52).

This is surely right, and a salutary corrective to some of the universalising tendencies that we have encountered elsewhere. McKenzie seeks to avoid those tendencies by showing that Performance Studies emerges from more than one model and although he emphasises the importance of liminal rites to modelling this emergence these have the status of '*a* (and not *the*) metamodel' (McKenzie 2001: 52). Nevertheless liminality is clearly so crucial to McKenzie's thinking that it has slightly distorting effects. In historical terms it is quite difficult to find performance scholars who were thinking about liminality in the 'sixties and early seventies'. Certainly the sixties had an impact on thinking about performance, as we've seen, but liminality barely figures as a concept in this work. The history as McKenzie tells it is made to service the liminal model. And, in theoretical terms, that model, for all McKenzie's caution, retains magical effects. It has, he says, shaped Performance Studies' image of itself but at the same time it indicates the dangers of generalising. It is difficult to know how it does the second job of work in circumstances where it has the ideological hold implied by the first. And of course it's also difficult not to see that comment about Performance Studies' self-image as itself a generalisation.

Astute as it is in showing how a particular concept of performance becomes privileged and widely adopted because of its ideological and institutional efficacy McKenzie's analysis is limited, I think, because he is also caught up in the ideological machine on which he comments. While he notes the dangers of generalisation, associated perhaps with Performance Studies' characteristic norms of thought, the same tendency to generalisation might be seen at work in the apparent purpose of his own book, with its attempt to create a general theory founded on the happy coincidence that the English word 'perform' has so many different uses (I am not sure how this is dealt with in translations beyond English). Furthermore many generalisations are made on the basis of selective evidence. The account of the concept of performance is more or less framed by the activities of New York Performance Studies, though McKenzie does make a point of mentioning other sites of development, including the route from oral interpretation. But this is a fairly restricted group. There is little time spent on institutions beyond the United States nor disciplines outside Performance Studies. I am not sure that cultural geography and religious studies, for instance, are quite so hung up on liminality in their concepts of performance. While the social science interest in performance tends to be presented by McKenzie as the journey towards the 'paradigm' of performance, it in fact continues simultaneously with the development of Performance Studies. It's this which reveals the nonsense in Carlson's definition of what performance 'is'. For a cultural geographer a car-boot sale could be analysed as performance, yet it is not separated from the rest of life nor is it clear that it is particularly liminoid, unless the boots are only half open.

As far as it goes, then, McKenzie's account of mainly New York Performance Studies is a deft and witty commentary, and it begins to open up the relationship of institutions and concepts of performance. But he passes rather fast over a number of points where there is more that can be productively said about the ideological work done by 'performance'. Because many of the currently dominant concepts of performance have been promoted and popularised within Performance Studies, this subject area will need to figure large in my own account as well. But I shall be attending to its different strands and also going outside it. This I shall do by looking at performance's relationships with three other terms: avant-garde, theatre, text. In the case of each, as McKenzie and several others have remarked, we see how current ideas of performance are shaped by its recent history.

That history makes itself most obviously felt in Richard Schechner's claim that 'If Performance Studies were an art, it would be avant-garde' (Schechner 2001: 2–3). We have already noted Bottoms' observations as to the contradictory nature of this claim (see p. 160). But we also need here to recall that phase in the history of so-called performance art when commentators were trying to establish a lineage for it, associating sixties' work with the early-twentieth-century avant-garde. Dissenting voices pointed out not only that this was a misleading connection but also, perhaps more importantly, that it limited the understanding of the work that was being done. Nevertheless that appeal back to the Modernist avant-garde functioned usefully, as Klein argues, to establish performance and live art as funded forms with their own infrastructure. The reference to avant-garde performance thus summons up the ideological associations with artistic heroism and mould-breaking while doing the material work of institutionalising and mould-forming. This argument is taken a stage further by David Savran when he notes the ideological potency: 'In the field of culture, the concept of an avant-garde is ineluctably tied to the modernist cultural hierarchy that opposes art and commerce, esoteric and popular, live and mediated, progressive and reactionary, avantgarde and kitsch. But this hierarchy no longer obtains. Or at least no longer takes the form it did for most of the 20th century.' Avant-gardism has become a sort of style, detached from any particular site of conflict, and as such easily co-opted by neoliberal capitalism. Thus 'the consecration of the avant-garde in the late 1980s and 1990s ... represented a *branding* of the avant-garde, the production of the label "avant-garde" as a kind of registered trademark' (2005: 35–36; my elision). Thus when Schechner says that if Performance Studies were an artform it would be avant-garde this ideological position could be taken as saying that it has investment value as a commodity.

If avant-garde is supposedly a positive point on the ideological compass, a negative one is 'theatre'. But, whatever it feels about it, performance can never free itself of the relationship with theatre. This unstoppable, niggling persistence stems, I suspect, from a basic confusion. When performance art opposed itself to theatre it did so sometimes on formal grounds – for example, theatre works with fictional representations – and sometimes on institutional grounds, in that it was organised, housed and funded differently. The latter are more clearly defined, whereas the formal distinction doesn't remain fixed. For instance the artist Tom Marioni said theatre created illusions while his immediate contemporary Terry Fox described the anti-Vietnam war performance in which he burned precious plants as 'theatrical', even though the burning was very far from illusory. When (New York) Performance Studies announced itself it simultaneously encouraged rejection of another discipline, theatre studies. But here there is no clarity of material difference: each is an academic programme within similar institutions and similar funding and staffing arrangements. As we have seen, there were some who thought that the claims for the new Performance Studies simply duplicated what was already happening in theatre studies, so that, for example, performance's battle with 'text' replays the 'rejection of textual sovereignty' that characterises much of the history of twentieth-century theatre (Reinelt 2002: 202). Clearly the proposed opposition of Performance Studies to theatre studies is predicated on assumptions about what theatre studies is – what it covers, what it argues about, how it is taught. These assumptions can vary across institutions. Schechner says that at New York University they were conscious that by including, for example, ethnographic work, they were in 1979–1980 teaching 'drama' in a way that was unlike any other institution. Meanwhile, elsewhere in 1985, Sally Harrison-Pepper (1999) had started incorporating ethnographic work into her teaching of drama, having read Victor and Edith Turner in 1982. There may have been accepted variability of practice, but New York found it necessary to call itself Performance Studies.

If the understanding of the remit of drama and theatre studies can differ across institutions within one national system, it can vary even more wildly across different national models. Some university systems separate off conservatoire training from theoretical analysis, some do analysis of dramatic texts only within literary departments while workshops happen elsewhere. The definition of the subject area is founded not on any inherent characteristics but on where the institutional lines are drawn. Thus one group of people might think they are doing Performance Studies while another group of people doing exactly the same thing might think of it as drama and theatre studies. For example Conquergood claimed that the transgressive energy of performance came from its mode of working, its workshop process. Within the discipline of oral interpretation that workshop process felt groundbreaking because it incorporated some basic changes to the traditional mode of teaching the literary text. Students were invited to engage with literary text not by analysing it on the page – which had been the dominant mode of 'New

Criticism' from the 1940s onwards – but by speaking it out loud or acting it out. In their volume *Teaching Performance Studies* Stucky and Wimmer describe this pedagogy. It takes its rationale from 'the place of Performance Studies as an interdisciplinary phenomenon' being composed of various different disciplinary strands, including those of ethnography and 'embodiment'. As an outcome of this pedagogy 'Students learn to perform before others, both in class and without, and in a variety of modes: cabaret; storytelling; speech-making; class presentations; improvisatory role-playing; dance pieces; and small and large, long and short, theatre pieces.' These performed activities offer the opportunity to 'learn how to evaluate speech elements of volume, pitch, tone, rhythm', among others. Stucky and Wimmer then add: 'In some Performance Studies courses, students are given the opportunity to learn to use, not simply evaluate, production elements in their performances as well: costume, make-up, sets, props, lighting, music, and movement' (2002: 5, 9). Now at this point our steps hesitate like travellers in thickening mist. For it has become very difficult clearly to discern the distinction here between Performance Studies and traditional theatre and drama education. Students learning to use movement are somewhere very different from those merely evaluating it. The word 'performance' as it's used here means 'doing performing'. Thus here Performance Studies seems to mean 'how to do performing'. The reconciliation of elementary craft practices to a broad-spectrum 'performance' might be thoroughly logical in a department with the specific history of, say, Performance Studies at Sydney. But it can look simultaneously pretty illogical against Schechner's insistence in 1992 that 'performance' departments should differentiate themselves precisely because they declined to offer training 'for the orthodox theatre'. Although Stucky and Wimmer may not be recommending training as such, their notion of 'production elements' would fit perfectly snugly, as would the distaste for training, with a fairly standard UK drama department.

There is an even more precise parallelism at work. This can be seen from another piece by Stucky, where he describes activity in the 'Performance Studies classroom'. He begins by noting that 'As an educational enterprise, especially as it is taught in the United States, Performance Studies participates in an ongoing experiment in social awareness and illuminates possibilities for social change.' The work of Augusto Boal is key, indeed *de rigueur*, in the curriculum. The pedagogy is characterised, he says, 'by an ethical social conscience, an active search for better ways to think and live, an objective to change the world' (2006: 262–63, 272). The 'critical performance pedagogy' described by Norman Denzin works in a similar way. Overall it 'resists the increasing commercialization and commodification of higher education' and in its specific subject area it 'implements a commitment to participation and performance *with*, not *for*, community members' (2006: 334). Now it's a little difficult to see here what is different from the doing of higher education drama. For example, Stucky's formulation of 'Performance Epistemology' as 'Performance Studies is interested in what we know through performance and how we come to know it' (2006: 273) could work equally well if you substituted the word 'drama'. But there is a more specific parallel. Later on in the same book as Stucky and Denzin, Jan Cohen-Cruz has an essay on 'community-based performance'. The author and essay topic would be associated, in the United Kingdom, with the specific subdiscipline of Applied Theatre, which had its origins in uses of theatre for education, particularly from the mid-1960s onwards. Stucky and Denzin too are both writing essays about something that could just as well, in a different part of the world, be called Applied Theatre. But while this particular crossover between Performance Studies and Applied Theatre may perhaps be explained as a specific effect of the oral interpretation strand of the subject, with its particular disciplinary values and history, such crossovers are not confined to it.

This is clear when we look at how an ambassador for New York Performance Studies plans to take the subject back to China. William Sun and Faye C. Fei's proposal as to how to embed Performance Studies in the Chinese educational system is, of course, an exercise fraught with diplomatic niceties, to which end they plan amalgamating 'Schechner's Performance Studies with the Confucian tradition of rites and Marxist theory of human nature. The result will be called Social Performance Studies (SPS), where the first two words 'refer to actions performed outside of the theatre that have a definite impact on a particular audience'. The difference of SPS from New York Performance Studies is that whereas the latter places 'more emphasis on individual freedom' the former emphasises 'social discipline and normative trainings'. This different emphasis is seen in the plan to insert 'theatre' into school curricula, which will downplay encouragement of individual creativity in order to maximise performing opportunities through learning 'imitative' theatre-making. One of the benefits of this is that it can 'train students to speak well'. And that sort of training seems key to the mission of SPS, which has observed that in the new times of 'open door policy' and 'market economy' many spokespeople did not know how to present to an audience. Its founders note that the manager of a luxury hotel discovered in a published paper by Sun that SPS was 'exactly what he needed to turn his employees into professional service people schooled in proper etiquette' (Sun and Fei 2014: 289–97). In the United Kingdom this would be called something like 'presentation skills training'. It is done as a money-making project both by professional theatre people and by conservatoires. It is therefore not without some irony that one encounters the border discipline which, having crossed the border into the particular circumstances of China, twenty or so years after Schechner inaugurated his version of Performance Studies happily returns the subject to proper theatre training and conservatoire skills, to mimesis and, as a bonus, etiquette. When the border-crossing discipline crosses some borders, perhaps when it strays beyond north-east America, Performance Studies concepts and practice turn into Applied Theatre or speech training without anything changing except the name.

The drift of my argument here is not particularly healthy. While the doing of Performance Studies in one place may involve the same activity as the doing of drama and theatre in another, it would not be correct to assume the next step and say that performance is always therefore more or less the same as drama and theatre. The seductiveness of this argument and its consequences are well illustrated by Erika Fischer-Lichte's *Routledge Introduction to Theatre and Performance Studies* (2014). She quite properly begins by observing how the concepts of theatre and theatricality have spread across the thinking of a range of disciplines. In this situation 'If everything is theatre . . . it raises the question why we need a separate discipline to study theatre at all' (my elision). The same point had been made about performance. So there is a need to 'set specific boundaries for our concept of theatre'. Performance is much more precise, as Fischer-Lichte sees it: 'we can define a performance as any event in which all the participants find themselves in the same place at the same time, partaking in a prescribed set of activities.' Following Max Hermann (1865–1942) performance is regarded as 'the most important element of theatre'. Hermann always conceived the performed doing as an important part of the remit of the subject, which is why in Germany, where the subject began, Theatre Studies 'was founded *as* Performance Studies' (2014: 10, 13). Even allowing for different institutional histories and developments in the United States, at base Theatre and Performance Studies are one discipline, where the Performance Studies part of it is concerned with analysis of what the performing body is doing. This analysis may deploy both semiotic and phenomenological models, and in doing so is able to accommodate analysis of body art within the unified discipline.

This argument might seem to be a usefully logical continuation and final sorting out of the vexed and restless relationship described by Worthen or Féral. But the disciplinary tidying up, so to speak, removes from view the fact that artists in the sixties and seventies thought what they were doing was separate from theatre. The distinction between forms that they were making cannot be conjured away simply by imagining that such a distinction only existed in the English language. For, as we know, there were German artists in the early seventies who were exploring non-theatrically inflected words for their practice, such as *Aktion* and *Handlung*. So too 'happening' was absorbed into German, for example, in the title of Sohm's 1970 *Happening & Fluxus*, as later was the word 'performance' itself, as 'Performanz'. Distinctions were therefore being made in various national systems, and they needed to be made because there were institutional battle-lines to be drawn.

But the art practices of the sixties are only a minor element of what the model of the unified theatre studies represses. More substantial are the concepts developed by sociology, folklore, cultural studies and anthropology. These are corralled off from the main body of the book into a short epilogue, and there is little exploration of their impact on aesthetic practice. While Brecht's 'street scene' is offered as an example of theatre's embrace of the everyday, this really won't fit the bill. The scale of the exclusion is marked in Fischer-Lichte's assertion that 'Current theories of performance were prompted by developments in theatre starting in the 1960s' (2014: 106). Although the book attributes almost every change to the 1960s, this assertion is quite patently wrong. Many current theories of performance, and many art practices of the sixties, were prompted by attempts to explain or change non-theatrical interactions. What vitiates the book's entire project is that it does not face up to, let alone try to answer, the straightforward historical question as to why at a particular juncture the word 'performance' became so popular and so potent. This omission seems so obvious that it compels speculation as to its cause.

Fischer-Lichte presides over a well-funded research institute, the name of which figures in one of the chapter titles. This coincidence, together with the heavy insistence on theatre studies' origin in Germany, makes this *Introduction* feel like an institution book. In that respect it recalls Schechner's *Introduction* to Performance Studies (you might, if you wish, also reflect on the agenda of the *Introduction* you are reading now). Indeed Fischer-Lichte's book might be seen as the antithetical mirror of Schechner's, with both employing similar rhetorical operations. Schechner has aesthetic theatre as a subset of performance, and Fischer-Lichte has performance as a subset of aesthetic theatre. While Schechner draws everything into Performance Studies, Fischer-Lichte shuts it out entirely as a separate discipline. While Schechner claims he is more or less the founder of Performance Studies, Fischer-Lichte tends to imply that the approach taken by her research institute underpins and guarantees the unified discipline. And finally both appropriate for themselves, strictly on their own terms, the concept of performance which begins with Goffman. Schechner attends to some of its ramifications while banalising and misrepresenting them, and Fischer-Lichte largely brackets it off. Here, speaking with what feels like a thoroughly institutional voice, the discipline of theatre and performance effectively distances itself from the concept of performance that was embraced by social science. Indeed that specific concept – or range of related concepts – is effectively reduced to a minor incident on the sidelines of the real business of drama and theatre.

For all the fuss and bluster, though, the relationship of performance to theatre seems to come down to a fetishism over institutional dividing lines. The practices often remain the same under different names, and as we have seen they can each quite cogently claim to embrace the other, which is nice and cosy. But the opposition to theatre contains another opposition within which is buried a much deeper ideological investment.

In the formal inaugural year of 1995 we know that Dwight Conquergood explained why 'text' was opposed to performance (see pp. 162–64). While text is a system for representing the world, performance actually happens in the here and now, so the argument goes. Performance doesn't represent anything. It is not communicated through a medium such as written text but is instead immediate. This refusal of dominant text is the source of performance's freedom and ability to make a difference in the world. Or so it is claimed. But in the same year as Conquergood's lectures, W.B. Worthen took apart this argument. His essay begins by showing that the assumed opposition between performance and written dramatic text was false, in that the two approaches were always tangled into one another, that not only performance but also the body was already textualised. From here he moved to address Performance Studies' separation of itself from theatre studies. As he incisively observed such an opposition runs contrary to the 'productive eclecticism' on which Performance Studies prides itself and operates to 'reinscribe Performance Studies with at least some of the analytical hierarchies its practitioners would contest' (1995: 21). Conquergood, as we've noted, locks the interdiscipline into a binarised territorial war.

Worthen's essay was published in *The Drama Review*, which called itself a journal of Performance Studies. Its publication in such a place shows that the journal, associated closely with Richard Schechner, had a liberal approach towards critics of the dominant views and hierarchy of Performance Studies. This liberalism was tempered somewhat by ensuring that a whole group of scholars also had the opportunity to respond, in the same issue, to Worthen. They did so in ways which were both supportive and bitchy, with the overall result that his intervention gets safely framed as a moment of 'dialogue' itself exemplifying the hegemonic inclusivity of

Performance Studies. But the problems around 'text' were much larger, and of longer time span, than a spat in a journal. They are locked into the history of that part of the supposed interdiscipline that comes from oral interpretation, which, after all, prided itself on the value of doing textual analysis. But what gives the anxiety around text its persistent energy is the desperation to establish the fact that performance is a practice that escapes from 'mediation'. Mediation here carries a sense of imprisonment within imposed systems and discourses, perhaps with its origins in the sixties' critique of mass media and indeed the spectacle. It frequently lingers behind the rhetoric that sees the actor as trapped within text written by another, or, to use Blau's phrase, 'slave to the ideological apparatus of reproduction' (1982/1983: 144). This anxiety doesn't seem to extend so readily to the use of video projection or sound amplification, or even simply artificial lighting, all of which mechanical devices come with their own protocols of use, which require the performer to rehearse into compliance with the kit. All of this stuff may thus be said to be 'textual', and indeed they are frequently celebrated as 'media', the more mixed and mediating the better. The difference from written mediation may simply be that in the history of performance thinking the use of technological media and the development of what Dick Higgins called 'intermedia' were in the sixties and early seventies ideologically marked as a sign of the new and, as against traditional theatre, the liberated.

Looking back on that period in 1982 Herbert Blau observed that 'There has been a serious effort over the last generation to eliminate the *as if*, to return performance to *unmediated* experience, as with The Living Theater, but with whatever measure of "truth" or "authenticity" it is at best only appearance. There is nothing more illusory in performance than the illusion of the unmediated.' Performance, theatrical or not, always has a consciousness of itself as performance: 'No sooner is it looked at with anything like performance in mind, the empty space is a space of consciousness.' So what scuppers any pursuit of the unmediated is that 'there is something in the very nature of performance which ... implies *no first time*, no origin, but only recurrence and reproduction, whether improvised or ritualized, rehearsed or aleatoric.' This is why, he concludes, 'a performance seems *written* even if there is no Text, for the writing seems imbedded in the conservatism of the instincts and the linguistic operations of the unconscious' (1982/1983: 143, 147–48). Although he invokes instincts and the unconscious, behind Blau's argument there is also the poststructuralist, and specifically Derridean, analysis of the illusion of expressive speech that is always actually citation of learnt language. Here is the influence of the Theory years, but in the context of what called itself performance theory in the nineties it was also a site for new struggle around text.

Performance scholars knew they couldn't avoid something as 'new' as poststructuralism, but Bottoms points out an interesting feature of the engagement with Derrida. In his essays on Artaud Derrida speaks of 'the theological stage', as a way of characterising Artaud's position. Derrida's own position is, as Bottoms puts it, that *'there is no non-theological stage to be had, no purely present performance in the moment, no escape from representation.'* And yet, says Bottoms, 'the theological stage is invoked to lend theoretical authority to reflexive prejudices against written drama' (2011: 26–27; for an account of Derrida's argument see Shepherd and Wallis 2004: 227–9). In other words the interesting feature of performance scholarship's engagement with Derrida is that it so often gets him back-to-front. This is not a randomly perverse misreading. Suspicion about poststructuralism is written into the history of the oral interpretation version of the subject. One of the presiding figures of the discipline, Wallace Bacon, just a couple of years after Blau said, in the house journal, that 'we' are not deconstructionists: 'Our center is the interaction between readers and texts which enriches, extends, clarifies, and (yes) alters the interior and even the exterior lives of students through the power of texts' (1984: 84).

Bacon has brought us to a parting of the ways. On the one hand there is text as enveloping citational system, the language that precedes speech; on the other hand there are texts as discrete verbal works interpreted by readers and performers. In much performance scholarship, and particularly that associated with oral interpretation, the first text is bad, and the second good. Ronald Pelias, he who announced the 'performance paradigm' in 1987, set out the position in an essay for a book that took its title from the new paradigm's inaugural conference, *The Future of Performance Studies*. He begins by noting the idea that the self 'is no more than a linguistic construct', relating it to Foucault's replacement of author by author-function. Against this Pelias sets 'our current performance practice', where 'Performers are actively engaged in authoring themselves, in demanding that their presence be acknowledged.' This is particularly seen in work on autobiographical and personal narratives, in performance of which, 'we see before us, most of all, not a subject position that serves certain discursive functions, but an individual who seems to desire an interpersonal response'. So too this individual is seen in 'our' work on 'performing theory'. This work is 'an interventionist strategy' in that it 'allows performers to make implicit theoretical assumptions explicit'. Once again the coherent self is apparent 'as it bends theory to personal and political interests' (1998: 15).

The contrasting positions are plain: on one hand the notion of the self as linguistic construct, as text so to speak; on the other, the writings, whether personal narrative or theory, through which selves make themselves present. Being authored is set against authoring. Not only is this a continuation of Bacon's attack on poststructuralism but it enlarges it into an assault on 'theory', not in the sense that theory is a bad thing – indeed it can provide 'interventionist' strategy – but in the sense that theory can, and should, be bent to 'personal and political interests'. Since it is usually assumed that what defines a theory is that it resists being bent to local interests, then, if performance can indeed do such bending, it must surely have a very special relationship with theory.

Chapter 22

The magic of performance

To clarify the assumption as to how theory usually operates I want to take a minor detour. All sorts of texts could be cited to demonstrate the proper function of theory, but I have chosen one on the basis of its date and its subject field. It comes from 1970, not especially significant in itself, but early in the engagement between theatre and social science. Its subject area is not that of performances and texts, aesthetic or otherwise, but anthropology. And about the doing of anthropology it raises some questions that predate the wholesale absorption of anthropology into performance.

When, in 1970, Jairus Banaji reviewed the state of British anthropology he suggested its problem was the persistence of functionalism. In its post-war manifestation this took the form of analysis of intersubjectivity, as opposed to structure, as the object of study. Both modes of study were faulty, he argued, because they not only look at but also primarily value the ideas about themselves that people consciously hold. Approaches based in phenomenology may be similarly faulty. As modes of study they are not looking for that which is 'unconscious', defined as that which shapes the formation of conscious ideas: 'The anthropologist's task is to penetrate a people's conscious representations, as embodied in their ideological productions (myth, ritual, marriage rules) and uncover a more fundamental, "unconscious reality".' This unconscious reality, or set of determinations, may well differ from those ideas which, although conscious, may nevertheless be illusory. Into this overall argument Banaji places, among others, Victor Turner, whom he sees, despite Turner's account of himself, as 'functionalist'. His model of liminality is abstracted from particular historical circumstances, and is thus a 'dehistoricised structure'. Furthermore it is a 'conscious' model (Banaji 1970: 75, 78). It reports on people's sense of what they are doing but it doesn't explore the deeper, unconscious, situation. So liminal process can feel consciously like change and mobility while in fact, in a way of which the participants are unaware, it functions as a mechanism for ensuring structural stability.

It is not, of course, just with anthropological work that one can see the distinction between conscious and unconscious modes of knowing. Back in that year when performance apparently entered the academy, 1979, Peter Gorsen made an analysis of contemporary practices which revealed a distinction between what people thought they were doing and what it seemed to him they were actually doing. In what he calls the 'subjective-thinker type' of performance practice he saw the work being motivated by a 'critical rejection of man as a "mere result", of his spontaneity being manipulated by economic, scientific, and technological norms.' This rejection of a notion that people are manipulated, or determined, by external 'norms' underwrote the frequent claims that performance art would liberate. Despite these claims, inspection of individual performances showed 'a tendency to imitate the alienated conventional behaviour and experiences springing from everyday life with irrational directness' (1984: 137–38). What people consciously thought about what they were doing differed from what they were actually doing. This distinction becomes especially important where performance claims for itself a capacity to break with norms and liberate. Those claims are written deep into the discourses of performance, as can be exemplified from a couple of moments taken from across the span of the development of today's dominant concept of performance. These will in turn lead us towards a summary of where I think we have been, and are going.

First, in the same year as Banaji's critique of anthropological thinking, Richard Schechner suggested that the crisis in North American society had produced 'yearnings' for alternatives, which triggered 'an interest in primitive peoples'. But he warns that such an interest, produced by engagement with anthropology, has led to sentimental fantasies about the 'primitive'. That warning offered, he then notes that the sorts of alternative experience for which North Americans yearn are 'fundamental to many oral-based tribal cultures'. Together these experiences amount to a 'special way of handling experience' which he calls 'actualizing': 'Actualizing is plain among rural, tribal peoples and it is becoming plainer among our own young and in their avant-garde art' (see p. 26). From here he looks at so-called new theatre experiments in the light of ancient practices (1988: 38–40). The argument moves very quickly away from scepticism about the 'primitive' in order to produce a generalised, and uncritical, invocation of something held in common amongst the 'rural'. It needs to be uncritical because this version of the 'rural' allows it to operate as a parallel to and reference point for the ethical earnestness of 'experimental' theatre. Its similarity to the 'rural' confirms that experimental practice is not constrained by, and confined to, the academy and professional arts practice but instead is dealing with really real, albeit handily generalisable, people. Anthropology offers a prized connection to the organic. But, although its absorption into discussion of art practice may be driven by a political urgency to describe alternatives to the present crisis, it simultaneously brings with it the uncritical thinking, the 'conscious' model, against which Banaji warns. Banaji, however, was writing as an anthropologist while Schechner writes as a theatre-maker. Theatre-making and, even more so, 'performance'-making had a particular requirement of anthropology. What they required was a language for justifying, for giving value to, the effectiveness of their own theatre experiments. New ways of doing theatre, or as it was later called 'performance', could seem to offer a way of escaping the dominant and constraining practices of the traditional theatre and academy by engaging with the alternative modes of thinking and feeling found among people who, while not being called 'primitive', could be seen as outside, other, different. In engaging with such alternatives it seems inappropriate to distrust their own consciousness and subject it to academic critique. Thus the apparently laudable political aim of challenging the dominant potentially brings with it a habit of mind that may well encourage 'immediacy, involvement and intimacy as modes of knowing', to use Conquergood's phrase, but at the same time piques itself on its abjuring of critique and history.

If Schechner was pushed in the direction of anthropology by his desire to validate (his own) experimental practice, a similar habit of mind emerges from the oral interpretation strand of Performance Studies. By the early years of the new century both anthropologically inclined and text-based Performance Studies had come together to form a new dominant concept of performance. The ideological claims of this dominant could be exemplified from a range of texts, but one that eloquently articulates them is Della Pollock's Introduction to her 1998 edition, *Exceptional Spaces*, which is my second example.

Pollock repeats a regular trope by defining Performance Studies as an 'interdiscipline' which draws 'diversely' on 'traditions of literary and anthropological performance'. As a consequence it 'generally cedes the object-status of the text ... to a sense of the text-in-performance as an always already intertextual rite'. This is what gives to performance some familiar characteristics, namely 'the vitality, erotics, and transformative dynamics of subject-subject exchange'. That exchange is based in dialogue, which, drawing on Bakhtin, is proposed as being at the heart of performance's efficacy. It thus positions the audience as 'more active than reactive'. With these 'transformative dynamics' based in dialogue, performance not only creates its audience as 'social agents' but also has its own capacity to be 'an important site of – even a paradigmatic trope for – cultural resistance' (Pollock 1998: 22, 26; my elision).

Much of this is heavily, if not well, trodden ground. Note the claim to being an 'interdisicpline' which seems to imagine that there is only one interdiscipline on the block. Note too that in this inclusive interdiscipline the 'literary' and 'anthropological' are foregrounded to the exclusion of the non-literary and cultural. Note again that the main mechanism for efficacy is dialogue, verbal exchange. In these respects, however 'interdisciplinary' the claim, the argument is actually shaped by Pollock's background in oral interpretation. That background also shows itself when the argument moves to propose a concept of agency. This proposition is based in the nature of performance which is not 'primarily, a specific genre of practice or speech protocol'. It is instead 'the alchemy of occurrence and recurrence through which agency (otherwise so deflated within the economies of the "postmodern") emerges qualified but cogent' (the antipathy to the 'postmodern', for which, here, we might read 'poststructuralist critique of agency' in particular, is, again, part of an established position). In the model of agency it's not quite clear what 'qualified' means but the following sentence shows at least what is being rejected: 'Displacing both narrowly idealistic (intentional) and deterministic models of act-agency with the affective, sensual, multivoiced, and multiperspectival activity of discursive exchange, performance figures agency as embodied action, as that which is generated in and as performance'. Coming back to this idea a few pages later, the argument has to acknowledge the weight of decades of analysis that show the effects of determination on agency so it has another go at defining the preferred version of performance in relation to this thinking: 'Performance is no more free of historical determination than other "products" of a capitalist system.' That's the concession; now here's the prestidigitation: 'But by its very evanescence, it retains the mark of process and the promise of change.' The very nature, the essence, of performance thus allows it an escape route from determination, and, as has already been argued, by doing performance one can become an agent. This ability to promise change is secured by what constitutes the essence of performance, dialogue. Dialogue, as we know, operates in such a way that each party may be affected by it: 'The effort to change an-other in and through dialogue redounds to the speaking self.' On this basis we are ready for the big assertion: ' The speaker who expresses her agency in the act of claiming rights and access to language use thus becomes the agent of her own transformation' (Pollock 1998: 22–23, 26).

   Here the decades of assumptions about the nature of performance, particularly as inflected by oral interpretation, pile up in order to construct an heroic model of agency. In the face of many more decades of arguments that agency cannot be seen as floating free of the circumstances in which it operates, the argument makes a neat sidestep that allows performance in particular to escape such determination on the basis of an essential 'evanescence'. Note that 'essential' quality which traces its heritage back at least to Phelan's fairyland if not before. So too the image of the speaker who becomes 'agent' of her own transformation tends to obscure, or downplay, the material circumstances which bear on that speaker. In a similar way Madison and Hamera uncouple agency from determination by redefining 'performativity': 'We may understand performativity as citationality, but we may also understand performativity as an intervention upon citationality and of resisting citationality.' Two uses of 'performativity' are carefully blended in this one sentence. But despite this alchemical suppleness it still remains difficult to see how performing can shake free of citationality. Nonetheless they press their argument on towards the moment when 'we rework performativity beyond a "stylized repetition of acts"' (Madison and Hamera 2006b: xviii–xix). By setting to one side what has to be seen as a partial or intermittently operating citationality, the argument can envisage a human agent or agents in control of the repetition. Despite Butler's insistence that interior self is an illusion produced by imitative practices, the re-installation of the individual as agent needs to happen as part of a discourse that eventually finds its homecoming in the figure of the performance scholar who is also a performance creator. In each of these cases, from 1998 and 2006, the speaker's act of claiming their right to speech and 'performative' intervention, thereby transforming themself, seems to be very similar to the 'narrowly idealistic (intentional)' model of 'act-agency' that Pollock says Performance Studies displaces. Although the language is scrabbling around, at a conscious level, to assert that performance really does have a different relationship to determination, what seems to be going on, at a less conscious level, is the same sort of thing that Peter Gorsen observed in performances in 1979, a desire to reject the idea that the human being is manipulated by norms in order to assert that performance is liberatory. As we have seen, however, this liberatory argument itself reproduces, and indeed depends on, a set of norms, the by-now established norms that pertain to what performance and Performance Studies are. The nature of performance enables Performance Studies to be an 'interdiscipline' which has its own agency to change the world.

That heroic vision is a culmination of an historical process that has, over time, established what now passes for an elaborated concept of performance. This shows the following features.

There is a tendency to universalise, drawing a range of different performed practices into equivalence. It seems to begin with the rhetoric of Happenings, as they sought to position themselves against dominant art practice. The new mode of 'performance' art then offered itself as a master category, not just in opposition to but also able to subsume previous and narrowly specific practices. The status as master category was assisted by early theorisations of so-called postmodernism, where 'performance' was a common denominator. Within the institutionalisation of performance study as a discipline the claim to be a master category was stated in terms of performance being an 'inter-discipline' or multidiscipline. This claim gave it ethical status, on the basis that the subject area had commitment to embracing not only divers disciplines but also, by extension, all forms of difference. It also of course justified the absorption of other subject areas and, by placing them all within a single, generously inclusive, master category, simultaneously facilitated the search for similarities and equivalences across differing practices. The universalising, often on the grounds of political radicalism, thus erases specificity of practice. The conception of a 'performance or performative turn' effaces concrete circumstances and abstracts performance from the stuff of historical process. Despite repeated critique from those studying or using performance in more social scientific areas, the tendency to universalise persists.

There is a tendency to romanticise agency, laying heavy stress on embodied experience and taking less interest in specifying the determinants upon both that experience and its romanticisation. This process seems to begin with the counterculture and oppositional politics of the sixties and early seventies. The proper stress on equality across gender, race and sexuality required attention to differences from assumed norms which, combined with arguments as to the need for liberating desires and emotions from learnt oppression, placed high value on the importance of the expression of individuality. This was given additional emphasis by the demonstrated distortions to which old-style political discipline and organisation seemed susceptible. The new way thus seemed to rely on liberating the individual, which was often imaged as the individual performing their liberation.

Despite the sceptical insights of people such as Gorsen performance was glamourised by the acquisition of an historical lineage tracking back to the heroic avant-garde individualists of the early twentieth century. The grip of these performance practices and their rhetoric seemed then to persist through the period when much of the arts academy was taken up by an interest in Theory. That interest was most strongly influenced by poststructuralism and by poststructuralist reworkings of, for example, Marxism or psychoanalysis and one of its overall consequences was a dismantling of assumptions around so-called human nature, the autonomous unified subject and any sort of 'essence'. Within many writings produced under the rubric of performance study, however, there was, as we have seen, a resistance to the drive of poststructuralism. Sometimes this resistance was explicit – Bacon rejecting 'deconstruction', Conquergood attacking Derrida, Pelias so revealingly saying

'I simply don't like the person Lacan would have me be' (1998: 18) – but more often it was an apparently consensual engagement which in the name of poststructuralism effectively rewrote it. This occurred most often in the invocations of the theory of performativity. But that habitual revision was underwritten, as it were, by the activity of the 'radical' performance classroom, with its emphasis on embodied individual experience as opposed to abstract critique. The combination of this history, political good intentions and pedagogic commitment had the result, in many many places, of substituting for poststructuralism's dismantled subject an autonomous agent, an individual freely engaging with other individuals. That engagement is carried out by those who inhabit a master discourse, the so-called interdiscipline, which works to guarantee the liberalism and good intentions of their dealings with all those diverse and dispossessed who are assimilated into that master discourse, assimilated, that is, like it or not – for there is a way of labelling everything they do, inescapably, as performance.

These seem to me tendencies in much of what I have heard and read. Of course there are critiques that are highly conscious of these shifts and effects in the dominant concept of performance, but the critiques don't appear to be in the majority. Yet, as is so often the way, the need for such critique seems to me more urgent than ever. For we are dealing here with something more than the regressive adaptation of poststructuralist theory or the reactive defensiveness around a young discipline. My sense is that the academic engagement with performance has taken place within, and contributed to the formation of, yet another 'turn'.

This is the 'turn' to neoliberalism. In his effort to give a concrete historical explanation of this so-called turn, David Harvey asks how it is that so many people could be persuaded to vote and act against their own self-interest, apparently willingly acceding to their own increased exploitation by the very rich, consenting passively to hand over yet more power to the increasingly few. To get to an answer Harvey first recalls Gramsci's distinction between 'common' sense – 'the sense held in common' – and 'good sense'. Common sense 'is constructed out of long-standing practices of cultural socialization' while good sense 'can be constructed out of critical engagement with the issues of the day'. This distinction is similar to, and perhaps lies behind, Banaji's separation of analysis that attends to the conscious as opposed to the unconscious. Being founded on uninspected practices if not prejudices common sense can be 'profoundly misleading', but it nevertheless lays a basis for consent. That consent to neoliberalist measures was obtained through various channels within which different forms of 'common sense' were articulated. Among these were the political upheavals of the late sixties which, as Harvey says, were 'strongly inflected with the desire for greater personal freedoms'. Whether it was campaigns around civil rights or opposition to war, the 'intrusive state' was the enemy. This was a position shared by neoliberalism, which needs to curtail the interventionist and regulatory activity of the state. It obtained the consent for doing so by benefiting from a culture that 'emphasized the liberty of consumer choice, not only with respect to particular products but also with respect to lifestyles, modes of expression, and a wide range of cultural practices', in which we may, or may not, wish to include performance. This may be seen to have happened in the case of New York where in the late seventies control over the city moved from its democratic organisations to the financial elites. These elites supported 'the opening up of the cultural field to all manner of diverse cosmopolitan currents'. These included what Harvey calls the 'narcissistic exploration of self, sexuality, and identity' which become 'the leitmotif of bourgeois urban culture'. The artistic freedom promoted by New York's cultural institutions, and this would presumably include freedoms around performance, 'led, in effect, to the neoliberalization of culture. "Delirious New York" ... erased the collective memory of democratic New York' (Harvey 2007: 39–41, 47; my elision).

Among the channels by which consensual common sense is formed are the universities. The most obvious role they play in the consolidation of neoliberal thinking is seen in their business schools and economics departments. But it is as well not to forget the existence of a more widespread common sense that, in Harvey's analysis, is part of the founding conditions for the 'turn' to neoliberalism. That common sense holds to the importance of individual expression and choice, often in defiance of imposed rules and traditions. The construction of the neoliberal culture required 'differentiated consumerism and individual libertarianism'. As such, says Harvey, this culture 'proved more than a little compatible with the cultural impulse called "postmodernism"' (2005: 42). In the universities' embrace of postmodernism, as we saw in the case of Wisconsin-Milwaukee in the mid-seventies, it was not the business schools at the forefront but the arts faculties. And, for some, at the forefront of postmodernism, exemplifying its common characteristics, was performance.

This argument is heading somewhere grim. It is necessary to repeat, therefore, that many people in performance departments were and are adamantly conscious of, and angry about, the depredations of neoliberalism, the loss of democratic rights and the creation of more impoverished and desperate underclasses. At the same time, and indeed to sustain this consciousness and anger, it is necessary to inspect the extent to which the writing and teaching about performance keep in place, albeit unwittingly, 'common-sense' assumptions which facilitate consent, at a very deep level, to the culture of neoliberalism. These assumptions circulate around a concept of performance that places great emphasis on individual expression, that promotes a fantasy of autonomous agency, that downplays the effect of material and ideological determination, and that regards discipline, or should we say regulation, whether by text or craft or tradition, as the enemy.

The attractiveness of this model of agency and its relationship to discourse and the determinants upon it constitutes its historical potency. It works to call back from exile and, to use Belsey's terms, reinstate once again in a position of dominance that efficient dispenser of a somewhat less than humane liberalism, the autonomous bourgeois subject. The appearance on the stage of this subject has been facilitated here by a simple mechanism, the concept of performance. In modelling a by-now fairly dominant concept of performance, commentators have resisted poststructuralism in general and reinterpreted poststructuralist performativity in particular. These intellectual manoeuvres, and the desire to deploy them, have their own specific history. Current ideas about performance, and in particular art performance, tend to derive in the main from an orthodoxy about the 'nature' of performance that settled into place after 1979. This established its claim to that place by tracing back a lineage to the early-twentieth-century avant-garde. That long view manages not simply to reinterpret but also to bracket off poststructuralist and materialist theories in order to install, in place of the culturally produced, constructed but fractured self, an image of the liberal bourgeois subject, the autonomous individual, now conflated, in all its magical glamour, with the heroic Modernist arts fighter.

These marvellous tricks of ideological disguise and transformation have been facilitated by a concept of performance that insists that it is truthful and 'relevant' because it is wise to, and rejects, the illusory practices of traditional theatre, that it has the capacity to provide universal explanations and a unique position of overview, that it is organically related to and able to speak about the realities of everyday lives, and that it is compassionate, accessible and earnest. Perhaps, above all, the importance lies, so to speak, in being earnest.

Closing note

The phrase 'performance theory' has not often been used. As I said in the Preface, I want to be cautious about overarching theories. Instead I have talked about 'concepts' of performance, ideas which appear at specific junctures, to do specific jobs of work, and not always related to each other. It is possible to describe these concepts specifically and to trace their origins and modes of operation. This I hope I have done. I have not articulated a general theory of performance, however.

This is because I am still not sure what such a thing would be. But, as is the way, I think I am clear what it is not. In the phrases 'literary theory' or 'critical theory' we speak of a set of theories, a set of approaches to reading literature or art, each with their own history and procedures, and each with their own name. 'Performance theory' is not yet confidently formalised in this way. For the purposes of analysing how performance works, however, these 'literary' approaches are often useful, as say in reading performance within a psychoanalytic frame. So too modes of analysis from theatre are useful, as say in describing processes of turn-taking or filling and emptying.

But these approaches have tended on the whole to assume that they know what the object to be read or analysed is. In terms of performance the substantial change, over the last sixty or so years, has been a new understanding of what it is that we are meant to be studying. A new object of knowledge has been identified, and it is with this process of definition that this book has been mainly concerned. I have thus made a major generalisation: the sort of performance designated here by the phrase 'performance theory' is not acting. Acting is a very fine ancient art, with a large set of theories all of its own. The 'performance' with which this book deals has often been defined as precisely that which is not acting.

In order both to clarify and secure in place the particular set of concepts with which I am dealing here I have aimed to tell a range of histories. Together these insist that a specific set of ideas came into being and were rapidly taken up. But there still hangs in the air the question as to why the word 'performance' gained such widespread status and credibility as to become a catch-all noun by 1979, and why then performance came to seem to be possessed of a 'theory'. My answer to this question has to do with the historical coincidence of the areas of 'art' performance and 'behaviour' performance. We know that in specific details they ventured into each other's domain: Goffman's social science used theatre as an analogy, various artists of the 1950s and 1960s became interested in using everyday life as a model, with some reading social science too. These crossovers are part of, and driven by, something deeper. In the 1950s, it seems, social science was beginning to break from its previous modes and protocols of fact-based knowledge, asking new questions about how we know what we know, interested not just in the datum but its communication. This intellectual development was given shape, in the western world, by political challenges to the 'facts' and the control over their communication maintained by governments fighting wars in Algeria and Vietnam, for example, and presiding over unequal societies. In Europe conditions of hard austerity immediately after the war gave way to economic growth, whereas the United States was already booming in the immediate post-war period. In both places, in different ways, there was a sense both of the need to rebuild anew and of scepticism about wealth as a guarantor of equality. For artists, students, political activists – for those as it were not tied into the existing economic institutions – opposition to dominant structures produced not only activism around the issues of war and civil rights but also a perception of how these issues were linked to the university and gallery infrastructure, which in turn supported a system which exchanged art as commodity. The attempted break from commoditised art and its institutions coincided with the social science break from fact-based knowledge. In each case what came to be called 'performance' was associated with the new space that was being opened up, whether the new non-positivist way of looking at human behaviours or the development of an art practice that was not tainted by the forms of existing commodities. It is these parallel developments that eventually not only shared a single word but also gave to that single word, 'performance', its power.

To account for the conceptual and indeed emotional power of performance is in some sense to develop a theory of it. Given the history of the word, however, there's a need for caution and discrimination in the business of coming up with a general 'theory'. That said, and by way of closing this book down, I shall risk the following observations based on the material I have covered:

Performance is both a practice and a mode of analysis. It is a communicative behaviour for which there is no other name (that's to say, if you can call it acting you treat it as acting). It is a mode of analysis that works by framing, thinking of, its material as if it were performed, which is to say as if it were a deliberate communicative practice.

The communicative behaviour claims to communicate truth rather than illusion. Theatre is a practice that explicitly uses enacted illusions in order to do its work. Performance, as understood here, does not present itself as dealing in illusions. Its techniques may, however, be analogous to those of theatre.

As communicative behaviour performance has various modes. These differ from one another in the degrees to which they mark, and call attention to, themselves as deliberate communicative acts. A person managing the impression they give to others in conversation may regard themselves as failing if they come across as too constructed, too deliberate or special. A group of children playing together agree to adopt certain rules in order to allow them to immerse themselves in the specially demarcated activity of play. A legal ceremony works by insisting that it is following historically enshrined, traditionally repeated, rule-bound procedures in order to get something done. A political demonstration may work by deliberately breaking agreed rules of communication, explicitly refusing historical usage, and spectacularly inventing its own.

As mode of analysis performance borrows ways of thinking and terminology both from theatre and from communicative behaviours. While not everybody thinks Goffman's elaborate 'dramaturgical' terminology is useful, the concept of 'role' has been widely applied to many social practices. So too the concepts of 'play' and 'ritual' have been widely used. These have been applied also to the analysis of theatrical work.

Performance has been useful to theatre while insisting on its difference from theatre. At the same historical juncture that social scientists were modelling their new concepts of communicative behaviour artists in various media were trying to develop modes of practice that were verifiably outside available institutions. This was in large part driven by a political or ethical rejection of dominant political ideas, economic practices and social alienation. One way of marking the difference of this practice was to show that it had no interest in making illusions. Indeed much of the communicative effort and its techniques went into a demonstration of not being illusory.

Some of this work was explicitly critical of theatre and it had the effects of provoking changes in theatre practice. Theatre absorbed some of the thinking and practices of those who, at least initially, began outside theatre. But so too the analysis of theatre absorbed ideas that were circulating around communicative behaviour. Just as did literary study, theatre study borrowed from other disciplines, for example drawing on the literature of play, in order to do its thinking.

Thus what I think we have observed in the materials under survey can be schematically summarised in the following way:

'Performance Theory' is the thinking which establishes a new field of study in the social sciences and arts, connected with human behaviour;

'Performance Theory' offers analytical models and procedures, based in the new field of study, which may be applied in a range of disciplinary areas, working by framing its objects of study as if they are performance;

'Performance Theory', as a set of concepts and analytical modes, provokes and enables an existing field of practice, theatre, to renew itself;

'Performance Theory', recognised as a field of study, with analytical models and terminology, becomes the rationale for disciplinary developments in the academy, and brings to those developments an historical anxiety around institutions and, indeed, discipline.

References

Altman, Dennis 1971 *Homosexual: Oppression and liberation* London: Allen Lane.

Augsburg, Tanya 1995 'Collaboration within the Field' *The Drama Review*, 39(4), 166–72.

Auslander, Philip 1995 'Evangelical Fervor' *The Drama Review*, 39(4), 178–83.

Auslander, Philip 1997 *From Acting to Performance: Essays in modernism and postmodernism* London and New York: Routledge.

Bacon, Wallace 1984 'Forum: Issues in interpretation' Literature in Performance, 5(1), 83–84.

Banaji, Jairus 1970 'The Crisis of British Anthropology' *New Left Review*, 64, 71–85.

Banes, Sally 'Institutionalizing Avant-Garde Performance: A hidden history of university patronage in the United States' in Harding 2000.

Barber, Bruce 1979 'Indexing: Conditionalism and its heretical equivalents' in Bronson and Gale 1979.

Battcock, Gregory (ed.) 1995 *Minimal Art: A critical anthology* Berkeley, Los Angeles, London: University of California Press.

Battcock, Gregory and Nickas, Robert (eds) 1984 *The Art of Performance: A critical anthology* New York: E.P.Dutton.

Bauman, Richard 1977 *Verbal Art as Performance* Rowley, MA: Newbury House Publishers.

Baxandall, Lee 1969 'Spectacles and Scenarios: A dramaturgy of radical activity' *The Drama Review*, 13(4), 52–71.

Baxandall, Lee 1970 'Happenings: An exchange' *The Drama Review*, 15(1), 147–49.

Bell, Catherine 1992 *Ritual Theory, Ritual Practice* New York and Oxford: Oxford University Press.

Bell, Catherine 1998 'Performance' in Taylor 1998.

Bell, Elizabeth 2008 *Theories of Performance* Los Angeles, London, New Delhi, Singapore: Sage Publications.

Belsey, Catherine 1985 *The Subject of Tragedy: Identity and difference in Renaissance drama* London and New York: Methuen.

Ben-Amos, Dan and Goldstein, Kenneth (eds) 1975 *Folklore: Performance and Communication* The Hague and Paris: Mouton.

Benamou, Michel and Caramello, Charles (eds) 1977 *Performance in Postmodern Culture* Madison, Wisconsin: Coda Press.

225

Benamou, Michel 1977a 'Preface' in Benamou and Caramello 1977.

Benamou, Michel 1977b 'Presence and Play' in Benamou and Caramello 1977.

Berghaus, Günter 1995 'Happenings in Europe: Trends, events, and leading figures' in Sandford 1995.

Bial, Henry 2014 'Performance Studies 3.0' in Citron, Atay, Aronson-Lehavi, Sharon, Zerbib, David (eds) *Performance Studies in Motion* London: Bloomsbury.

Blau, Herbert 1982/3 'Universals of Performance: Or, amortizing play' *SubStance*, 11/12 (4/1), 140–61.

Bottoms, Stephen 2003 'The Efficacy/Effeminacy Braid: Unpicking the Performance Studies/theatre studies dichotomy' *Theatre Topics*, 13(2), 173–87.

Bottoms, Stephen 2011 'In Defense of the String Quartet: An open letter to Richard Schechner' in Harding and Rosenthal 2011a.

Brake, Michael 1987 *Comparative Youth Culture: The sociology of youth culture and youth subcultures in America, Britain and Canada* London: Routledge & Kegan Paul.

Bronson, A.A. and Gale, Peggy (eds) 1979 *Performance by Artists* Toronto: Art Metropole.

Buchanan, Ian 2000 *Michel de Certeau: Cultural theorist* London: Sage Publications.

Burke, Kenneth 1945 *A Grammar of Motives* New York: Prentice-Hall.

Burns, Elizabeth 1972 *Theatricality: A study of convention in theatre and in social life* London: Longman.

Burns, Elizabeth and Burns, Tom (eds) 1973 *Sociology of Literature & Drama: Selected readings* Harmondsworth: Penguin.

Butler, Judith 1988 'Performative Acts and Gender Constitution: An essay in phenomenology and feminist theory' *Theatre Journal*, 40(4), 519–31.

Butler, Judith 1990 *Gender Trouble: Feminism and the subversion of identity* New York and London: Routledge.

Butler, Judith 1993 *Bodies that Matter: On the discursive limits of 'sex'* New York & London: Routledge.

Caillois, Roger 1961 *Man, Play and Games*, trans. M. Barash New York: Free Press of Glencoe.

Caramello, Charles 1977. 'Styles of Postmodern Writing' in Benamou and Caramello 1977.

Carlson, Marvin 1996 *Performance: A critical introduction* London: Routledge.

Carlson, Marvin 2004 *Performance: A critical introduction,* second edition New York and Abingdon: Routledge.

Carlson, Marvin 2011 'Performance Studies and the Enhancement of Theatre Studies' in Harding and Rosenthal 2011a.

Case, Sue-Ellen (ed.) 1990 *Performing Feminisms: Feminist critical theory and theatre* Baltimore and London: The Johns Hopkins University Press.

Case, Sue-Ellen 1992 'Theory/History/Revolution' in Reinelt and Roach 1992.

Case, Sue-Ellen 2002 'The Emperor's New Clothes: The naked body and theories of performance' *SubStance*, 31(2 & 3), 186–200.

CCCS 1975 *Resistance through Rituals* Working Papers in Cultural Studies 7 & 8 Birmingham: The Centre for Contemporary Cultural Studies.

Clarke, John 1975 'Style' in CCCS 1975.

Clarke, John 1978 'Football and Working Class Fans: Tradition and change' in Ingham, Roger et al, *'Football Hooliganism': The wider context* London: Inter-Action Inprint.

Cockburn, Alexander and Blackburn, Robin (eds) 1969 *Student Power: Problems, diagnosis, action* Harmondsworth: Penguin.

Cohen-Cruz, Jan 2006 'The Problem Democracy Is Supposed to Solve: The politics of community-based performance' in Madison and Hamera 2006a.

Connor, Steven 1992 *Postmodernist Culture: An introduction to theories of the contemporary* Oxford and Cambridge, MA: Blackwell.

Conquergood, Dwight 1989 'Poetics, Play, Process, and Power: The performative turn in anthropology' *Text and Performance Quarterly*, 1, 82–97.

Conquergood, Dwight 1991 'Rethinking Ethnography: Towards a critical cultural politics' *Communication Monographs*, 58, 179–94.

Conquergood, Dwight 1992 'Ethnography, Rhetoric, and Performance' *Quarterly Journal of Speech*, 78, 80–123.

Conquergood, Dwight 1995 'Of Caravans and Carnivals: Performance Studies in motion' *The Drama Review*, 39(4), 137–41.

Conquergood, Dwight 1998 'Beyond the Text: Toward a performative cultural politics' in Dailey 1998.

Coutts-Smith, Kenneth 1970 *The Dream of Icarus: Art and society in the twentieth century* London: Hutchinson & Co.

Coutts-Smith, Kenneth 1979 'Role Art and Social Context' in Bronson and Gale 1979.

Dailey, Sheron (ed.) 1998 *The Future of Performance Studies: Visions and revisions* Annandale, VA: National Communication Association.

Davis, Fred 1970 'Focus on the Flower Children: Why all of us may be hippies someday' in Douglas, Jack D. (ed.) *Observations of Deviance* New York: Random House.

Davis, R.G. 1966 'Guerrilla Theatre' *Tulane Drama Review*, 10(4), 130–36.

Davis, R.G. 1988 'The Politics, Packaging, and Potential of Performance Art: Reactionary and revolutionary elements in the avant-garde' *New Theatre Quarterly*, 4 (13), 17–31.

Davis, Tracy C. (ed.) 2008 *The Cambridge Companion to Performance Studies* Cambridge: Cambridge University Press.

Debord, Guy 2010 *Society of the Spectacle* Detroit: Black & Red.

de Certeau, Michel 1988 *The Practice of Everyday Life*, trans. Steven Rendall Berkeley, Los Angeles, London: University of California Press.

Denzin, Norman K. 2006 'The Politics and Ethics of Performance Pedagogy' in Madison and Hamera 2006a.

Derrida, J. 1988 *Limited Inc*, ed. Gerald Graff Evanston: Northwestern University Press.

Dews, Peter 1989 'From Post-Structuralism to Postmodernity' in Appignanesi, Lisa (ed.) *Postmodernism: ICA documents* London: Free Association Books.

Diamond, Elin (ed.) 1996 *Performance and Cultural Politics* London and New York: Routledge.

Dirksmeier, Peter and Helbrecht, Ilse 2008 'Time, Non-representational Theory and the "Performative Turn": Towards a new methodology in qualitative social research' *Forum Qualitative Sozialforschung*, 9(2), 1–10; www .qualitative-research.net (accessed June 2015)

Dirksmeier, Peter and Helbrecht, Ilse 2010 'Intercultural Interaction and "Situational Places": A perspective for urban cultural geography within and beyond the performative turn' *Social Geography*, 5, 39–48.

Dolan, Jill 1995 'Response to W.B.Worthen's "Disciplines of the Text/Sites of Performance"' *The Drama Review*, 39(1), 28–34.

Dolan, Jill 2001 *Geographies of Learning: Theory and practice, activism and performance* Middletown, CN: Wesleyan University Press.

Duvignaud, Jean 1973 'The Theatre in Society: Society in the Theatre', trans. Tom Burns in Burns and Burns 1973.

Dworkin, Dennis 1997 *Cultural Marxism in Postwar Britain: History, the New Left, and the origins of cultural studies* Durham and London: Duke University Press.

Edwards, Paul 2006 'Performance of and beyond Literature' in Madison and Hamera 2006a.

Emigh, John 2011 'Liminal Richard: Approaches to Performance Studies' in Harding and Rosenthal 2011a.

Erickson, Jon 1992 'The Spectacle of the Anti-Spectacle: Happenings and the Situationist International' *Discourse*, 14(2), 36–58.

Estrin, Marc 1969 'A Note on Guerrilla Theatre' *The Drama Review*, 13(4), 76.

Evreinoff, Nicolas 2013 *The Theatre in Life*, ed. and trans. A.I. Nazaroff Mansfield Centre, CT: Martino Publishing.

Féral, Josette 1982 'Performance and Theatricality: The subject demystified' *Modern Drama*, 25(1), 170–81.

Féral, Josette 2002 'Foreword' *SubStance*, 31 (2 & 3), 3–13.

Fischer-Lichte, Erika 2014 *The Routledge Introduction to Theatre and Performance Studies*, ed. Minou Arjomand and Ramona Mosse, trans. Minou Arjomand London and New York: Routledge.

Frascina, Francis 1999 *Art, Politics and Dissent: Aspects of the art left in sixties America* Manchester and New York: Manchester University Press.

Fried, Michael 1995 'Art and Objecthood' in Battcock 1995.

Geertz, Clifford 1972 'Deep Play: Notes on the Balinese cockfight' *Daedalus: Journal of the American Academy of Arts and Sciences*, 101(1), 1–37.

Geertz, Clifford 1980 'Blurred Genres: The refiguration of social thought' *The American Scholar*, 49(2), 165–82.

Gilson-Ellis, Jools 1995 'Say Just What You Mean', *The Drama Review*, 39(4), 173–77.

Goffman, Erving 1990 *The Presentation of Self in Everyday Life* London: Penguin.

Goffman, Erving 2005a 'On face-work' in *Interaction Ritual: Essays in face-to-face behavior*, intro. Joel Best New Brunswick and London: Aldine Transaction.

Goffman, Erving 2005b 'The Nature of Deference and Demeanor' in *Interaction Ritual: Essays in face-to-face behavior*, intro. Joel Best New Brunswick and London: Aldine Transaction.

Goldberg, RoseLee 1979 *Performance: Live Art 1909 to the present* London: Thames and Hudson.

Goldhill, Simon 1999 'Programme Notes' in Goldhill, Simon and Osborne, Robin (eds) *Performance Culture and Athenian Democracy* Cambridge: Cambridge University Press.

Gorsen, Peter 1984 'The Return of Existentialism in Performance Art' in Battcock and Nickas 1984.

Gottlieb, Vera and Jones, Nesta 1976 'Drama: A course, a process and a project' in Craig, David and Heinemann, Margot (eds) *Experiments in English Teaching: New work in higher and further education* London: Edward Arnold.

Gregson, Nicky and Rose, Gillian 2000 'Taking Butler Elsewhere: Performativities, spatialities and subjectivities' *Environment and Planning D: Society and Space*, 18, 433–52.

Gurvitch, Georges 1973 'The Sociology of the Theatre', trans. Petra Morrison in Burns and Burns 1973.

Hall, Stuart c.1968/69 *The Hippies: An American "Moment"* Birmingham: CCCS; http://www.birmingham.ac.uk/schools/historycultures/departments/history/research/projects/cccs/publications/stencilled-occasional-papers.aspx (accessed October 2015).

Hall, Stuart 1969 'The Hippies: An American "Moment"' in Nagel 1969.

Hamera, Judith 1986 'Postmodern Performance, Postmodern Criticism' *Literature in Performance*, 7(1), 13–20.

Hamera, Judith 2006 'Performance, Performativity, and Cultural Poiesis in Practices of Everyday Life' in Madison and Hamera 2006a.

Hansen, Al 1965 *A Primer of Happenings, & Time/Space Art* New York, Paris, Cologne: Something Else Press.

Harding, James M. 2000 *Contours of the Theatrical Avant-Garde: Performance and textuality* Ann Arbor: The University of Michigan Press.

Harding, James M. 2003 'From Anti-Culture to Counter-Culture: The emergence of the American avant-garde performance events' in Rathman, Thomas (ed.) *Ereignis: Konzeptionen eines Begriffs in Gesichte, Kunst und Literatur* Köln, Weimar, Wien: Böhlau Verlag.

Harding, James M. and Rosenthal, Cindy (eds) 2011a *The Rise of Performance Studies: Re-thinking Richard Schechner's broad spectrum* Basingstoke: Palgrave Macmillan.

Harding, James M. and Rosenthal, Cindy 2011b 'Introduction: The rise of Performance Studies' in Harding and Rosenthal 2011.

Harrison-Pepper, Sally 1999 'Dramas of Persuasion: Performance Studies and interdisciplinary education' *Theatre Topics*, 9(2), 141–56.

Harvey, David 2005 *A Brief History of Neoliberalism* Oxford and New York: Oxford University Press.

Hebdige, Dick c.1974 *Sub-cultural Conflict and Criminal Performance in Fulham: Towards a radical theory of role* Birmingham: CCCS; http://www.birmingham.ac.uk/schools/historycultures/departments/history/research/projects/cccs/publications/stencilled-occasional-papers.aspx (accessed October 2015).

Hebdige, Dick 1979 *Subculture: The meaning of style* London and New York: Methuen.

Heddon, Deirdre 2012 'The Politics of Live Art' in Heddon, Deirdre and Klein, Jennie (eds) *Histories and Practices of Live Art* Basingstoke: Palgrave Macmillan.

Hibbitts, Bernard J. 1992 'Coming to Our Senses: Communication and legal expression in performance culture' *Emory Law Journal*, 4, 1–46; http://faculty.law.pitt.edu/hibbitts/ctos.htm (accessed June 2015).

Higgins, Dick 1969 *Foew and Ombwhnw: A grammar of the mind and a phenomenology of love and a science of the arts as seen by a stalker of the wild mushroom* New York, Barton, Cologne: Something Else Press.

Hoffman, Beth 2009 'Radicalism and the Theatre in Genealogies of Live Art' *Performance Research*, 14(1), 95–105.

Home, Stewart 1991 *The Assault on Culture: Utopian currents from Lettrisme to Class War* Stirling: A.K.Press.

Howell, Anthony and Templeton, Fiona 1977 *Elements of Performance Art* London: The Ting: Theatre of Mistakes.

Huizinga, Johann 1949 *Homo Ludens: A study of the play-element in culture* London: Routledge & Kegan Paul.

Hunt, Albert 1976 *Hopes for Great Happenings: Alternatives in education and theatre* London: Eyre Methuen.

Hunter, Roddy and Bodor, Judit 2012 'Art, Meeting, and Encounter: The art of action in Great Britain' in Heddon, Deirdre and Klein, Jennie (eds) *Histories and Practices of Live Art* Basingstoke: Palgrave Macmillan.

Hymes, Dell 1964 'Introduction: Toward ethnographies of communication' *American Anthropologist*, new series, 66(6.2), 1–34.

Hymes, Dell 1975 'Breakthrough into Performance' in Ben-Amos and Goldstein 1975.

Jackson, Shannon 2004 *Professing Performance: Theatre in the academy from philology to performativity* Cambridge: Cambridge University Press.

Jackson, Shannon 2006 'Genealogies of Performance Studies' in Madison and Hamera 2006a.

Jackson, Shannon 2012 'Rhetoric in Ruins: Performance Studies, speech, and the "Americanization" of the American university' in McKenzie, Roms and Wee 2012.

Jansen, William Hugh 1957 'Classifying Performance in the Study of Verbal Folklore' in Richmond, W. Edson (ed.) *Studies in Honor of Distinguished Service Professor Stith Thompson* Bloomington: Indiana University Press.

Jappe, Anselm 1999 *Guy Debord*, trans. D. Nicholson-Smith Berkeley: University of California Press.

Jeffery, Tom 1999 *Mass Observation: A short history* MO Occasional Papers number 10 [first published as a CCCS Occasional Paper in 1978].

Jordan, John 1998 'The Art of Necessity: The subversive imagination of anti-road protest and Reclaim the Streets' in McKay 1998.

Kaprow, Allan 2003 *Essays on the Blurring of Art and Life*, ed. Jeff Kelley Berkeley, Los Angeles, London: University of California Press.

Kaye, Nick 1994 *Postmodernism and Performance* Basingstoke: Macmillan.

Kempton, Richard 2007 *Provo: Amsterdam's anarchist revolt* Brooklyn, NY: Autonomedia.

Kershaw, Baz 1997 'Fighting in the Streets: Dramaturgies of popular protest, 1968–1989' *New Theatre Quarterly*, 13, 255–76.

Kirby, Michael 1995 'The New Theatre' in Sandford 1995.

Kirshenblatt-Gimblett, Barbara 1975 'A Parable in Context: A social interactional analysis of storytelling performance' in Ben-Amos and Goldstein 1975.

Klein, Jennie 2012 'Developing Live Art' in Heddon, Deirdre and Klein, Jennie (eds) *Histories and Practices of Live Art* Basingstoke: Palgrave Macmillan.

Knabb, Ken (ed. and trans.) 1981 *Situationist International Anthology* Berkeley, CA: Bureau of Public Secrets.

Kostelanetz, Richard 1968 *The Theatre of Mixed Means: An introduction to happenings, kinetic environments, and other mixed-means performance* New York: The Dial Press.

Lebel, Jean-Jacques 1969 'Notes on Political Street Theatre, Paris: 1968, 1969' *The Drama Review*, 13(4), 111–18.

Lebel, Jean-Jacques 1995 'On the Necessity of Violation' in Sandford 1995.

Lefebvre, Henri 1995 Introduction to Modernity: Twelve preludes, September 1959–May 1961, trans. John Moore London: Verso.

Lefebvre, Henri 1996 *Writings on Cities*, selected, translated and introduced by E. Kofman and E. Lebas Oxford: Blackwell.

Loeffler, Carl E. (ed.) 1980 *Performance Anthology: Sourcebook for a decade of California Performance Art* San Francisco, CA: Contemporary Arts Press.

Lorimer, Hayden 2005 'Cultural Geography: The busyness of being "more-than-representational"' *Progress in Human Geography*, 29(1), 83–94.

Loxley, James 2007 *Performativity* London and New York: Routledge.

Lyman, Stanford M. and Scott, Marvin B. 1975 *The Drama of Social Reality* New York: Oxford University Press.

MacAloon, John J. 1984a 'Introduction' to MacAloon, John J. (ed.) *Rite, Drama, Festival, Spectacle: Rehearsals toward a theory of cultural performance* Philadelphia: The Institute for the Study of Human Issues.

MacAloon, John J. 1984b 'Olympic Games and the Theory of Spectacle in Modern Societies' in MacAloon, John J. (ed.) *Rite, Drama, Festival, Spectacle: Rehearsals toward a theory of cultural performance* Philadelphia: The Institute for the Study of Human Issues.

Madison, D. Soyini and Hamera, Judith (eds) 2006a *The Sage Handbook of Performance Studies* Thousand Oaks, London, New Delhi: Sage Publications.

Madison, D. Soyini and Hamera, Judith 2006b 'Performance Studies at the Intersections' in Madison and Hamera 2006a.

Manning, Phil 1991 'Drama as Life: The significance of Goffman's changing use of the theatrical metaphor' *Sociological Theory*, 9(1), 70–86.

Marranca, Bonnie 1996 'Introduction' and 'Afterword to the 1996 Edition' in *The Theatre of Images* Baltimore and London: The Johns Hopkins University Press.

Marsh, Peter 1978 'Life and Careers on the Soccer Terraces' in Ingham, Roger et al, *'Football Hooliganism': The wider context* London: Inter-Action Inprint.

Martin, Bradford D. 2004 *The Theater Is in the Street: Politics and public performance in sixties America* Amherst and Boston: University of Massachusetts Press.

Marx, Karl 1986 *Karl Marx: A reader*, ed. Jon Elster Cambridge: Cambridge University Press.

Maxwell, Ian 2006 'Performance Studies at the University of Sydney' *The Drama Review*, 50(1), 33–45.

McAuley, Gay 2012 'Interdisciplinary Field or Emerging Discipline? Performance Studies at the University of Sydney' in McKenzie, Roms and Wee 2012.

McKay, George (ed.) 1998 *DiY Culture: Party & Protest in Nineties Britain* London and New York: Verso.

McKenzie, Jon 1998 'Genre Trouble: (The) Butler did it' in Phelan and Lane 1998.

McKenzie, Jon 2001 *Perform or Else: From discipline to performance* London and New York: Routledge.

McKenzie, Jon 2006 'Performance and Globalization' in Madison and Hamera 2006a.

McKenzie, Jon, Roms, Heike, Wee, C.J.W-L. (eds) 2012 *Contesting Performance: Global Sites of Research* Basingstoke: Palgrave Macmillan.

Messinger, Sheldon E., Sampson, Harold, Towne, Robert D. 1975 'Life as Theater: Some notes on the dramaturgical approach to social reality' in Brissett, Dennis and Edgley, Charles (eds) *Life as Theater: A dramaturgical sourcebook* Chicago: Aldine Publishing Company.

Metzger, Gustav 1965 *Auto-Destructive Art* London: A.C.C.

Nagel, Julian (ed.) 1969 *Student Power* London: Merlin Press.

Nuttall, Jeff 2012 'The Situation Regarding Performance Art (1973)' *Contemporary Theatre Review*, 22(1), 175–77.

Parker, Andrew and Sedgwick, Eve Kosofsky 1995 'Introduction: Performativity and Performance' in Parker, Andrew and Sedgwick, Eve Kosofsky (eds) *Performativity and Performance* New York and London: Routledge.

Peariso, Craig J. 2014 *Radical Theatrics: Put-ons, politics, and the sixties* Seattle & London: University of Washington Press.

Pelias, Ronald 1998 'Performance Studies: Meditations and mediations' in Dailey 1998.

Pelias, Ronald and VanOosting, James 1987 'A Paradigm for Performance Studies' *Quarterly Journal of Speech*, 73(2), 219–31.

Peters, Sybylle 2012 'The Performance of Performance Research: A report from Germany' in McKenzie, Roms and Wee 2012.

Phelan, Peggy 1993a *Unmarked: The politics of performance* London and New York: Routledge.

Phelan, Peggy 1993b 'Reciting the Citation of Others, or, a second introduction' in Hart, Lynda and Phelan, Peggy (eds) *Acting Out: Feminist performances* Ann Arbor: The University of Michigan Press.

Phelan, Peggy and Lane, Jill 1998 *The Ends of Performance* New York and London: New York University Press.

Pinder, David 2005 *Visions of the City: Utopianism, power and politics in twentieth-century urbanism* Edinburgh: Edinburgh University Press.

Pollock, Della 1998 'Introduction: Making History Go' in *Exceptional Spaces: Essays in performance and history* Chapel Hill and London: University of North Carolina Press.

Pontbriand, Chantal 1979 'Introduction: Notions of Performance' in Bronson and Gale 1979.

Pontbriand, Chantal 1982 'The Eye Finds No Fixed Point on Which to Rest ...' *Modern Drama*, 25(1), 154–62.

Puchner, Martin 2006 *Poetry of the Revolution: Marx, manifestos, and the avant-gardes* Princeton and Oxford: Princeton University Press.

Ramparts, The Editors of (eds) 1971 *Conversations with the New Reality: Readings in the cultural revolution* San Francisco: Canfield Press.

Reinelt, Janelle G. 2002 'The Politics of Discourse: Performativity meets theatricality' *SubStance*, 31(2 & 3), 201–15.

Reinelt, Janelle G. and Roach, Joseph R. (eds) 1992 *Critical Theory and Performance* Ann Arbor: The University of Michigan Press.

Roms, Heike and Edwards, Rebecca 2012 'Towards a Prehistory of Live Art in the UK' *Contemporary Theatre Review*, 22(1), 17–31.

Rosenberg, Harold 1962 *The Tradition of the New* [London]: Thames and Hudson.

Rothenberg, Jerome 1977 'New Models, New Visions: Some notes toward a poetics of performance' in Benamou and Caramello 1977

Sainer, Arthur 1975 *The Radical Theatre Notebook* New York: Avon.

Sandford, Mariellen (ed.) 1995 *Happenings and Other Acts* London and New York: Routledge.

Saunders, Graham 2012 'The Freaks' Roll Call: Live art and the Arts Council, 1968–73' *Contemporary Theatre Review*, 22(1), 32–45.

Savran, David 2005 'The Death of the Avantgarde' *The Drama Review*, 49(3), 10–42.

Sayre, Henry M. 1989 *The Object of Performance: The American avant-garde since 1970* Chicago and London: The University of Chicago Press.

Schechner, Richard 1966 'Approaches to Theory/Criticism' *Tulane Drama Review*, 10(4), 20–53.

Schechner, Richard 1969 *Public Domain: Essays on the Theatre* Indianapolis: Bobbs-Merrill.

Schechner, Richard 1973 'Performance and the Social Sciences: Introduction' *The Drama Review*, 17(3), 3–4.

Schechner, Richard 1988 *Performance Theory* New York and London: Routledge.

Schechner, Richard 1998 'What Is Performance Studies Anyway?' in Phelan and Lane 1998.

Schechner, Richard 2001 *Performance Studies: An introduction* London and New York: Routledge.

Schneider, Rebecca 1997 *The Explicit Body in Performance* London and New York: Routledge.

Sell, Mike 1998 'The Avant-garde of Absorption: Happenings, Fluxus, and the performance economies of the American sixties' *Rethinking Marxism*, 10(2), 1–26.

Shepherd, Simon and Wallis, Mick 2004 *Drama/Theatre/Performance* London and New York: Routledge.

Shubik, Martin 2011 *The Present and Future of Game Theory* Cowles Foundation for Research in Economics, Yale University: http://cowles.econ.yale.edu/P/cd/d18a/d1808.pdf (accessed June, 2015).

Singer, Milton (ed.) 1959 *Traditional India: Structure and change* Philadelphia: The American Folklore Society.

Singer, Milton 1972 *When a Great Tradition Modernizes: An anthropological approach to Indian civilization* London: Pall Mall Press.

Smithson, Alison and Smithson, Peter 1967 *Urban Structuring: Studies of Alison & Peter Smithson* London: Studio Vista.

Sohm, H. (ed.) 1970 *Happening & Fluxus: Materialen* Koeln: Koelnischer Kunstverein.

Sontag, Susan 1966 *Against Interpretation and Other Essays* New York: Dell Publishing.

States, Bert O. 1996 'Performance as Metaphor' *Theatre Journal*, 48(1), 1–26.

Stedman Jones, Gareth 1969 'The Meaning of the Student Revolt' in Cockburn and Blackburn 1969.

Stegmann, Petra (ed.) 2012 *'The Lunatics Are on the Loose . . . ': European Fluxus Festivals 1962–1977* Berlin: Down with Art!.

Striff, Erin 2003 *Performance Studies* Basingstoke: Palgrave Macmillan.

Strine, Mary S., Long, Beverly Whitaker, Hopkins, Mary Frances 1990 'Research in Interpretation and Performance Studies: Trends, issues, priorities' in

Phillips, Gerald M. and Wood, Julia T. (eds) *Speech Communication: Essays to commemorate the 75ᵗʰ anniversary of the Speech Communication Association* Carbondale and Edwardsville: Southern Illinois University Press.

Stucky, Nathan 2006 'Fieldwork in the Performance Studies Classroom: Learning objectives and the activist curriculum' in Madison and Hamera 2006a.

Stucky, Nathan and Wimmer, Cynthia 2002 *Teaching Performance Studies* Carbondale: Southern Illinois University Press.

Sullivan, Rob 2011 *Geography Speaks: Performative aspects of geography* Farnham: Ashgate.

Sun, William H. and Fei, Faye C. 2014 'Social Performance Studies: A new PS school with Chinese characteristics' in Citron, Atay, Aronson-Lehavi, Sharon, Zerbib, David (eds) *Performance Studies in Motion* London: Bloomsbury.

Tambiah, S.J. 1979 'A Performative Approach to Ritual' *Proceedings of the British Academy*, 65, 113–69.

Taylor, Mark C. (ed.) 1998a *Critical Terms for Religious Studies* Chicago & London: The University of Chicago Press.

Taylor, Mark C. 1998b 'Introduction' in Taylor 1998a.

Thrift, Nigel and Dewsbury, John-David 2000 'Dead Geographies – and How to Make Them Live' *Environment and Planning D: Society and Space*, 18, 411–32.

Tilly, Charles 2008 *Contentious Performances* Cambridge: Cambridge University Press.

Tuan, Yi-Fu 1977 *Space and Place: The perspective of experience* Minneapolis and London: University of Minnesota Press.

Turner, Victor 1977 'Frame, Flow and Reflection: Ritual and drama as public liminality' in Benamou and Caramello 1977.

Turner, Victor 1982 *From Ritual to Theatre: The human seriousness of play* New York: PAJ Publications.

Turner, Victor 1984 'Liminality and the Performative Genres' in MacAloon, John J. (ed.) *Rite, Drama, Festival, Spectacle: Rehearsals towards a theory of cultural performance* Philadelphia: The Institute for the Study of Human Issues.

Turner, Victor 1992 *The Anthropology of Performance* New York: PAJ Publications.

Turner, Victor 1995 *The Ritual Process: Structure and anti-structure* New York: Aldine de Gruyter.

van Haaren, Hein 1966 *Constant*, trans. Max Schuchart Amsterdam: J.M. Meulenhoff.

Voeten, Teun 1990 'Dutch Provos' *High Times*, January: http://www.marijuanali brary.org/HT_provos_0190.html (accessed December 2013).

Walsh, Victoria 2001 *Nigel Henderson: Parallel of Life and Art* London: Thames & Hudson.

Wigley, Mark 1998 *Constant's New Babylon: The hyper-architecture of desire* Rotterdam: Witte de With.

Wollen, Peter 1989 'Bitter Victory: The art and politics of the Situationist International' in Sussman, Elisabeth (ed.) *On the Passage of a Few People Through a Rather Brief Moment in Time: The Situationist International, 1957–1972* Cambridge, MA, London: MIT Press

Worthen, W.B. 1995 'Disciplines of the Text/Sites of Performance' *The Drama Review*, 39(1), 13–28.

Worthen, W.B. 1998 'Drama, Performativity, and Performance' *PMLA*, 113(5), 1093–107.

Index

Cambridge Introductions to . . .

Authors

Topics